Contents

Chronology

All dates are BCE

The Spartan Hegemony

404/403	Thirty Tyrants rule Athens (Spartan garrison on Akropolis)
403	Thrasyboulos captures Peiraieus (democracy restored)
401	Rebellion of Kŷros the Younger, Battle of Koúnaxa (march of Ten Thousand – Xenophon's *Anabasis*)
399	Trial and execution of Sokrates, accession of Agesilaos II, Sparta intervenes in Anatolia (recruits Ten Thousand)
398	Persia builds fleet for Athens (led by Konon)
398/397	Dionysios I of Syracuse besieges Motya (first recorded use of catapults)
396	Agesilaos' campaign to 'liberate' the Greeks in Ionia, Battle of Sardis
395	Athens, Corinth, Thebes, Argos form coalition to break Spartan hegemony (start of Corinthian War), accession of Agesipolis I, Lysandros killed at Haliartos
394	Battles of Nemea River, Second Koroneia, and naval engagement off Knidos
392	Revival of Athenian naval power (Persia renews backing for Sparta), federation of Argos and Corinth
391	Rebellion of Evagoras of Salamis
390	Iphikrates defeats Spartan *móra* near Lechaion
387	Dionysios I captures Rhegion
387/386	Plato visits court of Dionysios I, Artaxerxes II terminates Corinthian War (King's Peace – autonomy for *all* Greek states *outside* Persian empire)

LEŪKTRA 371 BCE

Sparta's Twilight

Nic Fields

Helion & Company

Helion & Company Limited
Unit 8 Amherst Business Centre
Budbrooke Road
Warwick
CV34 5WE
England
Tel. 01926 499619
Email: info@helion.co.uk
Website: www.helion.co.uk
X (formerly Twitter): @Helionbooks
Facebook: @HelionBooks
Visit our blog at helionbooks.wordpress.com

Published by Helion & Company 2025
Designed and typeset by Mach 3 Solutions (www.mach3solutions.co.uk)
Cover designed by Paul Hewitt, Battlefield Design (www.battlefield-design.co.uk)

Text © Nic Fields 2025
Colour artwork drawn by Renato Dalmaso © Helion & Company 2025
Illustrations © as individually credited
Maps by George Anderson © Helion & Company 2025

ISBN 978-1-804517-69-7

British Library Cataloguing-in-Publication Data.
A catalogue record for this book is available from the British Library.

For details of other military history titles published by Helion & Company Limited,
contact the above address, or visit our website: http://www.helion.co.uk

We always welcome receiving book proposals from prospective authors.

Pre-Leŭktra

386/385	Agesipolis defeats Mantineia (a fledgling democracy)
382–379	Agesipolis defeats Olynthos (head of the Chalkidic League)
380	Agesipolis dies
382	Phoebidas captures Kadmeia
379	Sparta disciplines Phleious (apogee of Sparta's power)
379/378	Liberation of Kadmeia (emergence of Boiotia as superpower)
378	Sphodrias' unauthorised raid on Attica
378/377	Thebans 'liberate' Thespiai, re-foundation of Boiotian confederacy, formation of the Second Athenian Confederation
378, 377	Agesilaos twice invades Boiotia
376	Peloponnesian fleet defeated off Naxos
375	Iason of Pherai elected *tagos* ('overlord') of Thessaly; Timotheos' expedition to Korkyra and naval victory off Alyzeia in Akarnania; Sacred Band (under Pelopidas) defeat Spartans at Tegyra
375/374	Third 'common peace', *koinē eirēnē*, of Artaxerxes II (for the purpose of hiring Greek mercenaries to put down rebellion in Egypt)
373	Athenian interference on Zakynthos; Iphikrates' expedition to Korkyra
372	Thebans raze the walls (for the second time) of Thespiai
371	Athens and Sparta become allies, but latter is decisively defeated at Battle of Leŭktra (400 *Spartiātai* killed there)

Post-Leŭktra

370	Thebes dominate power in Greece, but lacks manpower to exploit its newfound position; formation of the Arkadian League, Iason of Pherai assassinated
370/369	Epameinondas' first invasion of Peloponnese, liberation of Messenia and re-founding of Mantineia
369	Epameinondas' second invasion reduces Sparta's effective allies to Corinth and Phleious
368	Diversion of Theban interest to Thessaly leads to revival of Sparta's power in Peloponnese, Dionysios I of Syracuse sends Iberian and Celtic mercenaries to aid Sparta (the first mention of Celts as

	mercenaries in Greece), foundation of Megalopolis by Epameinondas
368/367	Athenian alliance with Dionysios I
367	Dionysios I sends second force of mercenaries, Sparta wins 'Tearless Battle' (so called because allegedly not a single *Spartiātēs* was killed) against Arkadians, death of Dionysios I (son succeeds as Dionysios II)
367/366	Satraps' Revolt
367–364	Philip (later II of Macedon) hostage at Thebes, Persia backs Theban shipbuilding programme to counteract Athenian activity in northern Aegean
366	Plato invited to court of Dionysios II
366/365	Epameinondas' third invasion of Peloponnese and final collapse of Peloponnese League
364	Pelopidas killed in battle at Kynoskephalai; Thebes destroys Orkhomenos
362	Quarrels between Arkadia and Elis and between oligarchic and democratic Arkadians leads to decline in Theban influence in Peloponnese; Epameinondas' last invasion of Peloponnese and Battle of Second Mantineia (Epameinondas killed)
360	Agesilaos dies serving as a mercenary captain in Egypt (Sparta having recently adopted a model of state mercenarism)

Abbreviations

Ael.	Aelianus	
	NA	*De natura animalium*
	Takt.	*Taktiká*
	VA	*Varia Historia*
AHB	*Ancient History Bulletin* (Calgary, 1987–)	
AJA	*American Journal of Archaeology* (Princeton NJ, 1897–)	
Aiskh.	Aiskhylos	
	Ag.	*Agamemnon*
	PB	*Prometheus Bound*
	Seven	*Seven Against Thebes*
Alex.	Alexis	
Alk.	Alkaios	
Anakr.	Anakreon	
Andok.	Andokides	
Apoll.	Apollodoros, *Bibliotheka*	
Ar.	Aristophanes	
	Ach.	*Acharnenses* ('Acharnians')
	Av.	*Aves* ('Birds')
	Ekkl.	*Ekklesiazusai* ('Assemblywomen')
	Eq.	*Equites* ('Knights')
	Lys.	*Lysistrata*
	Nub.	*Nubes* ('Clouds')
	Ran.	*Ranae* ('The Frogs')
	Thesm.	*Thesmophoriazusai* ('Women Celebrating the Thesmophoria')
	Vesp.	*Vespae* ('Wasps')
Archil.	Archilochos	
Arist.	Aristotle	
	[*Ath. pol.*]	Ἀθηναίων πολιτεία ('Constitution of the Athenians')
	Nik. Eth.	*Nikomakhaian Ethics*
	Pol.	Πολιτά ('Politics')

Rh.	Ῥητοική ('Rhetoric')
Athen.	Athenaios, *Deipnosophistae* ('The Philologists' Banquet')
Bacch.	Bacchylides
BMC 8	B.V. Head, British Museum Catalogue of Coins, Vol. 8: *Central Greece (Locris, Phocis, Boeotia, and Euboea)* (London, 1884)
BSA	*Annual of the British School at Athens* (Cambridge, 1895–)
Cic.	Cicero
Div.	*De divinatione*
Inv. rhet.	*De inventione rhetorica*
Tusc.	*Tusculanae disputationes*
CQ	*Classical Quarterly* (Cambridge, 1908–)
CW	*Classical Weekly* (Baltimore MD, 1907–1957)
Dein.	Deinarchos
Dem.	Demosthenes
Diod.	Diodoros Sikoulos, *Bibliothēkē*
Eur.	Euripides
Andr.	*Andromache*
Bacch.	*Bacchae*
Hel.	*Helena* ('Helen')
HF	*Hercules furens* ('The Madness of Herakles')
Herakleid.	*Herakleidai* ('The Children of Herakles')
IT	*Iphigenia Taurica* ('Iphigenia among the Taurians')
Med.	*Medea*
Phoen.	*Phoenissae* ('Phoenician Women')
Supp.	*Supplices* ('The Supplicants')
Tro.	*Troades* ('Trojan Women')
FGrHist	F. Jacoby, *Die Fragmente der griechischen Historiker* (Berlin & Leiden, 1923–1958)
Fornara	C. W. Fornara, *Translated Documents of Greece and Rome I: Archaic Times to the end of the Peloponnesian War* (Cambridge, Cambridge University Press, 1983 2nd edition)
Frontin.	Frontinus, *Strategemata*
GBRS	*Greek, Roman & Byzantine Studies* (Cambridge MA, 1963–)
Gell.	Aulus Gellius, *Noctes Atticae* ('Attic Nights')
Gk.	Greek
G & R	*Greece & Rome* (Cambridge, 1931–)
Harding	P. Harding, *Translated Documents of Greece and Rome*, vol. 2. *From the end of the Peloponnesian War to the battle of Ipsus* (Cambridge, 1985)
Hell. Oxy.	*Hellenika Oxyrhynchia*
Hermes	*Hermes, Zeitschrift für Klassische Philologie* (Stuttgart, 1866–)
Hes.	Hesiod

	Th.	*Theogony* ('Birth of the Gods')
	Op.	*Opera et Dies* ('Works and Days')
Hdt.	Herodotos	
Hist.	*Historia, Zeitschrift für Alte Geschichte* (Stuttgart, 1952–)	
Hom.	Homer	
	Il.	*Iliad*
	Od.	*Odyssey*
IG	*Inscriptiones Graecae* (Berlin, 1923–)	
Isok	Isokrates	
JHS	*Journal of Hellenic Studies* (Cambridge, 1880–)	
Just.	Justinus *Epitome* (of Cnaeus Pompeius Trogus)	
Krit.	Kritias	
L	Latin	
Liv.	Livy	
Nep.	Nepos	
	Epam.	*Epameinondas*
	Iphik.	*Iphikrates*
	Pel.	*Pelopidas*
	Thras.	*Thrasybulos*
Paus.	Pausanias	
Pind.	Pindar	
	Olymp.	*Olympian Odes*
	Pyth.	*Pythian Odes*
Pl.	Plato	
	Lach.	*Laches*
	Leg.	*Leges* ('Laws')
	Symp.	*Symposium*
Plin.	Pliny, *Historia Naturalis*	
Plut.	Plutarch	
	Ages.	*Agesilaos*
	Alex.	*Alexander*
	Alk.	*Alkibiades*
	Apophth.	*Regum et imperatorum apophthegmata*
	Arist.	*Aristides*
	Artax.	*Artaxerxes*
	De garr.	*De garrulitate*
	Kleom.	*Kleomenes*
	Lyk.	*Lykourgos*
	Lys.	*Lysandros*
	Mor.	*Moralia*
	Nik.	*Nikias*
	Pel.	*Pelopidas*
Polyain.	Polyainos	
Polyb.	Polybios, *Historíai*	

P Oxy.	P.B. Grenfell & A.S. Hunt (eds.), *Oxyrhynchus Papyri* (London, 1898)	
Sage	M. M. Sage, *Warfare in Ancient Greece: A Sourcebook* (London: Routledge, 1996)	
SEG	*Supplementum Epigraphicum Graecum* (Amsterdam, 1923–)	
Soph.	Sophokles	
	Aj.	*Ajax*
Strab.	Strabo, *Geographia*	
Tod	M. N. Tod, ed., *A Selection of Greek Historical Inscriptions*, volume 2, *From 403 to 323 BC* (Oxford: Oxford University Press, 1948)	
Tyrt.	Tyrtaios	
Xen.	Xenophon	
	Ages.	*Agesilaos*
	Anab.	*Anabasis* ('March up Country')
	[Ath. pol.]	*Respublica Atheniensium* ('Constitution of the Athenians')
	Hell.	*Hellenika* ('Affairs of Greece')
	Hipp.	*Hipparchikos* ('Cavalry Commander')
	Kúr.	*Kúrou paideía* ('Education of Kŷros')
	Kyn.	*Kynegetikos* ('On Hunting')
	Lak. pol.	*Lakedaimoniōn politeia* ('Constitution of the Spartans')
	Mem.	*Memorabilia*
	Oik.	*Oikouménē* ('On the Household')
	PH	*Perì hippikēs* ('Art of Horsemanship')
	Por.	*Poroi* ('Ways and Means')

Glossary of Greek Terms

A brief description of some basic Greek words and technical terms that are used in the book. Where applicable, plural forms appear in parentheses.

Aeolians
: Those Greeks, found mainly in Boiotia (Boiotian Aeolic, e.g. Hesiod, Pindar), Thessaly, Lesbos (Lesbian Aeolic, e.g. Alkaios, Sappho) and a small part of the northern Anatolian coast, who spoke the Aeolian dialect and whose lives shared certain distinctive cultural and religious features

agōgē
: 'Raising'– the education system to which the young males of Sparta were subjected

acropolis
: 'High city' – original citadel of *polis* (q.v.); typically, it was the site of temples and shrines

antilabē
: Handgrip of *aspís* (q.v.) positioned near the rim; grasped with the left hand, it helped the hoplite manage the great weight of his shield and stopped it slipping down the forearm

árchōn (-ontes)
: 'Chief'– leading magistrate of the Boiotian confederacy

aspís (-des)
: 'Argive shield' – a soup-bowl shaped shield, some 80 to 100cm in diameter, held via *antilabē* (q.v.) and *pórpax* (q.v.)

aulós (-oí)
: 'Flute' – wind instrument akin to a pipe

boiōtarchēs (-oi)
: 'Leader of the Boiotians' – 11 (later seven) military commanders of Boiotian confederacy army

chōra
: Hinterland of *polis* (q.v.)

Corinthian helmet
: Full–face helmet formed out of a single sheet of bronze and lined with leather; close-fitting, being shaped to the skull with only small openings for the eyes, nostrils, and mouth

cubit
: Unit of measurement equal to the length from elbow to tip of middle finger (Attic cubit = 0.45m, Doric cubit = 0.49m)

Dorians
: Those Greeks, found mainly in the Peloponnese (except Arkadia), Libya, Crete, Thera, Rhodes, and

in the Dorian colonies of Sicily and southern Italy, who spoke the Doric dialect and whose lives shared certain distinctive cultural and religious features

dóru — 'Dorian spear' – long thrusting spear, 2.0–2.5m in length, armed with spearhead (bronze or iron) and bronze *sauroter* (q.v.)

drakhmē (-ae) — 'Handful' – standard weight as well as silver coin worth six *oboloí* (q.v.); in Athens, average daily wage of casual labourer (Attic-Euboic *drakhmē* = 4.3g, Aiginetan *drakhmē* = 6.1g)

éphoroi — 'Overseers' – highest magistrates, five in number, in Spartan state

enōmotia (-iai) — 'Sworn band', at full strength unit of 40 men commanded by *enōmotarchos*

gerontes — 'Elders' – 28-member principal deliberation and judicial council at Sparta, the *gerousia*

harmostēs (-ai) — 'fixer' – Spartan military governor abroad

hēgemonia — 'Leadership' – concept prominent in Greek interstate relations, *viz.* a *hēgemōn* controls subordinate allies without abolishing their separate identities

helots — 'Captives of war' – indentured serfs who worked land of *Spartiātai* and served as attendants and lightly armed troops on campaign

hippeīs — 'Horsemen' – bodyguard of Spartan kings

homoios (-oi) — 'Similars' – term used of full-blown citizens of Sparta, the *Spartiātai*

hoplite — Heavily-armed foot soldier accustomed to fighting shoulder to shoulder in phalanx

Ionians — Those Greeks, the Athenians believed that the Ionians had originated in Athens, who spoke the Ionic dialect and whose lives shared certain distinctive cultural and religious features; the language itself was divided into Old Ionic (e.g. Homer) and New Ionic (e.g. Herodotos), the latter includes Attic, the ordinary dialect of Athenian writers (e.g. Thucydides, Xenophon)

klāros (-oi) — 'Land plot' – Doric form of *klēros*, allotments assigned to *homoioi* (q.v.)

knēmídes — Greaves, bronze body armour for lower legs

kopis — Single-edged, heavy slashing-type sword shaped like a machete, hoplite's secondary weapon

lám(b)da — Greek letter Λ ('L')

lóchos (-oí) — 'War band' – at full strength unit of 640 men in Spartan army commanded by *lochagós (-oi)*; also used as tribal unit of various sizes in other Greek armies

linothōrax — Stiff linen corselet, lighter and more flexible (but more expensive) than *thōrax* (q.v.)

móra (-ai)	'Portion' – largest division of Spartan army; at full strength a unit of 1,280 men (Lazenby) or 640 (others) commanded by *polémarchos* (q.v.)
neodamōdeis	'New citizens' – helots freed *after* hoplite service in Spartan army
ōbá (-ai)	Four (later five) villages that made up *polis* of Sparta
obolós (-oí)	'Nail' – used both as weight and coin (Attic-Euboic *obolós* ≡ 0.72g); at Athens equalled one-sixth of *drakhmē* (q.v.)
ōthismos	'Shove' – pushing stage of hoplite battle
paiān	Collective war cry sung in unison, Dorian in origin but eventually adopted by other Greeks
panopliā	'Full armour' – panoply of hoplite (q.v.)
pentekostys (-yes)	'Fifties' – at full strength a unit of 160 men commanded by *pentekon(s)tēr(es)*
polémarchos (-oi)	'War leader' – commander of *móra* (q.v.), second level of field command closely associated with Spartan kings
polis (-eis)	Conventionally translated as 'city-state', term actually refers to autonomous political community of Greeks
pórpax (-kos)	Detachable armband of *aspís* (q.v.); left arm was put through this band, so securing *aspis* to forearm of hoplite
ptéruges	'Feathers' – stiffened leather or linen fringing on *linothōrax* (q.v.)
sauroter	'Lizard sticker' – bronze butt-spike; it not only enabled *dóru* (q.v.) to be planted upright in ground when not in use, but also could be used offensively in event of spearhead snapping off
stadion (-ia)	Unit of distance that varied from place to place; for this reason, generally consider it to be roughly equivalent to 200m
stratēgós (-oi)	General or commander of phalanx
sussítion (-ai)	Communal messes at Sparta
taxiarchos (-oi)	'Formation leader' – commander of *taxis* (q.v.)
thōrax	Bronze bell-shaped corselet, made up of front and back plates and flared at waist and neck
tálanton	Fixed weight of silver equivalent to 60 *minae* or 6,000 *drakhmae* (Attic-Euboic *tálanton* = 26.2kg, Aiginetan *tálanton* = 43.6kg)
taxis (-eis)	'Formation' – e.g. tribal unit in Athenian army, commanded by *taxiarchos* (q.v.)
triērēs (-ēis)	'Trireme' – oared ship rowed at three levels with one man to each oar, principal warship of the period.

Introduction

When something incomprehensible happens, it can be reassuring to fall back on old clichés. Antisthenes' description of the Thebans as 'no different from little boys strutting about because they had thrashed their tutor' summarises what many Greek leaders immediately thought after the battle of Leūktra.[1] The Sokratic philosopher's story may sound apocryphal, but in fact it was not until after their trouncing of the Spartans that the Boiotians considered training themselves in 'the craft of arms'.[2] As for the vanquished, an ability to lose is not, perhaps, the first thing people typically associate with Spartans. It is akin to Richard Cœur de Lion failing before a petty fortress and an unknown hand, and Leūktra was, in fact, a shameful defeat for the Spartans. So, there we are.

According to Plutarch, Epameinondas (†362 BCE), the renowned Theban *stratēgós* and victor of Leūktra who foreshadowed Philip II of Macedon (r. 359-336 BCE), held the firm belief that his citizen soldiers should have their bodies 'trained not only by athletic exercise but by military drill as well.'[3] Epameinondas' motive here is quite clear. At a time when formal military training for the citizen was not officially recognised by the state – Sparta being the notable exception of course – physical fitness and the ability to wield a weapon was the responsibility of the individual citizen.[4]

So how exactly did this thrashing come about? Epameinondas had deliberately broken with tradition by identifying the importance of applying mass to the proper point at the decisive moment – this would become the quintessence of Napoléon's style. This Epameinondas achieved by massing his 4,000 or so Theban hoplites on his left 'not less than fifty shields deep'

---

1   Source: Plut. *Lyk.* 30.6. Antisthenes (b. *c.* 446 BCE) in his youth had fought against the Thebans at Tanagra (426 BCE). He was a disciple first of Gorgias, and then of Sokrates. He was apparently still alive in 366 BCE (Diod. 15.76.4). In later times he is believed to have been the founded of the philosophical school of Cynicism (Diogenes Laertius *Vitae Philosophorum* VI §§1–2, cf. Thuc. 3.91).
2   Xen. *Hell.* 6.5.23, cf. 7.5.19.
3   Plut. *Mor.* 192E, cf. D, 788A, Nep. *Epam.* 2.4, 5.
4   *Vide* Xen. *Mem.* 3.12.4–5, where the author promotes the idea of exposing the body to regular physical exercise. Hard physical exercise still forms a major and vital part of a soldier's basic training; there is little point, for example, in being a marksman with a rifle if you are unfit to use it after a solid day's 'yomp'. Physical fitness, to this day, is still the keynote.

in the evocative words of Xenophon,[5] with the crack ἱερὸς λόχος; or Sacred Band of Thebes, an extremely tight-knit group even by Greek citizen-soldier standards, forming the front four ranks under his friend Pelopidas (†364 BCE). By doing so Epameinondas had it nailed by placing the very best of the Boiotians directly opposite Kleombrotos, the Spartan king (r. 380–371 BCE), and his 700 *Spartiātai*.

Epameinondas advanced obliquely to the left, refusing his right and centre, and screening his advance with Boiotian horsemen. The Lakedaimonian horsemen, also unusually in front of the phalanx, were pushed back into their own hoplites. The latter appear to have been attempting to deepen their 12-deep formation and to extend to the right in characteristic Spartan fashion. For the Sacred Band, standing right on the cusp of the storm, this was their moment to act, and so into this confusion they crashed at the double, cutting a swathe through the Spartan ranks. Kleombrotos fell, mortally wounded, and although the Spartans held their ground long enough to recover his body, perhaps all 80 files directly in front of the Theban mass following behind the Sacred Band were annihilated, including the king's tent companions and all 300 members of the *hippeīs*, the handpicked young men who served as the personal guard to the Spartan kings. The rest of the Spartan army (Lakedaimonians, allies, mercenaries) retired and left the field on seeing their right wing suffering a clear and unambiguous defeat. The battle was won, and the myth of Sparta's unchallengeable power had been fatally undermined.

---

5   Xen. *Hell.* 6.4.12.

Chapter 1

War, Greek Style

Plant foot by foeman's foot, press shield on shield, / thrust helm at helm, and tangle plume with plume, / opposing breast to breast: that's how to fight.

Tyrtaios fr. 11.32–34 West

War, in the ancient Greek world, was the central factor of political life and the dominating element in war was the hoplite,[1] heavily armoured citizen soldiers who fought shoulder to shoulder with spear and shield in a large formation that the Greeks knew as a phalanx.[2] With that, the armies of Greek *poleis* were based on a levy of those citizens prosperous enough to equip themselves as hoplites.[3] Except for the Spartans, whose soldiers were acknowledged as the 'craftsmen of war' because they devoted their entire lives to military training,[4] and a few state-sponsored units such as the famous homophilic unit, the Sacred Band of Thebes, 300 men who were paired in dyadic relationship and *in extremis* sworn to die for their partner, these citizen levies were untrained, part-time soldier farmers, owing their strength to numbers and determination rather than to martial skill or battle experience.

---

1   In Greek: ὁπλίτης / ὁπλῖται. It is wrongly believed by many scholars and commentators that it was from his shield that the hoplite derived his name. The noun ὅπλον / *hóplon*, in the singular, is in fact extremely rare in Greek in the sense of 'hoplite shield', the one exemplum I know of being found in Diodoros: 'called hoplites, from the shield they carried' (15.44.3). In truth, the common noun for hoplite shield is *aspís*. If, therefore, hoplites had been so called because of the shield they bore, they should be *aspístai*. Now, *hópla*, in the plural, is very frequent in the sense 'arms' and so it can be reasonably assumed that *hoplítai* means 'armed men'. Indeed, the noun *tà hopla* is often employed for *hoi hoplítai* (e.g. Thuc. 4.74.3). *Vide* Lazenby-Whitehead 1996.

2   In Greek: φάλαγξ / φάλαγγες, (in the plural) literally 'stacks' or 'rows' of men.

3   The problem of trying to estimate the value of hoplite equipment in modern monetary terms of ancient currencies is a difficult one. The best that can be done is to indicate contemporary wages and prices to give the reader some idea, a labourer earning between a *drakhmē* and a *drakhmē* and a half per day in the late fifth century BCE. It has been estimated that the cost of complete bronze panoply was in the order of 75 to one hundred *drakhmae*, the equivalent of about three months' wages (Hanson 1995: 294–301), though this does seem to be top of the range. There is an Athenian decree, which probably dates from the late sixth century BCE, listing regulations for an Athenian citizen colony on Samos. It contains the following ordinance: 'Each [colonist] is to provide arms himself to the value of thirty *drakhmae*' (Sage 38).

4   Xen. *Lak. pol.* 13.5.

For a citizen of a *polis,* it was his moral, social and, above all, political duty to fight on the behalf of his *polis* in times of crisis. Liable for military service at any time from the age of 20 years, citizens remained on the state muster rolls for at least 40 years – desertion or cowardice could lead to a loss of citizenship – and even a dramatist such as the Athenian Aiskhylos stood in the phalanx, and was, in fact, to be remembered on his grave as a warrior, not as a wordsmith.[5] It is a circular argument: hoplites were the citizens in battle, and citizens were the hoplites in assembly, ergo men who had a permanent stake in their *polis.*

The Hoplite

At first sight it may seem surprising that when Greek warfare emerges into the light of history, it not only soon becomes dominated by close-packed, heavily armoured amateurs, but also continues to be so for some three centuries (*c.* 675–350 BCE). It lasted so long because as time passed the system was maintained for the sake of tradition, shared values, and social prejudice. Since hoplites were expected to provide their own implements of war and keep them in a state of readiness, the majority of the population in any given *polis* was necessarily excluded. Yet the full rights of citizenship were only accorded to those who could afford to take their place in the phalanx fully equipped, so that the hoplites effectively were the 'nation in arms'. Besides, it would have been unthinkable to arm the *hoi polloí,* and for that reason citizenship was displayed in common military action.

It was only at Athens, whose true strength was at sea and for that reason the navy became paramount, that the poorest Athenian citizens, the *thētes* who rowed the triremes, came to have a significant military role. As Themistokles (a predecessor to Perikles) once told the Athenians 'that their future was on the sea', advice which they followed, and thus 'he [Themistokles] at once began to join in laying the foundations of their empire'.[6] Thence aggressive Athenian democracy,[7] or what the excessively cerebral Aristotle rudely called 'trireme democracy'.[8] Finally, as the events of the two Persian invasions of Greece (490, 480–479 BCE) were to prove, hoplites were extremely formidable.

---

5   Aiskhylos' tragedy *Persai* provides our earliest literary evidence for Xerxes' invasion, a war in which the citizen playwright was a participant. Late in life Aiskhylos retired to Gela, Sicily, where he died *c.* 456 BCE. Apparently, a tortoise dropped on his head by an eagle killed him, the bird having mistaken the bald shiny pate of the venerable playwright for a stone. His tomb was inscribed with the epitaph he wrote for himself: 'Aiskhylos, Euphorion's son / of Athens, lies under this stone / dead in Gela among the white / wheat lands; a man at need / good in fight / witness the hallowed field of Marathon, / witness the long-haired Mede' (*Vita Aeschyli* §11). He made no reference to his writings, which numbered some 70 plus plays (only seven survive); as he was responsible for the introduction of a second actor, thereby allowing for true dialogue, he is generally regarded as the real founder of Greek tragedy. Aiskhylos obviously prided himself more on his military services to Athens – with Marathon as the supreme day of his life – than on his dramatic art.

6   Thuc. 1.93.4.

7   In Greek: *dēmokratia,* from *dēmos* ('the people') and *kratei* ('rule').

8   Arist. *Pol.* 1291b.21, cf. 1304a.8, 1321a.2, Xen. [*Ath. pol.*] 1.2. It has been argued (Strauss 1996) that the experience of naval service itself fostered attitudes that were essential to the functioning

strength to a spearhead, increasing its effectiveness at piercing shields and armour during hand-to-hand spear play.

We have been speaking of the spear as δόρυ, but the noun initially meant a wooden shaft, plank or beam of wood; it is the material which forms the word, not its use. The word is rarely used by the Greek lyric poets, because it is a practical daily word in general use, but in the epic genre it is a specific word for the wooden handled, bronze tipped spear of the warrior. In Homer, for instance, it could be hurled or used in thrust, even swung sideways like an extended sword to slash with the broad cutting edges of the blade. The deadly life-taking spearhead, this is the Homeric warrior's weapon, as against 'effeminate' arrows, which belong to the 'degenerate' eastern powers.

Ash wood (as frequently mentioned in the epic verses of Homer)[24] was the most frequently chosen because it naturally grows straight and cleaves easily. What is more, it is both tough and elastic, which means it has the capacity to absorb repeated shocks without communicating them to the handler's hand and of withstanding a good hard knock without splintering. All in all, ash has a suitable modulus of elasticity for spear work, with enough density and weight to be thrown too, and these properties combined made it an excellent choice for crafting a spear.

The hoplite also packed a sword, but it was very much a secondary weapon – a far cry from its former predominance in the epoch of Homeric warfare – to be used only when his spear had failed him: it was the instrument of last resort. The introduction of the phalanx undermined the previous prestige of this arm. Besides, in the crush and squeeze of a phalanx, a shorter weapon was preferable so as to be more easily handled. It may have required special skills to handle a thrusting type sword, but with a meat cleaver it was almost impossible to miss in the cut and thrust of the tightly packed phalanx. One type was the Greek *kópis*, a strong, curved, one edged blade designed for slashing with an overhand stroke, not thrusting. The cutting edge was on the inside like a Ghurkha *kukri*, while the broad back of the blade curved forward in such a way to weight the weapon towards its tip, that is to say, making it 'point-heavy' – basically a hacking instrument for delivering 'butcher's blows' (κόπις literally means 'chopper' and was used of the domestic meat-clever too). Whatever the pattern, the sword was worn suspended from a long baldric from right shoulder to left hip, the scabbard being fashioned of wood covered with leather, with the tip strengthened by a small metal cap, the chape, usually moulded to the scabbard.

---

24 Ash tree, μελίη: Hom. *Il.*13.178, 16.767 Lattimore. Ash spear, δόρυ μείλινον: *ibid.* 5.655, 19.390, 22.225 Lattimore, et cetera Cf. Archil. fr. 229 Swift: 'the beech (ὀξύη) spear was flying'. Here Archilochos has used a vivid metaphor by using the substantive ὀξύη ('beech tree') to represent the spear itself, which may be a play on the Homeric epithet ἔγχεα ὀξυόεντα, 'sharp spear' (*Il.* 5.568 Lattimore).

The Advance

It is Thucydides who informs us too that the hoplite phalanx, as it advanced to contact, had a tendency to edge to the right.[25] In a compressed paragraph he gives us the essence of the matter, explaining that the right-hand man would drift in fear of being caught on his unshielded side, and the rest of the phalanx would naturally follow suit, each hoplite trying to keep under the protection of his right-hand neighbour's shield.[26] Each right wing therefore might overlap and beat the opposing left wing. Thucydides implies that this was a tendency over which *stratēgoi*, even in the Spartan army, had little or no control. At Thermopylai, for instance, this did not apply because the bare right spear-side of Leonidas' phalanx was suitably guarded by the sea, but at First Mantineia Agis' phalanx would employ this rightward shift to its advantage.

The practised Spartans, according to the impressed Thucydides, were noted for their slow and ordered advance, marching in step the whole way to the rhythm of *auloí* players – obsessive and monotonous to our ears probably – and singing awe-inspiring war songs, which contrasted with that of the enemy 'full of sound and fury'.[27] It was usual for summertime soldiers to be warmed up by a general's eleventh-hour harangue or some peak of bronze-banging bravado built up to by shouting, spear-waving, shield-pounding and the like. For the Spartans, on the other hand, there was no bluster and bronze banging. As they advanced into contact there were merely a few words of encouragement, the sort of words that are uttered in the din of battle, not distinguished individually but restoring confidence by the fact of being spoken.

And then, just before contact, so as to give themselves greater courage and strike fear into their opponents, the hoplites would raise, in unison, a collective war cry or a *paiān*. The Greek war cry sounded something like *éleleleū*,[28] the Greek equivalent to the Japanese battle cry *tennōheika banzai*, whereas the *paiān* was a chant – sometimes a mere yell – associated particularly with Apollo and sung,[29] amongst other occasions, before and after battle. The *paiān*, an invocation before battle or hymn of victory afterwards,[30] was a peculiarly Greek custom, Dorian in origin, but eventually adopted by the other Greeks. Aiskhylos describes it as: '…the strong cry of victory, / The shout of sacrifice familiar to all Greeks, / To inspire our men and make them fearless in the field.'[31]

---

25 Thuc. 5.71.1.

26 *Contra* van Wees 2004: 185–187.

27 Thuc. 5.70.

28 Xen. *Anab.* 1.8.18, Ar. *Av.* 364. In his *Stratēgikós* (§29.1–2), Onasandros advises the *stratēgós* to send his men into battle shouting and running to frighten the opposition.

29 The noun *paiān* (L *paeān*) derives from *Paiëon*, 'physician, healer', a title of Apollo (Hom. *Il.* 5.401, 899, cf. *Od.* 4.232 Lattimore), later as epithet (Aiskh. *Ag.* 146, Ar. *Ach.* 1212).

30 For example, Hom. *Il.* 22.391–2 Lattimore, Aiskh. *Seven* 1035.

31 Aiskh. *Seven* 268–70. The poet Alkman tells us that the singing of the *paiān* inspired comradeship and forged group cohesion: 'At feast and in the companies of the men's mess, it is well beside

Representation of hoplites in a phalanx, scene from the Nereid Monument (London, British Museum, inv. 868), panel from the lower frieze on the podium. The sculptured tomb, dated *c.* 390–380 BCE, from which this slab came, is at Xanthós in Lykia. It belonged to a local dynast who, like his master the Persian king, employed Greek mercenaries to stiffened native levies. The Greek *polis* was quintessentially a 'guild of warriors', and deployed its citizen body in a phalanx. This mass formation, broader than it was deep, was an effective way of expressing citizen military power. Note the *linothōrax*, and the double-gripped, concave hoplite shield, *aspís*, which was singular: the phalanx being calibrated by the depth of its cumulative shields – '8 shields deep', '12 shields deep', et cetera – not by counting spears or men. In the front rank, fifth from the left, is a hoplite with his head turned to the right and his raised right arm gesturing. He could be a *stratēgós* encouraging his men as they advance into contact. (©Nic Fields)

Aiskhylos, like many of his audience, was a hoplite and a veteran of Marathon. Unquestionably, the shout of Greek armies, reverberating under clear cobalt blue skies, often seemed to shake the gods from their slumber and, indeed, had such a quality of invocation that a foe of lesser vocal potency might well tremble involuntarily and look around him fearfully, as if anticipating the sudden arrival of an unseen host. The raw savage sound of thousands of men shouting in unison can be terrifying. It raises fear at a level below thought. Imagine, if you will, what frightening power there is in a cry roared out by only a few thousand throats to the tramp of marching feet. Fear, as much as spears, was a leading weapon.

The Spartans also wore garlands of foliage, at least up to the point where they halted to perform – much later than anyone else, and deliberately in sight of the enemy – their propitiatory blood sacrifice.[32] Undoubtedly, this last-minute halt provided a chance to dress the ranks again. This was obviously a matter of concern not only to Spartans. At Koúnaxa, when the line started to billow out, Xenophon, a former Athenian horseman turned mercenary, and his comrades shouted out to each other 'not to run at a headlong pace.'[33] Still, the slow steady march of the Spartans, their paralysing war songs and shrill reed flutes (Gk. αὐλοί / *auloí*) piercing through the din of battle, and their surreal fresh garlands must have been an unnerving sight in the eyes of those looking from the wrong side of the battlefield. More like a serene

---

them that sit at meat to strike up and sing the *paiān*' (fr. 87).

32   Xen. *Lak. pol.* 13.8, *Hell.* 4.2.18, Plut. *Lyk.* 22.2.

33   Xen. *Anab.* 1.8.19.

advance to a ritual sacrifice than a shambling advance to hard contact. We are ready: Are you? At this point it was common for the opposition to break and flee, that is to say, before actually coming 'within spear thrust' (εἰς δόρυ) of the Spartans. The alternative to breaking and fleeing, of course, was to surrender or die. In a way, this was to become rather a common failing amongst the Spartans – hard and well-officered, but much inclined to make too little of their adversaries. At Leūktra, as we shall discover, this habit was to be their undoing.

The Push

Tyrtaios exhorts the Spartans to 'hold the line',[34] maintaining by doing so they will 'die in less numbers'.[35] This is an abandonment of the heroic warrior code found in Homer, replacing it with a political goal, namely the defence of the *polis* through a unified effort and maintaining formation. The phalanx had replaced the fury (Gk. λύσσα / *lússa*) of the Homeric warrior with prudence (Gk. σωφροσύνη / *sōphrosúnē*): foolhardy daring could neither be tolerated nor rewarded with glory (Gk. ἀριστεία / *aristeía*), as Isidas, who truly believed this was his hour, defending Sparta against Epameinondas discovered.[36]

It was the hoplite shield that made the rigid phalanx formation viable. Half the *aspís* protruded beyond the left-hand side of the hoplite. If the man on the left moved in close, he was protected by the shield overlap, which thus guarded his uncovered side. Hence, hoplites stood shoulder pressing against shoulder with their shoulder-to-knee shields locked. Once this formation was broken, however, the advantage of the *aspís* was lost; as Plutarch says, the body armour of a hoplite might be for the individual's protection, but the hoplite's *aspís* protected the whole phalanx.[37] To lose one's shield in the battleline endangered all, while to throw it away in flight meant ignominy,[38] unless of course you were a sophisticated poet who could be laid back about *rhípsaspia* (ῥίπσασπια: ῥίπτειν, 'to throw' + ἀσπίς, 'shield'), the jettison of a shield.[39] The suppressing of one's instinct for safety is not easy, particularly at moments when your stomach turns over and will not go back into its place.

---

34 Tyrt. 10.15, 11.11 West.

35 *Ibid.* 11.12 West.

36 Plut. *Ages.* 34.6–8.

37 Plut. *Mor.* 220A.2, 241.

38 Kleonymos, an Athenian statesman not noted for his courage in battle, was known as a ῥίπσασπίς, 'shield-tosser' – he apparently did so at Delion (424 BCE) – and suffered at least a decade's worth of jokes and scathing comment in Aristophanes' comedies (*Nub.* 353–354, 670–680 [423 BCE], *Vesp.* 592–593, 822–823 [422 BCE], *Pax* 673–8, 1295–1304 [421 BCE], *Av.* 489–490, 1473–1481 [414 BCE]).

39 Archil. fr. 5, 115a Swift, Alk. fr. 401b West, Anakr. fr. 381 West, cf. Plut. *Mor.* 239B, Hdt. 5.95. The Augustan poet Horace (*Odes* 2.7.9–14) claims, in a sly reference to his undistinguished military career, to have shamefully thrown away his shield in a panic to facilitate his 'hasty retreat' from the horrors of the field of Philippi (42 BCE) where Romans had chosen to kill each other. Naturally, as spoils of war those of eminent people were greatly prized (Hom. *Il.* 8.191–193 Lattimore, Thuc. 4.12.1, Plut. *Nik.* 28.5, Diod. 15.87.6, cf. Paus. 1.15.5). Pausanias, when he visited Thebes a half millennium later, claims he saw 'bronze shields [*viz.* facings of] dedicated here which they say came from the Spartan officers who died at Leūktra' (9.16.3).

Obviously, when one was in fear of one's life, commonsense tells you your shield is the easiest part of the *panopliā* to drop, and the most burdensome. In the phalanx a hoplite's body armour was designed for fighting in such a compact formation, protected on each side by his comrades' shields, whereas his shield symbolised his commitment to the battleline and its abandonment was a mark of cowardice that endangered the wider group. Hence Plato thought the issue important enough for legislation.[40]

The phalanx itself was a deep formation, normally composed of hoplites arrayed eight to 12 shields deep, and occasionally even deeper.[41] In this dense mass only the front two ranks could use their 'death-dealing spears' in the mêlée, the men in ranks three and further back added weight to the attack by pushing to their front. This was probably achieved by shoving the man in front with the *aspís*. Thucydides and Xenophon, men who in their narratives both look back with a soldier's eye surely know far better than we can ever know, both commonly refer to the push and shove, *ōthismos*, of a hoplite mêlée.[42]

The opposing phalanxes collided head-on, and the resulting shock would have been tremendous: several authors familiar with hoplite combat mention the crash when contending phalanxes collided.[43] The two opposing lines of spears now crossed (and often snapped in the tremendous onrush), and the leading ranks were immediately thrust upon each other's weapons by the

---

40 Pl. *Leg.* 12.943e–945a.

41 For example, the Athenians were eight deep at Delion (Thuc. 4.94.1), and again at the Peiraeus in 403 BCE (Xen. *Hell.* 2.4.34); the Spartans at Mantineia were an average of eight deep (Thuc. 5.68.3), similarly Derkylidas, in Anatolia, 'ordered the divisional commanders and the captains to form up their men in a phalanx eight shields deep' (Xen. *Hell.* 3.2.16) as did Mnasippos with his men on Korkyra (*ibid.* 6.12.20), while at Leûktra the Spartans would opt for a phalanx 12 deep (*ibid.* 6.4.11), and Agesilaos, in Arkadia the year after, deployed his phalanx with a depth of 'nine or ten shields deep' (*ibid.* 6.5.19); the allies finally agreed on a maximum of 16 deep at the Nemea (*ibid.* 4.2.13, 18); the Syracusans before Syracuse had also formed up 16 deep (Thuc. 6.67.2). However, the Thebans stood 25 deep at Delion (*ibid.* 4.93.4), the first recorded use of a very deep phalanx, and at Leûktra their phalanx was beefed-up so as to stand 'no less than fifty shields deep' (Xen. *Hell.* 6.4.12). Curiously, Xenophon (*Anab.* 1.2.15) informs us that four deep was the 'customary order' of the Ten Thousand, though much later he has them 'fallen into a phalanx eight deep' (*Anab.* 7.1.23). Finally, for what it is worth, the late Hellenistic Asklepiodotos (*Taktiká* 2.1, cf. 7) theorises that the depth of a hoplite phalanx could be eight, ten, 12 or 16, although his ideal for the depth of the perfect phalanx, whatever that was, is 16. Curiously, Xenophon informs us here that four shields deep was the customary order of the Ten Thousand (*Anab.* 1.2.15, cf. 7.1.23) and Herodotos (6.112) hints at four deep for the Athenian centre at Marathon in 490 BCE. Also, if we can believe Diodoros (13.72.5, 72.6), the Spartans outside Athens in 408 BCE formed up a phalanx only four shields deep. Reasons for a phalanx deeper than eight can include, first, a lack of confidence (e.g. Xen. *Hell.* 2.4.34, 4.2.18), second, add weight to the push (e.g. Thuc. 4.93.4, 6.67, Xen. *Hell.* 6.4.12) and, third, the nature of the terrain (e.g. Xen. *Hell.* 2.4.11, 12). Whatever, there was a strong tendency amongst hoplite armies to form deep (Xen. *Hell.* 4.2.13, 18). Alternatively, reasons for a phalanx of less than eight shields deep can include, first, the desire to prevent outflanking by the enemy (e.g. Hdt. 6.112) and, second, by increasing the width of the phalanx the impression is created that there are more hoplites than there really were. This parade of the Ten Thousand, therefore, could be seen as an example of the latter with Kŷrus ordering the Greeks to double the width of their phalanx so as to impress the locals.

42 Thuc. 4.43.3, 96.2, 6.70.2, Xen. *Hell.* 4.3.19, 6.4.14.

43 Tyrt. fr. 19.18 West, Aiskh. *Seven* 100, 103, 106, Eur. *Herakleid.* 832, *Supp.* 699.

irresistible pressure from behind. In our mind's eye we can visualise the majority of front rankers in each phalanx going down in the initial crunch, 'While knees sink low in gory dust, / And spears shivered at first thrust'.[44] However, their comrades stepped forward – or were pushed from behind – over their dead and dying bodies to continue the struggle. Xenophon, in his eyewitness account of the Battle of Second Koroneia (394 BCE), laconically recalls his own experience of the clash and collision of the *ōthismos* as the Spartans 'crashed into the Thebans front to front. So, with shield pressed against shield (ὠθισμός ασπίδον) they struggled, killed and were killed'.[45] Elsewhere, in his panegyric to his princely patron, Agesilaos, he was happy to elaborate:

> There was no shouting, nor was there silence, but the strange noise that wrath and battle together will produce... Now the fighting was at an end, a weird spectacle met the eye, as one surveyed the scene of the conflict – the earth stained with blood, friend and foe lying dead side by side, shields smashed to pieces, spears snapped in two, daggers bared of their sheaths, some on the ground, some embedded in the bodies, some yet gripped by the hand.[46]

Our eyewitness Xenophon manages to make it sound as if it is happening right in front of you, and it is easy to picture the crows flocking overhead, implying the recent carnage still fresh on the field of the slain.

Euripides, who as an Athenian citizen would have had firsthand experience of this sort of horror, had used similar language to describe what happened when phalanxes of Athens and Thebes finally came to grips with each other on the red field of slaughter: 'All down the lines the fronts of battle clashed: / Men slew – were slain – a thunder of wild war cries / Rang, roared, of men on cheering each his fellow'.[47]

The image he portrays is striking and raw. Shaped by the world around him, Euripides here reflects the unvarnished emotions of real hoplites facing real danger for their *polis*.

When the masses of flesh and bronze had been pushing against each other for some time, their spears (if still intact) interlocked, matters were now held in the balance. In the dust and terror of the *ōthismos* at Delion (424 BCE), according to Thucydides, with terrific stubbornness the Thebans dug their heels in and eventually 'got the better of the Athenians, pushing them back (ὠθισμός ασπίδον) step by step at first and keeping up their pressure'.[48] Outside Syracuse (415 BCE) the Athenians and their Argive allies defeated both wings of the Syracusan army, by pushing.[49] Once experienced such things were never easily forgotten, and even Aristophanes' chorus of veteran Athenian hoplites, fondly reminisce about their great victory over the 'long-haired Medes' at Marathon (490 BCE), are made to say:

---

44   Aiskh. *Ag.* 66–67 Vellacott.
45   Xen. *Hell.* 4.3.19.
46   Xen. *Ages.* 2.12, 14.
47   Eur. *Supp.* 699–701.
48   Thuc. 4.96.2, cf. Tyrt. fr. 11.31–32 West, Eur. *Herakleid.* 836.
49   Thuc. 6.70.2.

> At once we ran up, armed with warlike spear and shield and, / drunk with the bitter wine of anger, / we gave them battle, man standing to man and rage distorting our lips. / A hail of arrows hid the sky. / However, by the help of the gods, we pushed off the foe towards evening.[50]

The pushing with these wide and weighty, bowl-shaped shields explains the famous plea of the Theban *stratēgós*, Epameinondas, 'for one more pace' at Leūktra.[51] We shall hear a lot more of Epameinondas hereafter. Indeed, on the subject of pushing Xenophon, who was certainly no admirer of the Thebans, minces no words, saying that the Spartan right at Leūktra was 'being pushed back'.[52] For this reason, Xenophon advocates that the best men should be placed in the front and at the rear of a phalanx so that the worse men in the middle, namely the cowards and the like, could be 'led by the former and pushed by the latter',[53] a disposition reminiscent of that of Nestor, who drove the cowards between two lines of good men.[54]

The pushing itself could go on for some time. Gelatinous with fatigue, it was now time for one side to crack. The crisis point of the contest had now been reached, when the decision would swing either way, depending on which side was most capable of delivering the last fearful push. Thucydides says that at the Battle of Solygeia (425 BCE), a village some 10 kilometres from Corinth, the Athenian and Karystian right wing 'with difficulty pushed the Corinthians back'.[55] However, time is master, always. Once one side finally crumbled and collapsed, all was up, and panic took hold, the vanquished suffering the most fearful losses in the initial rout. The mass of fugitives would have been more like the mob of Argives Xenophon describes, 'frighten, panic stricken, presenting their unprotected sides, no one rallying to his own defence.'[56] Soldiers in fear of their lives will flee. This is certain. However, long-range pursuit stood not within the lexicon of hoplite warfare. The victors asserted control of the battlefield by attaching a set of enemy arms and armour to a stake or tree as a trophy at the spot where the opposition had been routed.[57]

In hoplite warfare, therefore, the phalanx itself was the tactic. When one *polis* engaged another, the crucial battle would usually be fought on level ground with mutually visible fronts that were not more than a kilometre or so long and often only a few hundred metres apart. Normally, after a final battleline blood sacrifice, *sphagia*, by the *stratēgós*,[58] the two opposing phalanxes would simply head straight for each other at a fast walk, pick up

---

50   Ar. *Vesp.* 1081–1085.
51   Polyain. 2.3.2, cf. 3.9.27, 4.3.8.
52   Xen. *Hell.* 6.4.14.
53   Xen. *Mem.* 3.1.18.
54   Hom. *Il.* 4.297–300 Lattimore.
55   Thuc. 4.43.3.
56   Xen. *Hell.* 4.4.12, cf. *Hipp.* 2.7–9.
57   Defined by the Greeks as 'those tokens of victory, which we set up are named from the turning and pursuit of the enemy' (*Etymologicum Magnum* s.v. Tropaion = Sage 151), the *tropaion* was quite literally a 'turning point marker'.
58   Hdt. 6.112.1, Thuc. 6.69.1–2, Xen. *Hell.* 4.2.20, 6.5.8.

the pace of the advance into a swinging stride, break into a dogtrot for the last few metres, collide with a crash and then, blinded by the dust and their own cumbersome helmets, stab and shove until one side cracked. At this juncture, we should note that the role of the *stratēgós*, who himself fought (and often perished) in the front rank of the phalanx, was 'nearly exhausted with the choosing of a battleground to suit the phalanx.'[59] Few armies, except the Spartan, as we shall discover, had the structure needed to allow major changes after the initial dispositions on a suitable battleground had been made. Once these were made, therefore, the *stratēgós* fought in battle, often in the most dangerous and therefore honourable section of the battleline.[60] Leadership was an amalgam of one-third tactical ability and two-thirds encouragement through example. As Euripides impertinently points out, 'the *stratēgós* / – one man one spear among those thousands.'[61]

The Experience

Violent death at the 'sharp end' is an awful, messy business at the best of times, and the Greeks, with a stygian sense of humour, called hand-to-hand combat the 'law of hands'.[62] The mêlée itself was a 'toe-to-toe, man to man' affair,[63] when you were close enough to see the foe's retina and the tone of his skin, with the front two ranks of opposing phalanxes attempting to stab their spears into the exposed parts of their foes so as to cause the most unpleasant wounds, that is, to the throat or groin, which lacked protection. Usually this was executed over arm, driven by the full force of the right arm and shoulder across the rim of the shield. Euripides puts this danger in a broad perspective when he has Medea say: 'I would rather stand three times behind a shield than give birth once': the gods had ordained pain in childbirth immutable.[64] Every man was a murderer, breath coming in short gasps, teeth set, hands clenched round the grips of his spear and shield, nerves and sinews alive with life. He neither hated his foe nor wanted him dead, but he feared him.

While the opposing front ranks, their faces wholly hidden by shields and helmets, tried to butcher each other with a primitive energy, the ranks behind would push. Picture this, if you will, once a hoplite was down, wounded or not, he was unlikely ever to get up again. This short but vicious mêlée was resolved once one side had practically collapsed.

---

59 Snodgrass 1967: 62.
60 For *stratēgós* who fell in mêlée, *vide*: Hdt. 7.224 (Leonidas and Dithyrambos at Thermopylai); Thuc. 1.63.3 (Kallias at Potidaia); *ibid*. 2.79.1, 7 (Xenophon, Hestiodoros, and Phanamachos at Spartolos); *ibid*. 3.109.1 (Eurylochos at Olpai); *ibid*. 4.44.2 (Lykophron at Solygeia); *ibid*. 101.2 (Hippokrates at Delion); *ibid*. 5.10.8–11 (Brasidas and Kleon at Amphipolis); *ibid*. 74.3 (Laches and Nikostratos at First Mantineia); Xen. *Hell*. 1.3.6 (Hippokrates at Chalkedon): *ibid*. 6.4.13 (Kleombrotos at Leūktra); Plut. *Pel*. 32.7 (Pelopidas at Kynoskephalai); Diod. 15.87.1 (Epameinondas at Second Mantineia). Note, the renowned Athenians Sokrates and Alkibiades served at Potidaia, as rank-and-file hoplites, and Alkibiades distinguished himself in this battle (Pl. *Symp*. 219–20).
61 Eur. *Andr*. 695–696.
62 Hdt. 8.89.1.
63 Eur. *Herakleid*. 836.
64 Eur. *Med*. 250–251.

Sometimes, it appears, fighting went on until both sides had virtually wiped each other out. At the Nemea (394 BCE), for instance, where the citizens of Pellene opposed those of Thespiai, they each fought and 'stood their ground and fell where they stood'.[65]

There was no pursuit by the victors, and those of the vanquished who were still on their feet fled the red field of battle as fast as they were able. It was enough, as the philosophers noted, every so often to kill a small portion of the enemy in an afternoon clash, crack his morale, and send him scurrying in defeat and shame whence he came. That was the ruthless truth of war, Greek style.

Close quarter fighting denied participants the ability to distance themselves from conflict the way people today can do merely by observing the brutal business of war from the safety of their electronic devices. It is hard for us to visualise the copper-tasting fear just before hard contact and the wild cruel joy of being alive afterwards. Ancient combat would have made a profound impact on those participating in it, involving stabbing, slashing, bludgeoning, and hitting the enemy directly. Even distance weapons like bows and slings had a relatively short range so that it was possible to see their terrible effects.

The Cost

War for the Greeks was by gender and definition men's work (even today it is mostly a male habit). This is because the quality of courage, bravery, or pugnacity that was required to stand fast in the hoplite phalanx was in their vocabulary ανδρεία, manliness. It was therefore, strictly speaking, impossible for a Greek woman to be brave in the relevant martial sense, that is to say, courageous on the red field of hoplite battle. Today this might come across as misogynistic, but the entire male baggage of war, in the pithy phrase of the visionary Herakleitos of Ephesos (*fl.* 500 BCE), was 'the father of all, the king of all'.[66]

Still, there was a human dimension to Greek warfare that is too easily overlooked. At this remove in space and time, the lives of thousands of citizen soldiers are not easily accessible to us. Yet some means must be found to grasp the human reality of the miniscule battlefields on which so many Greeks fought, suffered and died. The sanguinary warrior god of war may have spared far more men than he slaughtered, nevertheless even for the victors the sight of the wounded and near dead littering the battlefield offered one of war's most horrifying realities. Let us take a slice of Tyrtaios' war poetry as an indicator as to how gruesome hoplite warfare could be. In particular, look at his snapshot of a casualty, a senior citizen no less, trying to stave off death:

---

65   Xen. *Hell.* 4.2.20.
66   Herakleitos of Ephesos fr. 22B53 Diels-Kranz.

> Do not desert your elders, men with legs / no longer nimble, by recourse to flight: / it is disgraceful when an older man / falls in the front line while the young hold back, / with head already white, and grizzled beard, / gasping his valiant breath out in the dust / and clutching at his bloodied genitals, / his nakedness exposed: a shameful sight / and scandalous.[67]

To put this into context, this was the similar fate of one of Xenophon's comrades, the Arkadian mercenary Nikarchos.[68]

A spear thrust into the lower stomach and groin – a hoplite was usually unprotected in this region – was almost always fatal, converting a comrade into a corpse. Death would generally result from shock, peritonitis, or other local infections, as the contents of the intestines spilled out into the abdominal cavity and the victim suffered from blood and fluid loss. In the Hippocratic corpus we read of a man who suffered a javelin wound deep into the lower back, which resulted in peritonitis, an inflammation of the thin membrane lining the abdominal cavity. Though initially not painful, by the third day the patient was in severe agony and suffering constipation.[69] Twenty-four hours later, constantly vomiting and convulsing, the patient became dazed and dehydrated. He passed away, five days after the original wound.[70] William Shakespeare was surely right when he penned the line, 'I am afeard there are / few die well that die in battle.'[71]

Here it is worth us revisiting Second Koroneia and witness once again for ourselves the bloody aftermath of a hoplite battle through the keen eyes (and the lively stylus) of Xenophon:

> Now that the fighting was at an end, a weird spectacle met the eye, as one surveyed the scene of the conflict – the earth stained with blood, friend and foe lying dead side by side, shields smashed to pieces, spears snapped in two, swords [ἐγχειρίδια, literally 'dagger'] bared of their sheaths, some on the ground, some embedded in the bodies, some yet gripped by the hand.[72]

Tribal conflict, and that is what we are looking at here, can go beyond what we would like to recognise as conventional limits. It can move beyond control or logic, so that the combatants lost any sense of guidance on the field and rendered blind by dust and blood, became wholly lost to reason, deaf to the inner plea for survival, and in primal fury went about slaughtering one another without pause. They did just that on this battlefield; Spartan and Theban stood toe-to-toe and stabbed wildly with spear and sword, or locked

---

67 Tyrt. fr. 10.18–26 West. Despite legends such as that he was a lame schoolmaster from Athens (Paus. 4.15.6, cf. Pl. *Leg.* 1.629a-b), Tyrtaios was almost certainly a Spartan, and had probably seen the 'sharp end'. Certainly, he never glosses over the horrors of close-quarter combat (e.g. fr. 18–23).

68 Xen. *Anab.* 2.5.33.

69 Cf. Hom. *Il.* 13.656–8 Fagles: 'Meriones speared him / between the genitals and the navel – hideous wound, / the worst the god of battles deals to wretched men'.

70 Hippokrates *Epidemics* 5.61, cf. 7.33.

71 Shakespeare, *Henry V* 4.1.126–127.

72 Xen. *Ages.* 2.14.

Attic grave stele (New York, Metropolitan Museum of Art, inv. 40.11.23), Pentelic marble, dated *c.* 390 BCE. This depicts an Athenian hoplite astride his adversary, a Spartan hoplite. The latter figure wears a *pilos* helmet and, having lost shield and spear, defends himself with an extremely short sword. Judging from his neatly trimmed beard, he may be an enrolled helot who been promised his freedom.

By the Peloponnesian War Spartan swords had become exceedingly short, more like daggers in fact, as is clear from the representational evidence depicting Spartan hoplites such as this one.

The sword was probably shortened to make it handier in the crush that ensued when two phalanxes collided, the up-close and personal style of combat the Spartans excelled at. Note the Athenian is wearing an *exōmis* but no body armour. (Metropolitan Museum of Art/Wikimedia Commons/CC0 1.0 Universal Public Domain Dedication)

arms and legs and teeth in total combat, prepared to hold on to one another until death.

Like Xenophon, Menander, acknowledged master of the genre of New Comedy, once saw fit to describe the disfigured remains of a battlefield, which included the blackened, bloated bodies that had been left to rot in the blistering sun for some three days.[73] An unending table of human corpses, fat feasts for carrion crows, and nourishment for a field. Or as the turbulent and fierce soldier (mercenary?)[74] poet Archilochos of Paros once

---

73   Menander *Aspis* 71, 109.

74   Archilochos was a split creature, part poet, part soldier, and his biographical tradition is built to a great extent around his own poetry. In the extant fragments the poet talks a great deal about the life of a soldier, if not a mercenary. 'And I shall be called a soldier of fortune like a Carian' (Archil. fr. 24 Edmonds, cf. Lassere fr. 27, Davenport fr. 169, Swift fr. 216). There are

sang in the aftermath of battle: 'I expect that fierce Sirius [the Dog Star] will dry up many of them as he shines.'[75] Napoléon himself was so moved by the carnage left on one of his many killing fields that he scribbled the following lines in a missive: 'The countryside is covered with dead and wounded. This is not the pleasant part of war. One suffers, and the soul is oppressed to see so many sufferers'.[76]

In the gruesome aftermath of hoplite combat, the wounded receive little attention in the Greek sources. Battle scars, such a source of pride in many warlike societies, hardly get a mention. 'A man who can cut out shafts and dress our wounds– / a good healer is worth a troop of other men', sings Homer.[77] 'Healers are working over them, using all their drugs, / trying to bind the wounds–', the bard continues elsewhere.[78] But only two men in the entire Greek army stuck outside Troy were specialist healers, Podalirios and Makhaon, both sons of Asklepios.[79] More or less the same situation prevailed in our period of study, most Greek armies lacked any sort of medical service, the Spartan army was the exception with its physicians attached to the king's staff.[80]

These physicians, who performed battlefield surgery as an empirical medical science even though procedures were accompanied by prayers and magic, were equipped with bags of medicinal herbs: hellebore, foxglove, euphorbia, sorrel, marjoram, and pine resin. They had compresses of linen,

---

many proverbial sayings in Greek which speak of the Karian as one of no value: 'For, as the proverb has it, the experiment should be made 'on the worthless Karian' not on the *stratēgós*' (Polyb. 10.32.11). Cheap to hire, paid by the month in the field, and dispose of them as needed in warfare, that was the role of the Karian. Ephoros of Kymē (*FGrHist* 70 F12, cf. scholiast on Pl. *Lach.* 187b), who wrote in the fourth century BCE, believed that the Karians were the first foreign mercenary fighters to serve for payment; they certainly make an appearance as such in the Bible (*Karī*: 2 Samuel 20:23, 1 Kings 1:38, 2 Kings 11:4, 19, Isaiah 22:5–7, cf. Hom. *Il.* 2.867 Lattimore). Non-Hellenic Karia had a wide reputation as a supplier of hoplite mercenaries (Hdt. 2.152, 163, 3.11, 5.111, Diod. 1.66.12, Strab. 14.2.28, Ael. *NA* 12.30, Plut. *Mor.* 302A) who hired themselves out to go in harm's way, so risking their necks for the sake of others by doing their 'dirty work' for them. So, if this is Archilochos' self-identity, then it needs two explanations. First, the noun ἐπίκουρος (*epíkouros*) in this early period were mercenaries, soldiers of fortune, and as such not only foreigners to the ethnocentric Greeks, but also hirelings. In Attic Greek (Thuc. 1.115.4, 2.33.1, 3.18.1, 34.2, 6.55.3, 8.25.2, Xen. *Hell.* 7.1.12, 23), alternatively, an *epíkouros* is a mercenary soldier as opposed to a citizen-soldier (Gk. πολίτης / *polítēs*) of a *polis*. Here we can add the more specialised term of δορυφόροι (*doruphóroi*), the hired bodyguard of hoplites that protected a Greek military tyrant or a Persian satrap (Hdt. 1.59, 64, 6.39, Xen. *Hieron* 5.3, cf. Thuc. 6.58.2). *Vide* Fields 1994: 106–8.

75 Archil. fr. 107 Swift. Sirius is associated with the scorching 'dog days' of summer, and the idea that it can dry out human flesh is found elsewhere (e.g. Hes. *Op.* 587–588).

76 *Correspondance de Napoléon Ier* [Paris, 1857–70], vol. XIV, no. 11813, a letter he wrote to Josephine after his pyrrhic victory at Eylau (8 février 1807). Apparently, after viewing the dreadful butchery left on the field of Eylau, with tears in his eyes he was overheard to mutter: 'What a massacre! And for what result? A spectacle well formed to inspire to inspire princess with a love of peace, the horror of war... A father who loses his children finds no charm in victory. When the heart speaks, even glory has no more charm in victory'. As *Maréchal* Ney described it in a hard-hitting idiom when he rode over the killing ground the following day: '*Quel massacre! Et sans resultat*' (source: Raymond de Montesquiou-Fézensac, *Souvenirs militaires de 1804 à 1814* (Paris, 1863), p.149.

77 Hom. *Il.* 11.606–607 Fagles.

78 *Ibid.* 16.31–32 Fagles.

79 *Ibid.* 2.834, 11.771, 995 Fagles.

80 Xen. *Lak. pol.* 13.7.

bronze 'dogs' to heat and jam into puncture wounds to cauterise the flesh, and 'irons' to do the same for surface lacerations. The medical treatment that a Spartan soldier might expect for his wounds and illnesses was rudimentary but by no means nonexistent. As for the other Greeks, with their militia armies, we can assume that wounded soldiers were either carried by their comrades, walked if they were ambulatory, or were left on the battlefield to await their painful deaths. Those with flesh wounds, simple fractures or concussions would have had a good chance of survival so long as infection could be avoided.

There is a famous illustration by the Sosias Painter on the tondo of a red-figure *kylix* from Vulci, dated *c.* 500 BCE,[81] which depicts Achilles binding the wounds of his comrade Patroklos, which suggests soldiers could care for each other if the injury was not too serious or life threatening. And then there is this from the *Iliad*:

> Pounding in his palms, he crushed a bitter root / and covered over the gash to
> kill his comrade's pain, / a cure that fought off every kind of pain… / and the
> wound dried and the flowing blood stopped.[82]

This may have been an onion, which is bactericidal, or *Achillea millefolium* (soldier's woundwort), or *Aristolochia clematitis* (birthwort), an herb used for the relief of birth-pangs. But the more seriously injured, with deep penetration wounds or severe blows to the head, especially where internal bleeding was involved, could not expect to survive. This applied to the Spartans as well, despite the rudimentary medical services provided by their professional army.

Playing by the Rules

According to Euripides, 'It is with the gods' help that wise / *stratēgoi* launch an attack, / never against their wishes.'[83] As an Athenian citizen who fought, the playwright was mindful of the fact that hoplite battles had a strong ritual character; the idea was to defeat rather than to annihilate. So, forget strategy and tactics. Hoplites fought a set piece battle on the flattest piece of terrain and physically pushed the opposition from the pitch, a point clearly made by Mardonios, son of the veteran general Gobryas and Dareios' sister, in a speech to his cousin Xerxes:

> The Greeks are pugnacious enough, and start fights on the spur of the moment
> without sense or judgement to justify them. When they declare war on each
> other, they go off together to the smoothest and flattest piece of ground they can
> find, and have their battle on it.[84]

---

81   Displayed in Berlin, Antikenmuseen, inv. F 2278.
82   Hom. *Il.* 11.1012–1015 Fagles.
83   Eur. *Erechtheios* fr. 352 Nauck.
84   Hdt. 7.9β.1.

As a polished Persian panjandrum, it was easy for Mardonios to believe that the Greeks pursued their unique style of warfare out of ignorance and stupidity, but what he says is incontrovertible. It was easy to laugh at people who collided head-to-head, but on the other hand it was not easy to defeat people who were willing to collide head-to-head. As it turned out, Mardonios was soon to suffer most directly from its effects, losing both his life and his army in the process.

Living as we do in a world inured to the routine obscenities of early twenty-first-century warfare, we may ask ourselves why did the hoplite-style of head-to-head open-terrain fighting last so long. For a start, the fighting was taking place on the hoplites' own ancestral fields, and the Greek people had a special affinity with the soil of their native land. In addition, as time passed, the system was maintained for the sake of tradition, shared values and social prejudice. Hoplite warfare was for prestige rather than for the survival of a *polis*. Sparta, whose citizens were acknowledged as the past masters of this style of warfare, was an exception to the rule – its hoplites were permanent and essential rather than occasional and ritual.

The aim of most hoplite warfare was not the destruction of the enemy but the winning of the possession of the field of battle. Indeed, there were implicit rules of engagement, the 'common customs', for Greeks fighting Greeks. These fixed and well-understood rules include the following:

1. War declared before hostilities.
2. Hostilities sometimes inappropriate (e.g. religious festivals).
3. Certain places are protected, and some persons (e.g. shrines, heralds).
4. Battlefield trophies are respected.
5. The return of the dead once hostilities have ceased.
6. Non-combatants not a legitimate target.
7. Fight in the proper season, *viz.* during the summer months.
8. In the span of a single day, the issue that precipitated the conflict to be decided.
9. A limited pursuit of defeated and retreating foes.

These rules did not apply to 'barbarians', non-Greek speakers, and they would break down during the Peloponnesian War,[85] a war unprecedented in scale, in duration, and in acts of unnecessary barbarity.[86] As Thucydides himself says, about the war he lived through: 'This was the greatest disturbance in the history of the Hellenes, affecting also a large part of non-Hellenic world, and indeed, I might almost say, the whole of mankind.'[87] Of course, Thucydides' claim directly challenges Homer (Trojan War) and Herodotos (Persian Wars).

The hoplites went into battle not for fear of punishment or in hopes of plunder and booty. The hoplites were the citizens of *poleis* who owned property – commonly farmsteads – and held certain political rights. They fought to defend their liberties and home and hearth. In the stench, filth, and

85 See especially, Krentz 2002.
86 Thuc. 1.50.1, 2.90.5, 3.50.1, 5.32.1, 116.4, 7.29.3–5, 87.3.
87 *Ibid.* 1.1.2.

gore of battle, they fought side by side with neighbours, brothers, fathers, sons, uncles and cousins. This meant that they did their utmost to demonstrate courage and self-confidence, side by side with their citizen comrades and that they had a vested interest in the outcome – they stood to lose everything. This was the unseen glue that bound the phalanx, and the *polis*, together. Moreover, being, in the main, farmers, meant citizens were available for military service only during the slack agricultural period between the grain harvest in May and the vintage in September, or the ploughing in November at the latest.

Hoplite battle was brutal and personal; it came like a summer hailstorm that mowed down a field of grain, and then was over for a year. Armed and armoured hoplites advanced in their phalanxes and fought to the death, pressed forward by those behind them into the anonymous strangers in that part of the enemy phalanx facing them. Their battlefields were scenes of furious fighting and carnage that usually consumed not more than an hour or two. Every man was pushed to the limits of his physical and psychological endurance – and then it was over, not to be repeated for a year or more.

Shifting the Tactical Calculus

Of the 'Great War' between Athens and Sparta something may be said here. The Peloponnesian War began not with a formal declaration of war but with a sneak attack by a few hundred Thebans. These men managed to infiltrate into Plataia in the murk of a cloudy winter's night aided by a group of oligarchic traitors from within. Plataia, the main Boiotian *polis* south of the river Asōpós, always looked towards Athens and its democracy: the connection went back to 519 BCE when Kleomenes I of Sparta told the Plataians to attach themselves to Athens.[88] Their close and long-enduring relationship with the Athenians earned the Plataians at a later time the title of 'Athenian Boiotians'.[89] Like Athens, but unlike Thebes, Plataia (along with Thespiai) refused to give earth and water (*viz.* tokens of submission) to the envoys of Xerxes.[90]

The Theban-backed oligarchic *coup d'état* against democratic Plataia failed, and the survivors of the infiltration were all rounded up and, without a trial, immediately put to death. Everything must have a beginning but, by the traditional touchstones of hoplite warfare, the opening event of war was not the done thing, and it indicated the kind of conflict the war would be. Both sides were pitiless, and there were death and cruel deeds by light and dark. It was a war waged to excess, with every means available. In peaceful and prosperous times both people and nations behave reasonably because

---

88 Hdt. 6.108. Kleomenes was unique in the fact that he understood that the world was much larger than the Peloponnese, which meant he was happy to interfere beyond the peninsula, while he also understood that Sparta was to avoid overreach.

89 Ἀθηναῖοι Βοιωτοί: Pseudo-Dikaiarkhos, *Description of Greece*, p.102. At the siege of Syracuse, true to the loyalty they had displayed at Marathon, Artemision, and Plataia, the Plataians were the only Boiotians fighting on the Athenian side (Thuc. 7.57.5).

90 Hdt. 7.132, cf. 8.66. It was the Persian Wars that the worst public blot fell upon the Theban name.

The inscribed Attic stele (Eleusis, Museum of Archaeology, inv. 5101) of Pythodoros, son of Epizelos, from the period of the great war between Athens and Sparta (431–404 BCE). Pythodoros served as *hipparchos*, cavalry commander at Athens, was one of the Athenian commissioners of the Peace of Nikias in 421 BCE (Thuc. 5.19.2, 24.1), and a *stratēgós* in the Argolid in the summer of 414 BCE (*ibid.* 6.105.2). In two zones, the stele depicts Athenian horsemen riding down Spartan hoplites. Sparta was justly famed for its professional hoplites, but not so for its amateur horsemen. The crack Spartan formation known as the *hippeís* ('horsemen'), despite their title, fought on foot, was an elite body of 300 handpicked men under the age of 30 who served as a battlefield guard to the Spartan kings. (©Nic Fields)

the tissue of material well-being and security that separate civilisation from brutal savagery has not been torn away and people reduced to brutal necessity. 'But war,' says Thucydides, 'which takes away the comfortable provisions of daily life, is a violent schoolmaster and tends to assimilate men's character to their condition.'[91]

One tragic incident will suffice to illustrate this allegation. Thracian peltasts, according to Thucydides, were deployed for the first time in 425 BCE by the Athenians at Pylos, on the west coast of Messenia.[92] Twelve years later, as the Athenians gathered reinforcements for their floundering armada in Sicily, 1,300 Thracian peltasts arrived in Athens too late to sail with the relief force headed for Syracuse under the *stratēgós* Demosthenes.[93] As the Athenians had no wish to incur unnecessary expenditure, they were sent packing. But to get some value from the homeward bound peltasts, they appointed another of their own *stratēgoi*, Diitrephes, and 'as they were to sail through the Eupiros, he was instructed to use them in doing whatever damage he could to the enemy on their voyage along the coastline.'[94] The knife carrying, fox-skinned Thracians had a wicked reputation for violence not always connected with events; they followed a rugged tribal code known as the 'Three Alls' – exterminate all, incinerate all, demolish all. Anyway, these particular Thracians were first used against Tanagra in a quick raid, and then against Mykalessos, both situated in Boiotia and whose inhabitants were defenceless. One morning at daybreak, the latter town was captured and what followed was one of the worst atrocities of the Peloponnesian War. The cat-footed Thracians: '…butchered the inhabitants sparing neither the

---

91 Thuc. 3.82.2.
92 *Ibid.* 4.28.4.
93 *Ibid.* 7.27.1, cf. Ar. *Lys.* 563.
94 Thuc. 7.29.1.

young nor the old, but methodically killing everyone they met, women and children alike, and even farm animals and every living thing they saw.'[95]

They then crowned their aimless exploits, to the horror of Greece and of the soldier historian who tells the tale, by storming a boys' school, 'the largest in the place, into which the children had just entered and killed every one of them.'[96] Certainly, the ethics of war was not a subject these murderous Thracians dwelt on, but Mykalessos was the shape of wars to come.

The Thracians may have added a new element of brutality to Greek warfare, but war, or the threat of it, is a constant theme in most of the plays of the contemporary Euripides. His tragedy, the *Suppliants*, produced at Athens within a year after its shattering defeat at Delion (424 BCE), was prompted by the barbaric Theban treatment of the Athenians left for dead on the battlefield.[97] This was obviously no escapist theatre where the audience were encouraged to leave their brains at home, and Euripides was noted for his ability to put in the mouths of his characters thinly veiled denunciations of crimes against humanity committed in the name of patriotism by those who might be sitting in the audience.[98]

Like his fellow citizen Thucydides (the two must have known one another), Euripides tossed away the glamorous views of war. Sometimes the dead were soldiers, and other times the dead were children: all were tragic and wasteful. The length and ferocity of this 'worldwide' struggle would transform warfare from a seasonal activity to one in which at least low-level conflict lasted throughout the traditionally inactive winter months. Low-level conflict was in fact characteristic of most of the war, on the Athenian side, including seaborne raids on the Peloponnese where fire and sword were visited upon it. Only two set pieces of hoplite warfare were ever played out – single battles on single days – Delion and First Mantineia.

During the Peloponnesian War, such battles may have been rare. Up to that point, the Greeks conformed to what has been labelled by Victor Davis Hanson the 'Western Way of War', a shadowy thesis that western civilisation has accepted the concept of an open, decisive battle without its ancient Greek corollary of 'battle by mutual consent'. Whether or not this was exclusively a Greek legacy, as Hanson assumes, hoplite battle was a head-to-head collision of citizen soldiers on an open plain in a magnificent display of demonic courage, physical prowess, virile honour, and fair play. There had been no interest in decoys, ambushes, sneak attacks, petty skirmishes or clever feints – the flashy manoeuvring we tend to associate with western military doctrine, although the attack that is heavy, clumsy, and in front is certainly not a thing of the past. Nor was there the involvement of non-combatants. There was also no honour

---

95   *Ibid.* 7.29.4.
96   *Ibid.* 7.29.5.
97   *Ibid.* 4.97–99. Few ancient battles were more renowned in antiquity than Delion, chiefly because Sokrates fought in it as a hoplite – he was to distinguish himself in the flight of the Athenian survivors – and Alkibiades, reputedly his young lover at the time, with the cavalry (Pl. *Symp.* 220e.7–221c.1, Plut. *Alk.* 4).
98   Eur. *Supp.* 522–527: 'I d not set war in motion / nor did I invade the land of Kadmos with these me. / But I judge it right to bury these lifeless corpses, / I bring no harm to your *polis* nor do I bring it man-destroying strife, / but I simply follow the custom of all Greeks. Where is the wrong in this?'

for the Greeks in fighting from afar. An archer or a javelineer who launched his weapon from a great distance was not held in high esteem because he could kill with little risk to himself. Only those who clashed with spear and shield, defying death and disdaining retreat, were deemed honourable.

Thucydides, like Herodotos before him, regularly describes stratagems. Herodotean examples, however, invariably involved 'barbarians' not Greeks, such as Kŷros' use of camels in order to throw Kroesos' cavalry horses into disorder.[99] Thucydidean examples are Greek and include the unwilling self-selection of helots for secret liquidation, probably down at the narrow promontory of Akrōtērion Taínaron,[100] and the bellows-powered flamethrower deployed by the Boiotians after their victory at Delion.[101] Indeed, devices to secure victory with minimum loss were highly esteemed by the Spartans. According to Plutarch, when the Spartans won by stratagem they sacrificed a bull to Ares; when in open battle a rooster; the distinction being intended to make *stratēgoi* not only warlike but also fit for command.[102] Plutarch also reports Agesilaos as saying that, while it is impious to wrong the other party to a treaty, it is sweet and profitable to mislead the enemy.[103] This was an attitude which Perikles in his Funeral Oration affects to scorn: 'This is because we [the Athenians] rely, not on secrete weapons, but on our own real courage and loyalty.'[104]

Similarly, Euripides offers his Athenian theatre audience a negative view of military deception with his classic denunciation of Spartan cunning.[105] On the other hand, there was one Athenian in favour, namely the pro-Spartan practical soldier of fortune, Xenophon. In one passage he recommends the constant practice of deception as appropriate to the situation:

> [F]or there is really nothing that offers so great a gain in war than deception… If one were to review the successes that have been won in warfare, one would find that the most numerous and the most important of them have come about with the help of deception.[106]

---

99 Hdt. 1.80.
100 Thuc. 4.80.3–4, cf. 1.128.1, Paus. 4.24.5, 7.25.3, 'the curse of Taínaron'. Pausanias says at Taínaron 'is a temple like a cave, with a statue of Poseidon in front of it. Some of the Greek poets state that Herakles brought up the hound of Hell [Kerberos] here, though there is no road that leads underground through the cave' (3.25.5, cf. 2.31.2, 9.34.5). Kerberos was, of course, the many-headed dog that guarded Hades – Hesiod calls him 'fifty-headed' (*Th.* 311), while Euripides (*HF* 24, 611) is satisfied with just three. As its fortunes waned, Sparta increased its stake in the international business of supplying mercenaries. So much so, that by the end of the fourth century BCE, Taínaron – the southernmost tip of Lakonia, ideally situated for sea traffic both east and west – became a flourishing international mercenary mart and served as such during the internecine wars of Alexander's Successors (Arrianus *Anabasis* 2.13.6, Diod. 17.108.6–7, 111.1–3, 18.9.1–3, 21.1, 20.104.2, cf. 14.44.2, 16.62.3, 19.57.5, 60.1). With its dead grey rocks, Taínaron was a naturally strong position: via land it could only be approached via Spartan controlled territory, plus it sat conveniently upon a narrow, rugged promontory. In a sense, Sparta perfected the technique of raising mercenaries in Lakonia and disowning them in Asia.
101 Thuc. 4.100.2–4.
102 Plut. *Mor.* 238F.25.
103 *Ibid.* 209A-B.11.
104 Thuc. 2.39.1.
105 Eur. *Andr.* 445–462.
106 Xen. *Hipp.* 5.9–11.

Elsewhere the author offers a précis on the theoretical justification and practical recommendations of military trickery in which success is said to require: '… a man who can plot, conceal his intentions, trick, deceive, steal, and snatch and be ready to take advantage of the enemy in every way.'[107]

In a pre-battle speech Thucydides puts into the mouth of Brasidas prior to the engagement outside Amphipolis (422 BCE) with the Athenians under Kleon, the Spartan commander justifies to his Peloponnesian allies the need for deception in warfare:

> It is, according to my calculations, because they [the Athenians] despise us and because they have no idea that anyone will come out [of Amphipolis] to fight them that the enemy have come up to the position in which they are and are now looking carelessly about them in no sort of order. But success goes to the man who sees more clearly when the enemy is making mistakes like this and who, making the most of his own forces, does not attack on obvious and recognised lines, but in the way that best suits the actual situation. And it is by these unorthodox methods that one wins the greatest glory; they completely deceive the enemy, and are of the greatest possible service to one's own side.[108]

The size of the two armies at this stage was about the same, but the Athenians were of a better quality; an assessment that Brasidas shared. As Thucydides says, his army's qualitative inferiority made Brasidas decide on military deception.

Brasidas' chance came when Kleon, who had never planned to fight a pitched battle without reinforcements, gave orders to retreat from Amphipolis. Thucydides' words are: '…he personally began to lead away the right wing, making it wheel round, and so exposing its unarmed side to the enemy'.[109]

Brasidas ordered 'the first gate in the long wall' to be opened and led his men at the double, his sudden attack falling on men already in confusion.[110] The hoplite's fear for his unshielded right side is described by Thucydides in his account of the drawing-up of the battle lines at First Mantineia (418 BCE).[111] About 600 Athenians were killed, Kleon included, 'but of their adversaries only seven'.[112] Among the latter was Brasidas, who was carried from the field still breathing, living long enough to hear he had won his final battle.[113] The Spartans had lost an outstanding commander and the Athenians a matchless opponent.

---

107 Xen. *Kúr.* 1.6.27.

108 Thuc. 5.9.4–5.

109 *Ibid.* 5.10.4.

110 *Ibid.* 5.10.6, cf. Diod. 12.74.1–2, who has Kleon advancing on Amphipolis and Brasidas coming out to meet him; the issue is decided by a large-scale, regular pitched battle, closely fought.

111 Thuc. 5.71.1.

112 *Ibid.* 5.11.2.

113 *Ibid.* 5.10.11. For an in-depth discussion on Brasidas' military actions at Amphipolis, see especially Howie 2012: 327–352.

Chapter 2

The Road to Leūktra

In times of peace and prosperity *poleis* and individuals alike follow higher standards, because they are not forced into a situation that they have to do what they do not want to do. But war is a stern teacher; in depriving them of the power of easily satisfying their daily wants, it brings most people's minds down to the level of their actual circumstances.

Thucydides 3.82.2

Ancient Greece was not a monolithic state in the modern sense, but a patchwork of competing city-states, *poleis*. The *polis* that we all know as Sparta lay in the northern part of the Eurotas valley in the region of the southeast Peloponnese called Lakedaimon.[1] The valley is still well watered and productive, but relatively narrow and broken by small hills and ridges. Homer, who chronicled the second fall of Troy, called the wealthy and fertile domain of Menelaos, king of Sparta, 'Lakedaimon's hollows deep with gorges'.[2] Certainly, the epithet was well chosen as a description of the valley, set as it is between the steep mountain barriers of Párnon (1,934 metres at its peak, Megáli Túrla) to the east, and of Taïygettos (2,404 metres at its peak, Profítis Ilías) to the west. Both these rugged mountain ranges run unbroken more or less north-south down two of the three prongs of land that terminate the Peloponnese, the first to tempestuous Akrōtērion Maléas, the second to the tip of gloomy Akrōtērion Taínaron, which is better known to the Anglophone world as Cape Matapan.[3]

'The *polis* was neither consolidated nor does it possess lavish temples and buildings, but consists of village settlements in the old Greek way.'[4] This

---

1   Laconia, in fact, was not a name in use among the ancient Greeks: it is a Latin coinage, appearing first in the works of elder Pliny (6.34.39, 17.18.30, cf. 25.8.53). From Laconia, of course, we get the adjective laconic. Lakedaimon, a son of Zeus and Taygétē, one of seven Pleiádes, was the eponymous king of Lakedaimon, which he renamed Σπάρτα in honour of his wife (and niece), Sparta (Paus. 3.1.2).

2   Hom. *Il.* 2.673 Fagles.

3   It was off this cape that a combined Royal Navy and Royal Australian Navy fleet under Admiral Sir Andrew Cunningham fought a successful engagement against an Italian Regia Marina fleet on the evening/night of 28 March 1941: the *Littorio*-class battleship *Vittorio Vento* was damaged; the *Zara*-class heavy cruisers *Pola* and *Fiume* sunk; the *Zara*-class heavy cruiser *Zara* crippled and finished off.

4   Thuc. 1.10.2.

The fertile Eurotas valley, looking northwest from the late eight-century BCE structure known as the Μενελάειον (sanctuary of Menelaos and Helen), some 5km to the southeast of modern Sparta, situated close to what was known in antiquity as Therapne (Hdt. 6.61.3, Polyb. 5.14.21, Paus. 1.35.1, 2.11.7, 3.9, 3.19.9). These Greek writers emphasise the fact that this dysfunctional couple were worshipped, along with Helen's divine brothers the Dioskouri, not as heroes but as gods. Sparta traces its origins in a group of village settlements dotted along the banks of the river Eurotas in the southeastern Peloponnese. It grew by subjugating or enslaving its

immediate neighbours in Lakedaimon, who thus became *perioikoi* (literally 'those who live about'), personally free but without citizen rights and subject to Spartan control, or helots (literally 'captives of war'), standing somewhere between serfdom and slavery. The Eurotas can be seen as the dried-up riverbed running from bottom left to centre of the photograph. (©Nic Fields)

View looking north across modern Sparta (founded 1834, following the Greek War of Independence). The slight, wooded rise on the edge of the modern town, seen here in the middle background, once served as the akropolis of ancient Sparta. The Athenian soldier historian Thucydides rightly said: 'For if the *polis* of the Spartans should be deserted, and nothing should be left of it but its temples and the foundations of its other buildings, posterity would, I think, after a long lapse of time, be very loath to believe that their power was as great as their renown' (1.10.2). Most Greek *poleis* possessed an akropolis, a walled citadel stoutly occupying an elevated position, which gave refuge to the populace in time of war, and which enshrined the temple of the presiding deity (e.g. Athena at Athens). The Spartan akropolis did not by any means conform to the usual type. (©Nic Fields)

description by Thucydides at the time of the Peloponnesian War is borne out by such archaeological evidence as can be gained from an area where a modern town occupies much of the original site. Even the location of the agora is not known. So, Sparta itself was never amalgamated as a *polis*,[5] the political process the Greeks called *synoikismós*, literally 'dwelling together (συν) in the same house (οἴκος)', but remained just an odd conglomerate of four un-walled village settlements (Pitana, Limnae, Mesoa, and Kynosoura),[6] known as *ōbaí*, with a fifth *ōbá* (Amyklai) having been added on at a later date, perhaps during the eighth century BCE. Its citizens were no fans of walls made of bricks and stone, boasting that they needed no fortification walls.[7] Certainly, its remoteness allowed Sparta to remain without an encircling wall until the second century BCE. Naturally, being Spartans, they affected to regard fortification walls as effeminate, and they were proud to rely purely on the masculine strength of their own militarily superb bodies for their self-defence. It was not an idle claim, as you shall hear anon.

Make War, not Peace

Before the Peloponnesian War, Sparta had been largely a status-quo power – unquestionably brutal in maintaining order at home, but generally conservative in expanding its alliances and responding to Athenian impingement. It began the Peloponnesian War with the mission 'to liberate Hellas',[8] which meant the destruction of the Athenian empire and the liberation of the *poleis* it ruled. The words had, of course, to be judged against Sparta's actions.

To state the obvious: the Peloponnesian War ushered in a style of politics where truth was, at best, an inconvenience: truth was not a value in itself, but a subset of power. Fast forward three decades, and Sparta batters Athens into submission, tearing down its walls 'to the music of flute girls'.[9] Mission

---

5   The *polis* was the characteristic form of Greek urban life. Its main features were small size, political autonomy, social homogeneity, and a real sense of community and respect for law. The *polis* was always defined in terms of its members (e.g. the Athenians not Athens, the Spartans not Sparta), rather than geographically or by way of 'bricks and mortar'. Here we witness the fundamental conception of man as subordinate to the main focus of the *polis*, which was broadly politically. The *polis* was, in essence, a 'guild of warriors' (hoplites), in which the military power of the community controlled the political and institutional life (*viz.* magistracies, council, and assembly): in the words of Aristotle, 'man by nature is a political animal' (*zoon politikon: Pol.* 1252b.29–30). As an agrarian based society, the *polis* controlled and exploited a territory (*chōra*), which was delimited geographically by mountains or sea, or by proximity to another *polis*. Border wars were thus common, as were inter-*polis* agreements and attempts to establish religious rights over disputed areas. Autonomy was jealously guarded, but the necessities of collaboration made for a proliferation of foreign alliances, leagues, and hegemonies – a treaty between two *poleis* did not end the basic enmity between them, but their common interest at the time was greater than their differences. There was also constant interchange and competition between *poleis*, so that despite their separate identities a common culture was always maintained.

6   Paus. 3.16.9, cf. Strab. 8.5.3.

7   For example, Plut. *Mor.* 210B.29, 30, 217E.7.

8   Thuc. 2.8.4, cf. 1.139.3: 'give the Hellenes their freedom'.

9   Xen. *Hell.* 2.2.23.

accomplished, Sparta now happily elbowed the truth aside and helped itself to the revenues that came to it from the maritime states of the Aegean archipelago.[10] 'To liberate Hellas' was a neat little slogan, a classic of the genre that packed nothing but a world of lies in three words, and the emptiness of this war cry of liberty was visibly demonstrated when a victorious Sparta slipped neatly into the imperialistic role wrested from Athens.[11]

That may have been sure enough, but the new shoes were a size larger than those which Sparta comfortably and usually fitted. On this dilemma the cerebral Aristotle gave the proper verdict:

> The charge which Plato brings, in the *Leges* [1.630], against the intention of the legislator, is likewise justified; the whole [Spartan] constitution has regard to one virtue only – the virtue of the soldier, which gives victory in war. And so long as they were at war, their power was preserved, but when they had attained empire they fell, for of the arts of peace they knew nothing, and had never engaged in any employment higher than war.[12]

The very completeness of that victory caused Sparta serious constitutional problems. According to Herman Kahn (1922–83), Cold War military strategist and highbrow futurist,[13] the natural tendency of an empire is to expand, and there is no limit to that expansion save running up against another empire of equal or greater strength. There have been exceptions to that rule; the most notable in our period of study being Sparta post-Peloponnesian War. Having 'liberated' (a word that was to do some heavy lifting in Spartan politics) the Greeks only to bring them more fully into subjection, the Spartans found that their state lacked the political, administrative, ideological, and economic machinery for running such a widespread empire. Profoundly conservative, the Spartans were stuck mentally in the era in which they had conquered their neighbour Messenia and turned its erstwhile citizens into helots some three centuries before.

So psychologically, the Spartans lacked the makeup to be successful empire builders. The occasional episodes of stick-wielding Spartans in our literary sources say it all. In 411 BCE, at the height of the naval war against Athens, a Spartan by the name of Astyokhos was nearly lynched when he raised his walking stick, the Spartan *baktēriōn*, against Dorieus, a high-ranking Rhodian exile who was speaking up for his own men – sailors who were owed arrears of pay, 'free men' as Thucydides is at pains to point out.[14] Again, after Athens was defeated, the Spartan governor, *harmostēs*, Kallibios holds sway from the sacred heights of the Athenian Akropolis. This arrogant brute raised his *baktēriōn* to strike Autolykos, an Athenian wrestler, but the

10 Diod. 14.10.1–2.
11 According to Thucydides, the planning of Sparta's imperial ambitions can be dated to 413 BCE after the Athenians' disaster in Sicily, for the Spartans believed that 'when the power of Athens had been destroyed, they themselves would be left secure in the leadership of all Hellas' (8.2.4).
12 Arist. *Pol.* 1271b.34.
13 Herman Kahn was one of the historical inspirations for the eponymous character of Stanley Kubrick's *Dr Strangelove* (1964), a black comedy satirising the Cold War.
14 Thuc. 8.84.2. Incidentally, this is the only occurrence of the word βακτηριᾱ in Thucydides.

champion threw Kallibios to the ground. His boss, Lysandros, showed no sympathy with Kallibios' rage at this unseemly behaviour, but reprimanded him and said, 'you do not know how to govern free men.'[15] Like his fellow Spartan Astyokhos, Kallibios had made the mistake of treating free Greeks as if they were helots. This unedifying behaviour against those they were supposed to liberate partly explains why Spartan liberation was both a sham and stillborn in practice.

To tell the truth, the Spartans acted with their habitual cold-blooded craft, and their empire was doomed from the outset. They too extracted tribute, imposed governments and garrisons, and maintained a navy,[16] but whereas the Athenians' empire had been conceived and largely maintained as anti-Persian and pro-democratic, the version hammered out by the Spartans was a dictatorship that did not even pretend to be a democracy. Anti-democratic and pro-despotic, they unashamedly showed how hollow their talk of liberation had been. As Aristotle mused, the Spartans, bred in the *agōgē* and trained up in the arts of war, failed as imperialist because 'like unused iron they lose their edge in time of peace.'[17] To be successful, it required the leopard to change its spots.[18] The post-Peloponnesian War 'peace' was a semi-frozen conflict pending renewed war.

Changing Enemies

It is no surprise that great power rivals fear losing their friends while being keen to acquire new ones. During the Peloponnesian War (431–404 BCE), Thebes had been one of the most active and persistent of the opponents of Athens, but later it joined Athens, Corinth, and Argos to overthrow the Spartan domination of Greece. Nine years on, the Corinthian War (395–387/386 BCE) turned the Greek world upside down again. The war was evidently brought about through the exploitation of Theban and Corinthian fears over Sparta. Athens, who had no care for Sparta, naturally sought for an excuse to escape the shameful settlement enforced upon it by the Spartan victory of 404 BCE. This came with a caveat: 'to follow Sparta by land and sea.'[19]

---

15 Plut. *Lys.* 15.7. Xenophon makes Autolykos the principle character in his *Symposium*. Sadly, as Plutarch tells us in the same passage, the Thirty Tyrants 'soon afterwards put Autolykos to death, to please Kallibios'. As a boy, in 422 BCE, Autolykos had won the *pankration* at the Greater Panathenaia of that year, the festival in honour of Athens' patron deity Athena, which was held quadrennially and open to all Greeks. The *pankration* was not for the fainthearted, for it not only involved wrestling-style holds, but punching, kicking, choking, finger breaking, and blows to the genitals were allowed too, only biting and eye gouging being prohibited. Bouts continued until one athlete gave up or was incapacitated. Stories tell of deaths and even a posthumous victory: before he died in a stranglehold, the *pankratiast* Arrhikhion is said to have broken his opponent's toe, forcing him to give up (Paus. 8.40.1–2).

16 Diod. 14.10.2.

17 Arist. *Pol.* 1334a.22.

18 As Napoléon explained: 'Peace is a marriage that depends on a union of wills' (*Correspondance de Napoléon Ier* [Paris, 1857–70], vol. XV, no.12408, p.91, to the King of Naples, Finkenstein, 18 avril 1807.

19 Xen. *Hell.* 2.2.20, cf. 3.1.4, 3.2.21–23.

force of 10,000 men.'[48] He continues, implying that because the allies were hesitant to provide their quota of men, Sparta decided to allow those who wished to substitute money, at a rate of three Aiginetan (four Attic) *oboloí* for each hoplite, or four times that amount for each horseman.[49] Presumably, although he does not say it outright (he calls this money μισθός, 'wages'), this money allowed Sparta to hire mercenaries.

Despotism, if it seeks to regulate what men think and say, expects them to say and think things that are pleasing to it. It is an authoritarian system where everyone defers to the boss out of cowardice and fear. The despotism of Sparta was the swan song of its greatness. It was during this Spartan pinnacle of success that the recovery of Boiotia begins. By 378 BCE, renewed tensions between Thebes exploded in another war. This time, as we shall discover, Sparta was decisively defeated and, although no one knew it at the time, was about to be reduced to the status of a second-rate power.

The Persian Factor

A small country, if we can call ancient Greece such, which survives under the shadow of a heavyweight champion, becomes quite naturally suspicious, sensitive, and fiercely jealous regarding its neighbour. It fears them, but cannot help imitating them, and being drawn to them. Invariably, the larger inevitably attracts the smaller. And from its position of superiority, it is natural that Persia would tend to overlook its tiny neighbour, and take Greece very much for granted. Indeed, to Persia, Greece was an appendage. Yet it must not be thought from this that the Persians underrated the Greeks. Far from it. They may have forgotten or ignored Greece from time to time, but when the Greeks came to their attention, they reserved a higher respect than they showed to anyone else. They recognised the Greeks as formidable, and were secretly just a little frightened of them, especially so after the disastrous events of Xerxes' grand adventure in the Greek homeland. So, the Persian factor in the fourth century BCE should not be seen as a struggle between an imperialist aggressor and a smaller nation fighting for its sovereignty.

---

48 Xen. *Hell.* 5.2.20.
49 *Ibid.* 5.2.21. By way of a comparison, the Thracian peltasts hired by Athens in 414 BCE who were considered too expensive a luxury to be kept for the war in Attica: 'they received a *drakhmē* a day each' (Thuc. 7.27.2). Indeed, Aristophanes' 'two *drakhmae* a day Thracians' was probably a joke directed against the lavish expenditure of Athenians on military pay (*Ach.*159–61). According to Xenophon, the standard rate of pay (μισθός) for the Ten Thousand was either one Daric or one Cyzicene per month per soldier (both were worth 25 Attic *drakhmae*), and this wage was reckoned from the first of each month and paid at the end of that month (Xen. *Anab.* 1.2.11–12, 3.21, 5.6.23, 31, 7.6.1, 7, 2.36, 3.10). Therefore, each hoplite was technically receiving five Attic *oboloí* per diem, there being six Attic *oboloí* to the Attic *drakhmē*. The *lochagoí* and *stratēgoi*, on the other hand, received double and quadruple the standard rate respectively 'as was customary' (*ibid.* 7.3.10, cf. 3.1.37). As for the fourth century BCE, Griffith (1984: 308) assumes this was the epoch of the 'four-*oboloí* recruit' (τετρωβόλου βίος) as mentioned by the Attic dramatist Menandros (*Perikeiroménē* 261–3, 273, *Olynthia* fr. 357 Kock), which is very much like the eighteenth century notion of hiring soldiers for *cinq ou six sous*, a common theme in the letters and works of Voltaire.

After 479 BCE, Persia, now cautious and time-serving, thought it wise to change its policy towards Greece, basing itself consistently on the time-honoured principle of 'divide and rule'. It is needless to go into the intricate complications of Graeco-Persian affairs, suffice to say that Greek leaders were learning that the same policy could be easily applied to the Persians themselves. The prime exemplum was of course the Ten Thousand, the Greek mercenaries (the Athenian military adventurer Xenophon included)[50] who had supported the rival claims of Kŷros the Younger (†401 BCE) to the Achaemenid Persian throne on the death of his father, Darios II Ochos (r. 424–405/404 BCE).[51] There is evidence to suggest that Sparta, now free from its preoccupation of the previous three decades, namely its titanic tussle against Athens, unofficially backed and aided the pretender's rebellion against his elder brother, Artaxerxes II.[52] This was certainly done in return for the gold Persia had paid for Sparta's victory over its Greek superpower rival in 404 BCE.[53]

Kŷros in fact was calling in a debt owed to him by Sparta. For Sparta, while posing as a liberator of the Greeks from Athenian tyranny, had been obliged to rely on generous monetary handouts from Persia, and the man most responsible for securing and channelling this vital Persian gold into Sparta's hollow war chest had been none other than Kŷros himself.[54] According to Andokides, the Persian treasury gave the Spartans no less than 5,000 talents for the war against Athens.[55] Furthermore, it is highly likely that the Spartans knew the actual motive for Kŷros' recruitment of hoplite mercenaries, that is to say, they would be used to unseat Artaxerxes, in accordance with the ancient and famous principle of displacing the superior to make room for the inferior. Indeed, if Diodoros Sikoulos is to be believed, Kŷros' whole operation had the full blessing of the *éphoroi*, who were shrewdly 'concealing their purpose, waiting the turn of the war'.[56] On the one hand, Sparta was merely abiding by the biblical maxim not to let the left hand know what the

---

50 The subject of his splendid *Anabasis*, where he weaves together his personal and professional experiences.

51 Kŷros the Younger was the second son of Dareios and Parysatis. Passed over the succession on his father's death, he nevertheless claimed by right of *porphyrogenitos* instead of primogeniture, for, unlike his elder brother, Artaxerxes, he had been 'born in the purple' (Ktesias *FGrHist* 688F15).

52 E.g. Xen. *Hell*. 3.1.1.

53 *Ibid*. 3.1.1.

54 Thuc. 2.65.12, Xen. *Hell*. 1.4.2–3, 5.3–7, 2.1.14, 3.8.

55 Andok. 3.29. The laws of Lykourgos did not permit coins. The closest things to coins were iron spits; even a fistful of such did not get you very far and did not buy very much. The idea was to discourage Spartans from accumulating portable wealth. This very much reminds us of that argument of Adam Smith, '[D]efence… is of much more importance than opulence', and praises the virtue of the soldier who is willing to defend his country at the cost of sacrificing his life (source: Adam Smith, *Wealth of Nations* [London, 1776], IV.ii.30). One of the giants of the Scottish Enlightenment, was the political economist and social philosopher thinking of Sparta when he penned this? Possibly.

56 Diod. 14.21.2, cf. Just. 5.11.6–7. See also Xen. *Hell*. 3.1.1, where Kŷros had asked the Spartans to 'show themselves as good friends as he was to them in the war against Athens'; Isok. 5.104, 8.98, where the pamphleteer reckons that Sparta sanctioned Klearkhos' command of the Ten Thousand officially; and Plut. *Artax*. 6.3, where the biography says that the *éphoroi* ordered Klearkhos to give Kŷros 'every assistance'.

right was doing. Equally, Kŷros was acting as a proxy to advance Sparta's own political-military interests abroad. And so, Sparta's shrewdness extended as far as giving the prince pretender military aid in the form of 700 hoplite mercenaries under the command of Kheirisophos, a *Spartiātēs*, and the *naúarchos*, Pythagoras, was ordered up with 35 *triērēis*.[57]

The anonymous author of the *Hellenika Oxyrhynchia*, on the other hand, claims that the Corinthian War was not the result of Persian money, with which it was bribing the enemies of Sparta, but of the internal politics of Greek states.[58] This could be true, but the mission of Demainetos would have reminded individuals from Athens, Corinth, Thebes, and Argos that others thought similarly as they did. Again, such a mission would also have reminded them that Persia was also a potential enemy of Sparta. Moreover, we must remember that the internal politics of these *poleis* did revolve around pro- and anti-Spartan factions, especially in Athens and Thebes.

Finally, the cause of the Corinthian War, much like any other human conflict throughout history, involved a certain amount of bluff. To adduce but two examples out of many, take Hitler and his unprovoked attack on Poland in September 1939. Britain and France had already swallowed his excuses for attacking Czechoslovakia in the previous year, so why not those offered for Poland as well. Indeed, a combination of satanic violence and astute bluffing had won for Hitler victory after victory destroying the new states of post-Versailles Europe: first Austria, then Czechoslovakia, and now Poland. Equally, accustomed to Spartan over caution, during the 460s BCE Athens fancied that it would get away with attacking Sparta's allies without Sparta responding militarily. Although Sparta, as an oligarchy, was firmly opposed to democratic governance on principle, Athens knew it eschewed ideological crusades.

Athens found out its mistake, and the conclusion was, of course, the first Peloponnesian War (461–446 BCE). Again, in 432 BCE who would have thought that Sparta would be forced into war over Korkyra, a *polis* on the periphery of the Greek world. In this respect it is worth looking at the Spartan ultimatum to the Athenians; there is no mention of Korkyra whatsoever, the Spartan envoys simply state that 'Sparta wants peace. Peace is still possible if you will give the Hellenes their freedom',[59] (giving people their freedom, where have you heard that infuriating nebulous concept before?). As we all learn sooner than expected in our lives, there is seldom such a thing as outright settlement in human affairs; there are adjustment and compromise, and a semblance or promise of solution, but at best all that can be hoped is life will go on without too much disturbance, and immediate crises are avoided. Unfortunately for the Greek world, as it was drawn into conflict on one side or the other, it was not to be this time around.

---

57 Xen. *Anab.* 1.2.21, 4.2, 3.
58 *Hell. Oxy.* 6–7.
59 Thuc. 1.139.3, cf. Hdt. 6.11.2, 8.143.1, where the Hellenes *do* fight for the freedom of Hellas.

Chapter 3

Kleombrotos, King of Sparta

[T]he king's might is greater than human, and his arm is long

Herodotos 8.140β.2

Sparta was unique in its retention of the kingship as a living force; unique also in the institution of double kingship, that is, the Spartans had not one but two kings. Indeed, the most peculiar fact about the Spartan state was its dual kingship, a phenomenon that has never been satisfactorily explained. As Moses Finlay wrote: 'The one phenomenon which remains a complete puzzle [in Sparta] is the survival of kinship, worse still, of a dual kingship. I have no explanation to put forward, but I will suggest that "survival" may not be the precisely correct term.'[1]

Riddle or not, every royal line has to start somewhere, and that of Sparta was no exception. Whereas most dynasties have a propensity to start with merciless pirates, or fortunate soldiers, or barbarian invaders, Herodotos claims that the two royal families of Agiadai and Eurypontidai shared a common ancestor, both of them proud to trace their lineage back to the demigod Herakles (whom we shall meet anon).[2] The Spartan king, says Thucydides (in the singular, but it was true of both), is 'the seed of the demigod son of Zeus'.[3] Zeus being not just a god, but king of the gods, ruler of Olympus.

With the invasion of the sons of Herakles, the Herakleidai, and the elimination of the Atreids – the house of the warrior kings Agamemnon and Menelaos, which had held the sceptre of Zeus – the Herakleidai were the last Greek dynasty that could claim power by devolution from the Olympian supreme ruler. In ancient Greece there was no sharp line drawn between the secular and the sacred as in our own society. The displeasure of the gods was not to be risked. So, Zeus was not a figure to be acknowledged as and when the worshipper needed, but a living, breathing fixture in your *polis*, who breathed down your neck as you made your oaths, his itchy trigger

---

1   Moses Finley, *Economy and Society in Ancient Greece* (London, 1981), p.39.
2   Hdt. 6.52.
3   Thuc. 5.16.2, cf. Tyrt. fr. 2.4 West: 'Zeus, gave the sons of Herakles this state'.

finger tapping against his thunderbolt. More to the point, all things, Sparta included, begin and end with Zeus.

A less fanciful modern suggestion is that the two kings stem from a time when there were two tribes, each headed by a tribal chieftain. Eventually, these tribes combined, and the two chieftains shared the leadership. We have in Pausanias an interesting story about the quarrel that arose between pairs of *ōbaí*, the four villages originally constituting Sparta. The story, of course, may be no more than hearsay, but he suggests that Pitana and Mesoa paired off against Kynosoura and Limnae, the rivalry resulted in bloodshed but was solved through ritualising the feud at the shrine of Artemis Orthía (Upright Artemis).[4]

Anyway, peculiar or not, if the principal function of the old Greek kings, much like those found in Homer, were those of a war leader, chief representative of the people before the gods, and magistrate, then the Spartan kings fulfilled all these functions, but especially that of a war leader. The other organs of rule in the Spartan polity where the *éphoroi* (chief magistrates), the *gerousía* (council of elders), and the *apélla* (citizen assembly). The most extensive description of the rights and duties of the Spartan kings is given by Herodotos. He tells us that both kings shared equal powers, privileges and duties – so that one could not act against the power and political enactments of his colleague – and were the commanders-in-chief of the army for life.[5] In other words, Sparta's dual kingship was a form of hereditary but non-monarchic military leadership, what Aristotle describes as 'a sort of plenipotentiary generalship (*stratēgia*), irresponsible and perpetual'.[6]

Ergo, on military campaigns, the kings take command. They lead on the march, issue the orders of the day, decide the place of encampment, and (in principle) battle. Needless to say, in battle they risked their life in the forefront of the phalanx,[7] which may explain why the kings were occasionally called *hēgemōnes*, leaders.[8] The strategists in war, the kings' judicial powers were also total in this context: they held court on all matters of dispute, booty,[9]

---

4   Paus. 3.16.9. Ὀρθία: with reference to the phallus, or because her statue stood erect.

5   Hdt. 6.56–59.

6   Arist. *Pol.* 1285a.4. The rule that only one king should accompany an army was established after the fiasco of Demaratos' jealous disagreement with Kleomenes during the invasion of Attica in 506 BCE, thus reversing earlier practice (Hdt. 5.75.2). Perhaps the Spartans came to realise that too many kings, like too many cooks, may spoil the feast. As Napoléon would later explain to Carnot during the first Italian campaign (1796), 'One bad general would be better than two good ones', an opinion he reiterated almost verbatim on Sainte-Hélène (*Correspondance de Napoléon Ier* [Paris, 1857–1870], vol. 1, no.421, to Carnot, 14 mai 1796, *ibid.* vol. XXIX, no.107, 'Oeuvres de Sainte-Hélène, Campaigne d'Italie'). Anyway, Kleomenes eventually got the better of his co-king Demaratos, whose disposition he contrived with the aid of the Delphic oracle. Shortly before Xerxes' invasion Demaratos went over to the Persians and accompanied Xerxes to Greece. He must have been an acute embarrassment to Sparta, but in Herodotos' narrative he always remains a dignified figure, faithful at heart to his old motherland Sparta, but loyal to his new master Xerxes.

7   Both in the *Hellenika* (4.3.19) and the *Agesilaos* (2.12–13), for instance, Xenophon (an eyewitness) reports that Agesilaos was severely wounded at Second Koroneia during the *mêlée* with the Thebans.

8   Xen. *Lak. pol.* 11.9, cf. 13.6.

9   Spartan kings customarily (according to Phylarkhos) claimed one-third of the booty (*apud* Polyb. 2.62.1).

and so forth, arising on campaigns. As Aristotle points out, though a king did not possess 'the power of life and death' at home, it was a very different matter when he was on campaign: Aristotle makes a neat Homeric analogy at this point, saying: 'For Agamemnon is patient when he is attacked in the assembly, but when the army goes out to battle, he has the power even of life and death. Does he not say? – "When I find a man skulking from the battle, nothing shall save him from the dogs and vultures, for in my hands is death".'[10] The fact that Spartan discipline permitted rank-and-file criticism of a commander's tactical decisions during battle, however, merits note.[11]

Although they were not above censure, we should not lose sight of the simple fact that individual kings were very powerful figures in their day through the force of their personality. In a society devoted to the art of war and so duteous of warrior-like prowess, a king with a good record of success in war would gain great glory and would be the focal point of his fellow warriors' esteem. What is more, the Spartans firmly believed that the blood of the gods ran through their kings' veins. Kings such as Kleomenes I and Agesilaos II, for instance, could and did transcend the Aristotelian notion that they were mere hereditary *stratēgoi* for life.

Kleombrotos (r. 380–371 BCE) was of the Agiadai, becoming king after the untimely death of his brother Agesipolis,[12] who died without issue.[13] Very little is known about the personality of the king; we have just one anecdote from Plutarch with reference to Kleombrotos: 'When some stranger was arguing about virtue with his father, Kleombrotos son of Pausanias [Agiadai king, 408–395 BCE] said, "My father will always be superior to you – until you have had sons".'[14]

Kleombrotos himself had two sons, and both became kings: Agesipolis II (r. 371–370 BCE),[15] and Kleomenes II (r. 370–309 BCE).[16] As the Spartans were notorious for the 'secrecy with which their affairs are conducted',[17] it could explain the relative silence of literary sources on Kleombrotos.

This we do know. Some seven years prior to Leūktra, in the midwinter of 379/378 BCE, when news of the uprising at Thebes reached Sparta, Kleombrotos was dispatched to Boiotia at the head of an army.[18] He crossed Mount Kithairon by destroying a small force of Thebans guarding the pass near Plataia but then encamped at the Kynoskephalai hills south-west of Thebes. After spending 16 days in Theban territory without engaging the

---

10 Arist. *Pol.* 1285a.4–5, paraphrasing Hom. *Il.* 2.391–3 Lattimore: 'But any man whom I find trying, apart from the battle, / to hang back by the curved ships, for him no longer / will there be any means to escape the dogs and the vultures'.

11 Thuc. 5.65.2 (Agis II at First Mantineia), Xen. *Hell.* 4.2.22 (unnamed *polémarchos* at the Nemea River).

12 Diod. 15.23.2, Plut. *Ages.* 24.2, Xen. *Hell.* 5.3.19.

13 Plut. *Agis* 3.3.

14 Plut. *Mor.* 223A.

15 Diod. 15.60.4, Paus. 3.6.1.

16 Diod. 20.29.1, cf. 15.60.4.

17 Thuc. 5.68.2.

18 Apparently Agesilaos avoided taking command, pleading old age: he was by now over 60 years of age. Actually, Xenophon (*Hell.* 5.4.13) says he feared incurring blame from his fellow citizens if he campaigned on behalf of 'tyrants', namely those ousted Thebans who had supported Sparta.

Thebans, the king then returned home, leaving Sphodrias, one of his friends, as *harmostēs* at Thespiai.[19] Although his show of strength in Boiotia panicked the Athenians, who put on trial the two *stratēgoi* who had aided the liberators of Thebes, executing one and exiling the other,[20] his lacklustre conduct earned Kleombrotos disapprobation back home.

In the late spring of 378 BCE, another army under his fellow king Agesilaos was dispatched to deal with the Thebans. Sphodrias' harebrained attempt to capture the Peiraieus in a surprise night march from Thespiai had propelled the Athenians back into an alliance with the Thebans. His actions were as self-defeating as they were brainless. For, on arriving in Boiotia, Agesilaos found himself facing the Athenians as well as the Thebans and their Boiotian supporters. However, the allies prudently refused to meet the Spartans in open battle, instead digging trenches and throwing up stockades outside Thebes, which they manned, preventing the Spartans advancing on the *polis*. For the next two summers, Agesilaos laid waste to the countryside, but eventually departed, leaving the newly liberated Thebes independent.[21]

In 376 BCE, on account of the illness of Agesilaos – a vein in his leg had ruptured – the command was restored to Kleombrotos, who then again achieved nothing, but returned to Sparta following a slight repulse at the hands of the Thebans and Athenians in the passes of Mount Kithairon.[22] Once more the king faced censure, and not long afterwards a congress of the Peloponnesian League was convened at Sparta. It was decided to prosecute the war by sea, the Athenians having organised a naval alliance, commonly called the Second Athenian Confederacy,[23] against Sparta. The Athenians were to gain victories at Naxos (376 BCE) and at Alyzeia (375 BCE).[24]

In the spring of 374 BCE, Kleombrotos was sent across the Gulf of Corinth into Phokis, which had been invaded by the Thebans, who, however, retreated into Boiotia on his approach.[25] He was to remain in Phokis until the spring of 371 BCE, the year of Leūktra.

---

19 Xen. *Hell.* 5.4.14–18, Diod. 15.27.1–3, 29.5–6, Plut. *Ages.* 24.1.
20 Xen. *Hell.* 5.4.19, 22, Plut. *Pelop.* 14.1.
21 Xen. *Hell.* 5.4.35–55, Diod. 15.34.1–34.2, Plut. *Ages.* 26, *Pel.* 15.
22 Xen. *Hell.* 5.4.58–59.
23 *Vide* Harding 35 for the charter of the Second Athenian Confederacy drawn up in the spring of 377 BCE.
24 Xen. *Hell.* 5.4.60–66.
25 *Ibid.* 6.1.1, 2.1.

Chapter 4

Epameinondas, *boiōtarchēs* of Thebes

> I cannot lack offspring; for I leave as my daughter the battle of Leūktra; which
> is certain, not only to survive me, but even to be immortal.
>
> Epameinondas to Pelopidas, Nepos *Epaminondas* 10.2

Epameinondas is remembered – if he is remembered at all – only for the crushing blow he had struck at Leūktra. Now, for the sake of completeness, there was more to Epameinondas' heavily stacked phalanx. Some of his activities were relatively orthodox in an oligarchic way. But it is difficult to get beyond his triumph on the field of Leūktra. True, he had no ordinary talent for war – well, at least the Greek style of war – but he was also the dominate figure of his age in the judgement of both contemporaries and of posterity.

Strategy, of course, comes from the word the Greeks used for their generals, *stratēgós*. A *stratēgós* was not solely concerned with winning battles – the tactics. He was, in the later words of Clausewitz, concerned with the use of battle to further the political ends of his *polis*. In other words, the *stratēgós* had to keep the long-term goal in mind and ensure that the tactics worked to further that goal. For this reason, Epameinondas crafted the Theban army into a force to be reckoned with. In this regard, he was an innovator who defied the tactical convention of the times, though whether this was the stuff of genius or simply one of necessity is a matter for conjecture. Thinking outside the box, his signature tactic was to mass his best hoplites to unusual depths under his own leadership on the left wing as opposed to the right, the traditional position of honour (and decision) in battle.

Plutarch has told us that for the first four decades of Epameinondas' life he lived in relative obscurity.[1] In fact, little is known of his life before Leūktra, other than formal philosophical schooling and his idealised friendship with Pelopidas. Diodoros Sikoulos informs us that Epameinondas was deeply

---

1   Plut. *Mor.* 1129C.

at the time of its disastrous war with the Aiolian League (245 BCE), Polybios mulls over its decline:

> The Boiotians had long been in a very depressed state, which offered a strong contrast to the former prosperity and reputation of their country. They had acquired great glory as well as great material prosperity at the time of the battle of Leūktra; but by some means or another from that time forward they steadily diminished both the one and the other.[22]

Without the guiding hand of Epameinondas, Thebes was to squander its limited manpower resources fighting the protracted, bitter, and useless Third Sacred War (356–346 BCE).[23] The importance of this decade-long war against the Phokians can hardly be exaggerated, for it was what brought Philip II of Macedon into Greece proper in the first instance. Since Sparta's *hegemonia* was long gone, the Athenian empire a dim memory, and Thebes currently moribund, neither of these exhausted states was in a position to challenge Philip and his 'new model' army. As a hostage of Thebes during his formative years (367–364 BCE), Philip had been exposed to the innovations of Epameinondas: profiting from his lessons, Philip 'quick to appreciate the Theban efficiency in the art of war and generalship'.[24]

Although we have unhappily lost Plutarch's *Epameinondas*, and presumably he would have written favourably of his fellow Boiotian, Ioannes Tzetzes (†1180), Byzantine poet and grammarian, performed a great service to classicists by preserving much valuable information from a range of classical literary, mythological, and historical subjects. The most influential of his many works is *Chiliades* ('Thousands'), 12,674 lines of political verse. This he has to say concerning Epameinondas:

> Epameinondas, who was a Theban general,
> Was the most incorruptible of all free souled men.
> When someone once brought him money,
> Not only did Epameinondas refuse, but said:
> 'Find a crook-footed cripple, or one driven out of his mind,
> And such a bribe would befit him.
> But it can never befit Epameinondas, general of the Thebans'.
> This general once noticed a household soldier
> Demanding gold from a prisoner.
> He immediately expelled his own soldier.
> And told him: 'Give me my own shield back,
> And as for you, go buy yourself a merchant's stall'.[25]

---

22 Polyb. 20.4.1–2, cf. Strab. 9.2.5: 'From that time on they [the Thebans in 316 BCE|] have gradually declined to our own day [*viz*. the reign of Augustus], and Thebes now does not have the character of a noteworthy village'.

23 Diod. 16.23–60.

24 Plut. *Pel.* 26.3, cf. Diod. 15.67.4.

25 Ioannes Tzetzes, *Chiliades* 10.46.

To come to still earlier times, there is this curious little gem from a work of late antiquity (third to fourth century CE) called *Parallela Minora*, falsely attributed to Plutarch but now known not to have been written by him:

> Epameinondas, the Theban general, when he was waging war against the Spartans, returned home at the season of the elections, giving orders to his son Stesimbrotos not to engage the enemy. But the Spartans learned of Epameinondas' absence and taunted the youth with lack of manliness. He became indignant and, forgetting his father's command, engaged the enemy and conquered. But his father being deeply offended, crowned the youth [*viz.* with a victory wreath] and cut off his head. This Ktesiphon relates in the third book of *Boiotian History*.[26]

Ktesiphon was a fourth century BCE Athenian orator, the one for whom Aischines, the arch-rival of Demosthenes, wrote his work *Against Ktesiphon* (330 BCE). Otherwise, he is unknown. As for Epameinondas having a son, well as far as we know that was not the case. Did not Epameinondas explain to Pelopidas (the two were justly celebrated for their friendship), as quoted above, 'I cannot lack offspring; for I leave as my daughter the battle of Leūktra'?[27]

---

26   Pseudo-Plutarch, *Parallela Minora* 12.1.

27   Nep. *Epam.* 10.2. Ioannes Tzetzes repeats this boast of Epameinondas with an addendum: 'Thebans, I do not die childless, but blessed with children / Because I leave behind my two daughters / The victory at Leūktra and the one in Mantineia' (*Chiliades* 12.16). Pelopidas of course had fallen in 364 BCE, two years prior to Second Mantineia.

Plate A: A Noontime Nip

(Illustration by Renato Dalmaso© Helion & Company 2025) See Colour Plate Commentaries for further information.

Plate B: Arming for Battle

(Illustration by Renato Dalmaso© Helion & Company 2025) See Colour Plate Commentaries for further information.

Plate C: Head-to-Head, Toe-to-Toe

(Illustration by Renato Dalmaso© Helion & Company 2025) See Colour Plate Commentaries for further information.

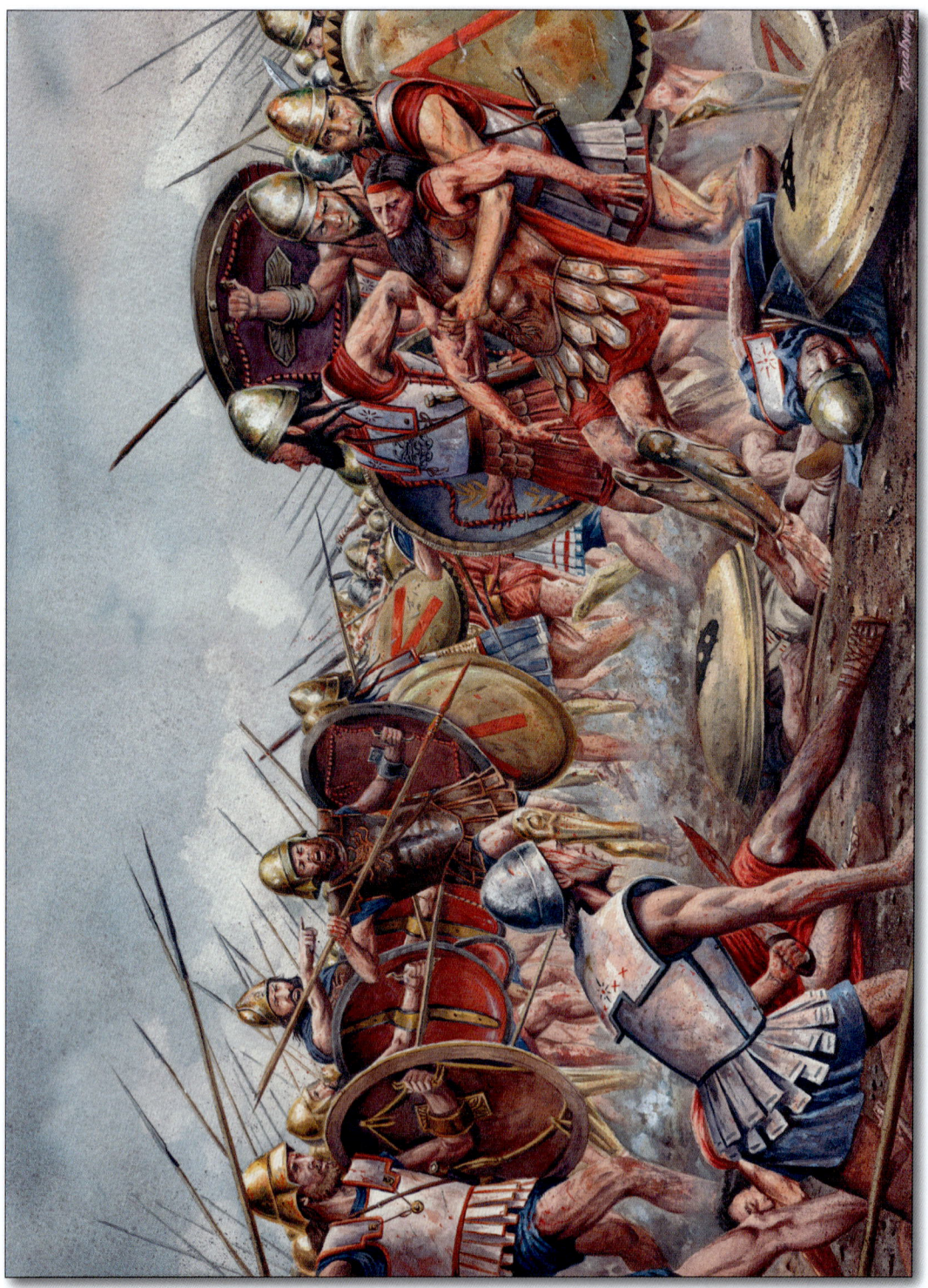

Plate D: The Death of a King

(Illustration by Renato Dalmaso© Helion & Company 2025) See Colour Plate Commentaries for further information.

Chapter 5

The Spartan Army

In short, all orders are required to pass in the same way and quickly reach the troops; as almost the whole Spartan army, save for a small part, consists of officers under officers, and the care of what is to be done falls upon many.

Thucydides 5.66.4

It should come as little surprise to those with knowledge of Spartan affairs that the Spartan army does not appear to have suffered any significant defeat in pitched battle between the disastrous engagement against the Tegeans, which took place some time early in the sixth century BCE,[1] and Leūktra in the summer of 371 BCE,[2] the subject of this monograph. It is clear the Greeks themselves were well aware of the main reason for the innate superiority of Spartan hoplites – what Thucydides calls, in one illuminating passage, their 'practised skill' or 'experience'.[3] It was under Perikles that Athens would become a cultural showpiece, and elsewhere Thucydides, whose account of the Peloponnesian War (431–404 BCE) contains a treasure trove of detail about the nature of warfare, has Perikles compare the Athenians and their opponents, the Spartans. More precisely, the Athenian wartime statesman contrasts their differing conceptions of child rearing, publicly sneering at the laborious system employed in Sparta to train its boys.[4] This conclusion is coloured by an understandable dislike of Sparta, and so it does not constitute a sober and subjective analysis. Herodotos, who produced the first historical analysis of the Persian Wars (492–449 BCE), comes nearer to the truth when he describes the Spartans as 'men who understood war' and the Persians, just by way of a contrast, as 'lacking in professional skill'.[5]

Unlike most Athenians, who thought the Spartans a pretty dreadful lot, Xenophon (†354 BCE), an Athenian historian and former mercenary who speaks as an eyewitness and enthusiastic admirer of all things Spartan,

---

1   Hdt. 1.66.
2   Xen. *Hell.* 6.4.8–15.
3   Thuc. 4.33.2.
4   *Ibid.* 2.39.1, cf. Xen. *Mem.* 3.5.15.
5   Hdt. 7.211.3, 9.63.2, cf. 7.107.

Early sixth century BCE terracotta metope (Sparta, Museum of Archaeology) depicting Spartan hoplites. Every picture tells a story. A *Spartiātēs*, all caparisoned for battle, slowly advancing to contact, spoke of reassuring discipline and obedience. But the blood-coloured tunic and oiled tresses, a terrifyingly beautiful sight in its own right, also evoked a more primitive world of hunting and death. In his right hand he held a spear, a well-loved object, big and sinister. Little wonder, therefore, the Spartan army was a complex fighting system, and so much more dangerous enemy than, let us say, the Athenians. Hard men. Dangerous men. The Spartans struck an excellent, grim fighting form in the field of battle, and knew well that they were the only hoplites in Greece who, when their phalanx was broken, could reform and fight just as well at the side of a stranger. They were trained to perform the commonplace under uncommon conditions and not for themselves alone, as Achilles or the solo champions of yore, but do it for one's brothers-in-arms. That was the Spartan way. (©Nic Fields)

Marble bust of Xenophon (Bergama, Arkeoloji Müzesi, inv. 784). Born into a well-to-do Athenian family, as a youth he served in the Athenian cavalry corps before abandoning his place of birth to seek fame and fortune by the spear. Having done so, he had little hesitation as to where to seek a career. As a soldier of fortune, he saw much rough service abroad with the Persians and the Spartans. Initially serving the younger Kŷros in the ranks of the Ten Thousand, feeling the need for new battlefields and a new paymaster to serve he later fought for Sparta under various Spartan bosses, including king Agesilaos. If he was anti-Athenian, he was by ill-chance anti-Boiotian too. But Xenophon never turned his spear against the democratic *polis* which had given him birth. In his *Anabasis*, which plays as a war diary, Xenophon writes with conviction and firsthand knowledge about the perils of life as a foreign mercenary. His *Hellenika*, on the other hand, is more problematical as a source. (©Nic Fields)

regarded the Spartans as 'the only true craftsmen in matters of war'.[6] Such is Xenophon's diagnosis of the key point in Spartan military professionalism, but it is left to Aristotle to put his finger on the heart of the matter. He explains that it is not so much the methods the Spartans used to train their young men that made them superior on the red field of battle, as the fact that they trained them at all.[7] It must be emphasised, however, that it was not the skill-at-arms of the individual Spartan that was important, as his training as part of a unit, for the simplicity of hoplite battle left little scope for the display of personal skills. Effectively, the specialised military training of Sparta probably took the form of 'square-bashing'. Nevertheless, it produced the right results, even for non-Spartans. To take just one example: in 381 BCE Agesilaos gave money and arms to the oligarchic *émigrés* from Phleious, a *polis* northwest of Argos, and instructed them to set up military messes along Spartan lines and whip themselves into shape: ergo, they were to train and equip themselves for war. Prudently, the exiled Phleiousians did so, and the outcome resulted in a large contingent of men 'in splendid condition of body, well disciplined, and extremely well armed'.[8] Now the Aristotelian truth had moved from the realm of philosophical hypothesis to that of common experience.

Our two principal literary sources for Spartan society are Xenophon's *Lakedaimoniōn politeia*, a contemporary albeit uncritical eulogy – he hated democracy and could therefore be biased – and Plutarch's *Lykourgos*, much of whose basis is the narrative of Xenophon into which has been fitted a plethora of antiquarian facts, some bona fide, others fabricated. From these two works we gather that the full citizens of Sparta, the *Spartiātai*, were wholly at the service of the state. In order to enable the *Spartiātēs* to overcome any mental impasse precipitated by man's natural fear of death, he had to be trained to think of himself as a man whose life was not his own. Hence, the *Spartiātēs* had to be always prepared for a sudden and violent end. This conditioning began in infancy.

The Making of a Spartan

At birth, the elders of the state, men over the age of 60 known as *gerontes*, decided on grounds of health if a newborn child should be reared, the grim alternative being exposure on a nearby mountainside. This was the terrible law of Sparta: no male child who was deformed, and so could not become a warrior, was allowed to live.[9] The boys who passed inspection were deliberately toughened from an early age, by bathing them in wine, feeding them with plain fare and getting them accustomed to harsh conditions.[10]

6   Xen. *Lak. pol.* 13.5.
7   Arist. *Pol.* 1338b.27–30, cf. Xen. *Hell.* 7.1.8, 10, 11, *Lak. Pol.* 11.7, 13.5, Plut. *Pel.* 23.3.
8   Xen. *Hell.* 5.3.17.
9   Plut. *Lyk.* 16.1.
10   Wine was reputed to induce convulsions in weak babies while tempering the strength of healthy ones.

In most societies, it is the parents' task to teach the rules of society to their children. The role of the child is to learn, or more commonly rebel against those rules. This was not the case in Sparta. Possibly from the age of seven years (Plutarch) and certainly from the age of 14 (Xenophon) there began a state-organised upbringing, the *agōgē* ('raising', as of cattle), aimed at preparing boys for their future role as warriors. The boys were organised into 'packs' (*agelai*, the same term that was used in Crete) under pack-leaders, whose orders the boys had to obey, which in turn were supervised closely by magistrates. An important magistrate, the *paidonomos* or Warden of the Boys, was appointed to take charge of the *agōgē*, and his authority over the boys was no less than that of a general over an army. He was assisted in the enforcement of discipline by citizens called Whip-bearers, and we may assume that this title was no empty one.[11]

Existing in the twilight zone of innocence and experience, the boys were brutally initiated into communal living, providing, for example, their bedding from reeds ripped up by their own hands from the banks of the shallow, sandy Eurotas. They were also prohibited everyday luxuries such as footwear, allowed only one cloak to wear throughout the year, and survived on a diet that was deliberately inadequate. The punitive logic of the latter hardship was clear. It promoted the stealing of food as an adventurous duty, to develop ingenuity in war, which in turn led to a retributive punishment if a boy was caught in the act: he was given a severe thrashing. Physical pain had to be endured without betraying the slightest emotion. The fate of these boys existed in that tension between rules and rule breaking.

Formal education was kept to a minimum, but did include music, gymnastics, and fierce games embracing what the Spartan viewed as the principles of warfare.[12] They were also 'taught to express themselves in a style, which was at once sharp, yet at the same time attractive and suited to concise exposition of a variety of points'.[13] By the fourth century BCE this spare style of speaking had acquired a name for itself, 'laconic'.[14]

Many definitions of the term education have been advanced by scholars, both past and present. All these definitions may be conveniently reduced to

---

11 The first real mention of the term *agōgē*, however, is by Polybios (1.32.1) when he talks of Xanthippos, the Spartan *condottiere* who aided Carthage during the early stages of the First Punic War (264-241 BCE). It is used, rather vaguely, in another (now lost) source, Demetrios of Skepsis, but the question remains, did he write before or after Polybios? We do know for certain that the term was not used by Herodotos, Thucydides, Xenophon or Aristotle, our principal sources for this period. Nonetheless, this should not unduly worry us because the *Lakedaimoniōn politeia*, which we attribute to Xenophon, mentions many of the elements equated with the training of Spartan boys.

12 Xen. *Lak. pol.* 2–3, Plut. *Lyk.* 16–18.

13 Plut. *Lyk.* 19.1.

14 Arist. *Rh.* 2.21.8. A good *exemplum* of the dry, biting wit of Spartans features Philip II of Macedon (r. 359–336 BCE), the father of Alexander the Great. After invading the Peloponnese and receiving the submission of other key *poleis*, he turned his baleful eye towards Sparta, which was no longer the power it once was, and asked menacingly whether he should come as a friend or a foe. The reply was 'Neither' (Plut. *Mor.* 233E). Never one to be patient or mince words, he sent a message, 'If I invade Lakonia, I shall turn you out'. The *éphoroi* wrote back with the single word 'If' (Plut. *De garr.* 17). The Spartans were, it must be said, masters of verbal combat along with the standard, sweaty, sanguine kind.

two major attitudes. The first is active and embraces all those definitions that refer to education as an intellectual search for and within new or expanding fields of knowledge. The second is passive and embraces all those definitions that consider education as training in the mastery of various skills. The former type of education (therefore, of knowledge) embraces the entire range or as many aspects as possible of humanity's reality, thus becoming an independent inquiry into the unanswered dilemma its reality proposes at almost every turn. The latter type of education concentrates mainly upon a few, supposedly known and established aspects of that existence which it reiterates and reconfirms. One reaches out into the unknown and in every possible direction, while the other revolves around the familiar and, therefore, moves in one direction alone. In this context, it will be understood that the *agōgē*, by its very nature and emphasis upon producing warriors who based their very existence upon the regularity and rigid discipline of military life, concentrated upon the second type of education, which it defined, quite conservatively, as the repetition of orderly and expected patterns of thought and behaviour, according to a precise sequence leaving little or no room for improvisation. Spartan education was the most thorough system in the Greek world, but it was designed to produce cogs for a machine.

And so it was, for the next 14 years (if we choose to follow Plutarch) of his life, that a boy worked his lonely way up through the increasingly brutal and brutalising pedagogy. In brief, it was an elementary education that was entirely determined for the purpose of inuring him to bear all manner of hardships indifferently, to despise the niceties of food and drink, to train him to endure an exacting discipline, to make his body an instrument as of forged iron, and to instil into his heart a sentiment of devotion to Sparta.

Failure, of course, meant utter disgrace, for it often entailed (in characteristically Spartan fashion) social ostracism. Even in his day, Thucydides could compare the easy living to be had by the Athenians to the laborious life of the Spartans 'from their very cradles'.[15] And, like most peoples in most ages, the Athenian assumed that a culture different from their own must be inferior. The militaristic Spartan in turn was equally prejudiced; proud of their own culture and heritage, they had no doubt that it was superior to that of the decadent, soft-living democratic Athenian. Indifferent to cold and toughened to scarcity, he proudly belonged to a military caste, in which the individual was rigidly subordinated to the *polis*. He was a soldier, and his education, marriage, and the details of his daily life were all strictly regulated with a view to the maintenance of professional military efficiency.

By way of a fitting finale to education Spartan-style, we can remark upon the fact that adolescent Spartan girls underwent an upbringing quite similar to the boys. The regime for girls was far less brutal, of course, but physical all the same being centred on dancing and gymnastics, the latter pursuit involving running, wrestling, javelin and discus throwing. They also mixed freely with boys and like them, according to Plutarch and depicted as such in the art of early Sparta, exercised either completely naked or partially nude in full public

---

15   Thuc. 2.39.1.

view.[16] Little wonder such disregard of the normal sexual inhibitions shocked outside observers. The derogatory epithet 'thigh-flashers' was coined just for them by one such tourist, although ultimately such 'exhibitionism' was done so as to attract suitors. The Athenian comic Aristophanes raised a laugh from his audience with a bawdy joke about gymnastic exercises practised by Spartan women, while his fellow, albeit more highbrow, dramatist Euripides readily condemns Spartan women for running around with 'bare thighs and loose clothing!'[17] The sexual powers of women could disturb the world of men, and Greek men outside of Sparta were clearly frightened of this, even if only subconsciously.

Big Units, Small Units

Although the literary evidence can be somewhat confusing at times, and when is it not, we must begin at the end and start with Xenophon, the contemporary historian who has provided us with the most information about the Spartan army and its tactical organisation. Presumably he was drawing upon his extensive experience of fighting alongside the Spartans, particularly in Asia under Thibron and Derkylidas (399–397 BCE),[18] and under the new king Agesilaos, to whom he became greatly devoted (396–394 BCE).[19] Xenophon's Spartan army was divided in six *mórai* (sg. *móra*),[20] and even though he does not mention the *pentekostyes*, he does imply of their existence when acknowledges that the Spartan officers who attended a conference outside Haliartos in 395 BCE,[21] or those in the plain of Lechaion in 390 BCE included the *pentekostēres*.[22] So, in Xenophon's Spartan army the *móra* was at least divided into *pentekostyes*.

This now leads to the first question, namely were the six *mórai* divided into *lóchoi* (sg. *lóchos*)? Xenophon only mentions such units three times in the *Hellenika*, and all three occur after the killing field of Leūktra in 371 BCE.[23] In his references to Spartan officers attending conferences and war

---

16 Plut. *Lyk*. 14.4, 15.1. There are some very fine bronze figurines manufactured in Sparta in the late sixth century BCE depicting adolescent girls or young women in athletic poses, e.g. a bronze figurine of a running Spartan girl in breast-exposing tunic, *c.* 520/500 BCE. It was found at Prizren, Kosovo (then Serbia), was possibly made in or near Sparta, and is now at the British Museum (inv. GR 1876.5–10.1).

17 Ar. *Lys*. 82, Eur. *Andr*. 598. Incidentally, Aristophanes' *Lysistrata* is the first known comedy to have been named after its heroine, played of course by a male actor, in drag. It is a brilliant drollery, citizen women from both sides of the Peloponnesian War conflict revealing their ultimate strength by refusing to lay with their war-mad men. This collectivist sex strike, they trust, will bring their men kicking and screaming to the negotiating table. Their dastardly plot is ultimately successful. At first glance this play is extraordinarily modern in its concept, but the joke lies in the complete reversal of the laws and is therefore impossible.

18 Xen. *Hell*. 3.1.4–7, 3.1.8–10, 1.16–2.11, Diod. 14.36–37.4, 38.2–3, 39.5–6.

19 Xen. *Hell*. 3.4.1–3, Diod. 14.79.1.

20 Xen. *Lak. pol*. 11.4. The term *móra* literally means 'portion'. Xenophon mentions such units three times in the *Hellenika* (2.4.3, 4.3.15, 5.12).

21 Xen. *Hell*. 3.5.22.

22 *Ibid*. 4.5.7.

23 *Ibid*. 7.1.30, 4.20, 5.10. The term *lóchos* literally means 'war band'.

councils, the *lochagoí* are not mentioned at all. There are those scholars, such as Hans van Wees, who reckon that the *móra* replaced the *lóchos*. On the other hand, if we return to Xenophon, he does provide a list of Spartan officers in his *Lakedaimoniōn politeia*, and this list does include the *lochagoí*.[24] Of course, Xenophon could have nodded in the references to the officers in his *Hellenika*, or *lochagoí* simply did not attend conferences of war councils, but if we look at the passages in which Xenophon does refer to *lóchoi*, none really suggest that we are dealing with a brand-new unit within the Spartan army. On balance, therefore, the *lóchoi* were part of the army's tactical organisation early on.

The second question is how many subunits made up the *móra*? Historians are not agreed on exactly how the *móra* were constituted. The only precise evidence comes from Xenophon's list of Spartan officers: 'Each hoplite *móra* has one *polémarchos*, four *lochagoí*, eight *pentekostēres* and sixteen *enōmotarchoi*'.[25] Scholars and commentators universally accept that each *móra* contained eight *pentekostyes*, but there is some dispute over the four *lóchoi* and 16 *enōmotiai*. Let us deal with the number of *lóchoi* first. In his *Hellenika* Xenophon implies not four *but* two *lóchoi* per *móra*,[26] which gives us a total of 12 not 24 *lóchoi* for the Spartan army. It has been suggested that the figure of 12 *lóchoi* came about because of the appalling loses suffered at Leūktra, that is to say, immediately after the *débâcle* there was a military reform by which the number of *lóchoi* was halved from 24 to 12, while the organisational level of *móra* was simply abolished altogether (van Wees). True, in his *Lakedaimoniōn politeia* Xenophon does say each *móra* contained four *lochagoí* (λοχαγοὺς τέτταρας),[27] and this passage clearly implies that there were four *lóchoi* per *móra* not two. Numbers are, however, notoriously prone to corruption in ancient texts, and in this case, there could be a manuscript corruption, numbers being second only to proper nouns in susceptibility to miss-transmission. John Lazenby suggests δύο ('two') may have been misread as δ΄, τέτταραρς ('four'),[28] that is to say, the two *lóchoi* per *móra* as given in the *Hellenika* is correct, the four of *Lakedaimoniōn politeia* not so. As expected, other scholars argue the opposite.

Like *lóchoi*, Xenophon does not mention *enōmotiai* in the *Hellenika* until Leūktra, but they surely existed throughout.[29] The *enōmotiai* were crucial as they were the smallest tactical subunit of the Spartan army, and at full strength numbered 40 hoplites.[30] The number 40 probably represents the 40 age groups 20 to 60 years, with one man from each group making up the full

24 Xen. *Lak. pol.* 11.4, cf. 10.
25 *Ibid.* 11.4.
26 Xen. *Hell.* 7.4.20, 5.10, cf. 1.30.
27 Xen. *Lak. pol.* 11.4.
28 Lazenby 1985: 7.
29 Xen. *Hell.* 6.4.12, 17. In his *Anabasis* Xenophon certainly features the *enōmotia* as a tactical subunit of the Ten Thousand.
30 Thucydides (5.68.3, cf. 64.3) gives the size of the *enōmotia* as on average 32 men (*viz.* 4 x 8) at First Mantineia, with the rest in the role of home defence. Xenophon (*Hell.* 6.4.12 with 17) has 35 men per *enōmotia* at Leūktra, *viz.* those up to 54 years of age, plus an extra five mobilised for home defence in the emergency that followed, *viz.* those aged between 55 and 59 years.

strength of the *enōmotiai*. If we assume that the numbers given by Xenophon in his *Lakedaimoniōn politeia* are correct, then the nominal strength of a *móra* was 640 (16 x 40), which in turn means that the entire Spartan army only amounted to 3,840 hoplites (6 x 640) plus the 300 *hippeīs*.

The Spartan army that Thucydides believed he knew was not made up of *móra* but apparently of *lóchoi*, in each of which 'there were four *pentekostyes*, and in the *pentekostys* four *enōmotiai*'.[31] Ergo Thucydides thought each *pentekostys* was formed of four *enōmotiai* not two, as given in the *Lakedaimoniōn politeia*. However, he does, much like his fellow Athenian Xenophon, provide us with a helpful list of Spartan officers, namely the Spartan chain of command at the battle of First Mantineia in 418 BCE: 'He [the king] gives the word to the *polémarchoi*,[32] they to the *lochagoí*, these to the *pentekostēres*, these again to the *enōmotarchoi*, and these last to the *enōmotiai*.'[33]

It is evident from Xenophon that the command of a *polémarchos* was a *móra*, and Thucydides' *lóchoi* are in fact *mórai*. So, whichever evidence we choose to believe, and historians are only good as their sources, orders in the Spartan army, much like today's western European armies, were passed down the line to commanders of increasingly smaller units.

Age Groups

As for citizens of other *poleis*, *Spartiātai* were liable for military service between the ages of 20 and 60, consequently making up the 40 age groups,[34] which probably accounts for the nominal strength of the smallest tactical subunit, the *enōmotia*. However, Xenophon speaks of 'the ten from manhood', namely the age groups 20 to 30, or 'the fifteen from manhood', namely the age groups 20 to 35, 'the age groups up to thirty-five from the minimum', namely the age groups 20 to 55,[35] which does suggest that for ease of mobilisation the age groups were split into eight and in this way five men were drawn from each of these eight groups in order to make up the total of 40 men. This certainly makes good sense if the *éphoroi* could not find, for sake of argument, a 26-year-old for one of the *enōmotiai*. Furthermore, if theoretically an *enōmotia* deployed for battle five across and eight deep, the young men were easily detailed to the front rank, each rank thereafter containing progressively older men.

Thus, we hear from Xenophon, for example, that the younger *Spartiātai* could move like greased lightning and even catch peltasts – highly mobile javelineers unencumbered by body armour – when 'within a javelin's throw of Spartan hoplites'.[36] This organisational system, with its handy blocks of 40

---

31 Thuc. 5.68.3.
32 Closely associated with the king on campaign, the *polémarchoi*, six in total, served on the king's council of war (Xen. *Lak. pol.*11.4, 13.1, 4, 9, Plut. *Lyk.* 12.3).
33 Thuc. 5.66.3.
34 Xen. *Hell.* 5.4.13, 6.4.17, Plut. *Ages.* 24.3.
35 Xen. *Hell.* 4.5.14, 16, 6.4.17.
36 *Ibid.* 4.4.16.

men, enabled the Spartans to tailor-make an army of any strength according to need. Nothing like this existed in any other Greek *polis*. For the campaign of 418 BCE, to use a convenient example, the *éphoroi* mobilised all the age groups for a march to the border, at which point the oldest and youngest were left behind to serve as a home guard, while those aged 25 to 54 years carried on and ended up fighting at Mantineia.[37] Tyrtaios' Spartan warrior 'with white hair and grey beard' was no poetic licence.[38]

The Chosen Ones

It is at Leūktra that we encounter the 300 *hippeīs* who, according to Xenophon, were selected by the three magistrates known as the *hippagretai*, each of whom chose one hundred men.[39] In all probability each *hippagretas* and his chosen one hundred were selected from each of the three traditional tribes of Sparta. Conventionally, these elite *Spartiātai* would have been in the prime of their lives, undoubtedly chosen from age groups 20 to 30, and in all probability young worthies from well-connected families too. Still, we must resist the temptation to think of these young blades as pretentious chinless wonders or petted carpet soldiers; the 300 *hippeīs* formed a crack unit despite their origins, a fighting royal guard in truth.

The *hippeīs* only took the field when one of the kings did so, fighting on foot either before or beside the king.[40] The unit itself actually appears for the first time in the historical record in 479 BCE, providing a splendid escort – an honour never before bestowed upon a foreigner – for Themistokles as he travelled home to Athens in 'the most beautiful chariot that could be found in Sparta'.[41] Themistokles, of course, was the architect of the naval victory over the Persians in the Salamis Straits.

Serve to Win

It is always dangerous to generalise, and one hesitates to state too dogmatically what the difference was between the Spartans and the rest. They were not, to put it tactfully as possible, the most immediately amiable people in Greece. The Spartan himself, who said nothing and asked less, was small and spare, physically robust and capable of ignoring personal discomforts. He was made of muscle, tough-as-nails. He could march, if he must, some 230km in three days, a steady, almost brutal pace, in an effort to prepare him for worse hardships to come – for battle itself. He carried a heavy load and war gear in which he fought. He was silent during the advance and made no noise during the battle. He fought as well on minimum rations, and those included

37   Thuc. 5.64.2–3.
38   Tyrt. fr. 10.19–27 West.
39   Xen. *Lak. pol.* 4.3.
40   Thuc. 5.72.4.
41   Hdt. 8.124.

nothing inviting, warm, and lush. As a heavily battle-scarred veteran, he had the instinctive adroitness and flexibility of a wild animal. Ahead of him was blood and sweat, but no tears. Tried and tested in battle many times, he knew his job, thought himself good at it, and believed that his superiors thought so too. In sum, he was tougher and dourer than his fellow Greeks and would stick it out however hard the fight. No doubt there were Spartans who were flamboyant, frivolous folk, and Sparta probably had its quota of fawning, polished sophisticates: but fortunately, they were in a tiny minority. Most Spartans gave off an air of such brute virility and barely contained violence, and an enemy who dared present himself on the field of battle to them was in very serious trouble.

That the Spartans were brave goes without saying, the enormous social pressures made sure of that. The story of Thermopylai is the *locus classicus* for the iron discipline and diehard bravery of the Spartans, and Herodotos recalls that the lone survivor of that three-day battle was shunned by his peers back home. Some five decades prior, the lone survivor of the quasi-legendary Battle of the Champions went home and hung himself, thereby avoiding questions about how he was able to survive such a holocaust.[42] This was nothing like a criminal attempt by a pusillanimous malingerer to evade the tender mercies of the battlefront, bullets, shrapnel and suchlike.

Courage is nothing to laugh at, not if it is proper courage and exercised by men who know what they do is proper. Proper courage is wise courage. It is acting wisely, acting wisely when fear would have a man act otherwise. It is the endurance of the soul in spite of fear – wisely. Plato, in the dialogue called *Laches*, has Sokrates with pointed questions whittle down the definition of courage to a mere wise endurance.[43] For courage, according to Plato, is one of the four parts of virtue. It is there with temperance, justice, and of course, wisdom, and all parts are necessary to make the sublime human being. In fact, Plato says, men without courage are men without temperance, justice, or wisdom, just as without wisdom men are not truly courageous. Men must know what they do is courageous, they must know it is right, and that kind of knowledge is wisdom and nothing else.

As well as wise endurance, courage is the product of self-confidence too, and this has a snowball effect. Thucydides provides a good example of this in his splendid account of First Mantineia. He describes how during the pre-battle warm up that whereas the confederates were fired up by their haranguing *stratēgoi* the Spartans were 'well aware that the long training of action was of more use for saving lives than any brief verbal exhortation, though ever so well delivered'.[44] Here we have a brilliant comparison between

---

42 *Ibid.* 1.82.
43 Pl. *Lach.* 192b–193d.
44 Thuc. 5.69.2. Before any clash, as was customary, the two opposing commanders strode through the ranks, and are said to have made oratorical harangues to stiffen up the sinews of their own soldiers. But these pre-battle speeches, if not made up by the author, perhaps meet the eye rather mended. We can hardly suppose each could extend his eloquence, let alone his voice, to a hundred odd lines in folio. Such speeches, as is often the case with speeches, contain some truths, some falsehoods. What probably happened was that the two chiefs strode up and down the lines before battle, speaking reassuringly to their soldiers, reminding of the basics of

the high-octane discipline of the Spartans and the shambling amateurism of the confederates facing them. It is hardly surprising then, that the Spartans trounced them soundly. Even the disaster on the Lechaion road may have been the product of Spartan overconfidence.[45] There are indications that the wounded of the first encounter were carried away safely by the helot attendants and that the *polémarchos* (unnamed by Xenophon) could have easily formed square and moved out of danger. However, over confidence and brashness decided that the *polémarchos* would stick around and thrash Iphikrates, the Athenian *stratēgós*.[46] There was also the tiny Spartan cavalry force, which did what every incompetent cavalry force in history does: they lost cohesion and got overwhelmed by infantry. The horses charge at different speeds, some not at all, so they get separated. And they have no cavalry commander to speak of, no clear objective worth the trouble. And their horses were probably not battle conditioned, so when they saw a swarm of humans ahead of them, screaming and throwing javelins at them, they stopped. With the horses stopped dead, the cavalry is doomed. Cavalry that is stopped is dead cavalry.

Spartans on foot, on the other hand, were famous for their discipline too. It goes without saying that the efficiency and courage of an army depends on discipline, and without discipline an army is a reed swaying in the wind. Discipline is, obviously, a virtue that applies to individuals, but it has its greatest application in the context of a group, and the military context sees the pinnacle of its relevance. Discipline in this context is in part a product of drill and training, what we can call the 'muscle memory' that kicks in when orders are shouted, or contact is made with the enemy. Herodotos records that even at the climax of Plataia the Tegeans advanced without orders but the Spartans coolly waited for Pausanias' command.[47] Earlier in the day Kallikrates, 'the handsomest man in the Greek army', was killed by an arrow before battle was joined as he 'was sitting in his place',[48] the implication being that the Spartans simply sat down and suffered the arrow storm directed against them by the Persians. From the beginning of history, discipline is one of those basic qualities that distinguish armies from mobs.

But discipline or even skill or physical courage was not the whole answer. Spartans could suffer just like their fellow Greeks. Xenophon recalls that Agesilaos once sent fire in earthenware pots to his men anaesthetised by cold atop a tempest-torn mountain.[49] Thucydides, in his account of Sphakteria,

---

weapon-handling, which, like the sensible injunction to 'wait until you see the whites their eyes', might be forgotten in the heat of battlefield emotion, and telling them of the justice of their cause.

45 Xen. *Hell.* 4.5.12–17, Diod. 14.91.2.

46 Of Thracian origin (Hdt. 7.75, 89, Thuc. 4.28.4, 7.29.1, Arist. fr. 498 Rose, Ar. *Lys.* 563, Xen. *Anab.* 7.4.4, *Mem.* 3.9.2), Iphikrates had seen the potential of peltasts (for the so-called Reforms of Iphikrates, *vide* Nep. *Iphik.* 1, Diod. 15.44.2–4, cf. Xen. *Mem.* 3.5.27) and used them with considerable success against the Spartan hoplites outside Lechaion. Peltast could not hope to defeat hoplites in pitched battle, but if they managed to keep their distance, they could wear them down by missile fire. In the fourth century BCE most peltasts were of Greek origin.

47 Hdt. 9.62.

48 *Ibid.* 9.72.

49 Xen. *Hell.* 4.5.4.

has the Spartans 'thrown into consternation',[50] and even Spartan hoplites could show their heels as at Lechaion when the shattered scraps of the *móra* broke towards the sea in hoped-for safety.[51] The rarest kind of news thus far in the history of Sparta; its hoplites, *Spartiātai* no less, were in full flight.

Yet individual fitness, courage, discipline, or skill, were not fundamentally important in hoplite clashes. In one of his dialogues Plato has a young man being shown *hoplomáchia* (ὁπλομάχια), but the Athenian *stratēgós* Nikias reckons such skills were of little use except when the phalanx cracked and then it was a case for each man for himself. He does concede, on the other hand, that the physical exercise derived from *hoplomáchia* did increase a soldier's strength, 'since it is as good and strenuous as any physical exercise'.[52] Xenophon, through the mouth of Polydamas of Pharsalos, reckons few citizens 'keep constantly in good physical training',[53] and he recommends training with heavy burdens so as to be able to bear arms.[54] The Athenian soldier of fortune was undoubtedly familiar with *hoplomáchia*, which was the art of fighting or dancing in full hoplite panoply and is believed to have originated sometime in the middle of the sixth century BCE in Arkadia, the nursery of Greek hoplite mercenaries.[55] In 401 BCE, passing through Anatolia, he had encountered an expert in *hoplomáchia*, a Greek mercenary named Phalinos, who was advising a Persian satrap.[56] All the same, Xenophon himself held a contemptuous opinion of those who taught *hoplomáchia*

---

50   Thuc. 4.34.2.

51   Xen. *Hell.* 4.5.17.

52   Pl. *Lach.* 182a-d.

53   Xen. *Hell.* 6.1.5.

54   Xen. *Kúr.* 2.3.14.

55   Athen. 4.154d, Ephoros *FGrHist* 70F54, cf. Xen. *Anab.* 6.1.11, Polyb. 4.20.4–12. For Arkadian hoplite mercenaries, *vide* Fields 2001.

56   Xen. *Anab.* 2.1.7. A true mercenary's sole motivation is financial gain, the acid test being whether he would switch sides for more money. In other words, a mercenary such as Phalinos, we would guess, does not discriminate between political causes or states to which he offers his services. His work simply goes to the highest bidder. On the other hand, most people who are labelled mercenaries are actually adventurers who *do* discriminate between political causes they support. So, in Xenophon's case, he supported Kŷros and not his brother the Great King, a far wealthier employer, and authoritarian Sparta and not his homeland of democratic Athens. He was an adventurer, not a mercenary in the truest sense of the word. The adventurous aspect of the soldier of fortune has been immortalised in the lines Alkaios addresses to his brother Antimenidas, a political exile, returning from mercenary service under Nebuchadnezzar II during the Babylonian king's Palestinian campaign of 604 BCE, which culminated in the siege of Askalon: 'So you are back from world's end, with an ivory / sword-hilt fastened with gold... / great achievement, and you rescued them from distress / by dispatching a huge giant, just one palm off / five imperial cubits!' (fr. 350 West, cf. Arist. *Pol.* 1285a.9–10). It is known that the aristocrats of Lesbos were notorious as drinkers, horse-breeders, adventurers, and mercenaries. They were also proud, luxury-loving, bravura, and self-assured (Athen. 14.624e); and perhaps we should add tellers of tall tales too, when you consider Antimenidas' opponent was some 2.22m tall. Only Goliath could figure in the kind of tale Alkaios tells. As for that fancy sword-hilt, Alkaios clearly views this as a bit of foppery typical of a wandering adventurer. The Icelander Bolli Bollason proudly carried his father's sword, *Fótbítr* (Foot-biter or Leg-biter) and used it to avenge his father's killing. This was a particularly fancy sword, 'now inlaid with gold at the top and shank, and gold bands wound about its hilt' (*Laxdæla Saga* 77), though we are told that when *Fótbítr* was in the possession of Geirmundr *gnýr* it had 'a hilt of walrus ivory... no silver overlay' (*ibid.* 29), which does suggest Bolli had dandified it, most probably when he was in Constantinopolis serving with the Varangian Guard.

(along with *taktiká*), mere drillmasters whose expertise could have little use outside of the parade ground.[57]

Perhaps a rather frivolous example of this sort of 'nonsense' comes from Herodotos. Xerxes, having heard how brave the Spartans were, challenged Demaratos to fight 20 of his men, to which the deposed king replied that it was not as individuals but as a team that Spartans are the 'best of all men'.[58] Finally, the answer does not lie in the training or skill of Spartan officers, junior and senior alike, most of whom owed their position to their social standing. One doubts these officers received any formal tactical or strategic training in the modern sense, except perhaps at the very simplest level, that is to say, the 'square-bashing' mentioned earlier. So where does the answer lie?

All Spartans are Brothers

The smallest tactical unit in the Spartan army was the *enōmotia*, of which mention has been made, with a nominal strength of 40 hoplites and, perhaps, a campaign strength of 30 to 35 hoplites. In modern terms, this was a small, nimble, platoon-size force. With such articulation it is no wonder the Spartans, albeit professionals anyway, developed the vital ingredient of *esprit de corps*. The *enōmotia* itself was probably formed using the 15-man *sussítion* as the basic subunit, the communal messes (συσίτια) to which all adult *Spartiātai* had to belong.[59] For the *Spartiātai* membership of the military mess was the basic criterion of full citizenship and formed the basis of all military training. Full citizens were held to be equal or *homoioi* (literally 'those alike'), subject only to distinctions of age and honour due to achievement. The *esprit de corps* would have been that much stronger as members of the same *susstion* were accustomed to eat, sleep, live, and train together. Likewise on campaign, these messmates dined together and in battle fought side by side in the same *enōmotia*. Social and spiritual as well as military and political, the messes were miniature communities, sticking together through thick and thin as long as they survived, so they formed the strongest of ties.

The Athenian army, by way of a good comparison, was very much simpler (and also less powerful) in its military organisation. The democratic reforms of Kleisthenes (508 BCE) had transferred most of the military and political functions of the old tribes into 10 newly created tribes and 147 so-called demes (urban wards, rural districts). Athenian hoplites were now mobilised by deme and local levies combined to form 10 tribal units, *taxeis*, each commanded by a *taxiarchos*, elected on an annual basis.[60] Nonetheless,

---

57   Xen. *Mem.* 3.1, *Kúr.* 1.6.12–14.

58   Hdt. 7.104.4, cf. 211, 9.62, Thuc. 4.33.2, Xen. *Hell.* 4.5.15–16.

59   Plut. *Lyk.* 12.2.

60   Theophrastos, nephew of Aristotle, talks of that proverbial character, Cowardice, having 'his messmates' (*toùs sussítous*, 25.3) next to him in the phalanx. The craven hoplite also stands alongside his 'fellow demesmen' (*toùs demótas*, 25.4) and his 'fellow tribesmen' (*toùs pulétas*, 25.5), which does suggest that in an Athenian phalanx, at least, citizens who knew each other fought together as hoplites. The forensic speeches of Lysias provide at least four other exempla of this phenomenon. The first (20.23) involves the eldest son of Polystratos, who is speaking

the *taxis* ('formation') was a unit of some 1,000 hoplites, and even though it was divided into a small number of subunits called *lóchoi* (with their *lochagoí* appointed by the *taxiárchoi*) this is as complex as Athenian military organisation ever became, their tactical articulation stopping at this second tier and going no further.[61] In modern terms, it is as if the Athenian army was composed of 10 British regiments (or 10 American battalions), which were only subdivided into companies, each commanded by a major (or a captain), with no platoons and sections (or squads), no lieutenants, sergeants and corporals. And so, when Thucydides, in his marvellous contemporary account of Mantineia, describes how the Spartan army was organised, he remarks on the command structure, the implication is that this was surprising and even interesting for his Athenian audience.

The glue that holds armies together has a complex and variable composition, which includes not only major components like hostility towards the enemy, but small, and often more powerful ones, like the bonds that link men in their units. Today we would say that no commander should ever suffer a defeat from lack of drilling and training. In assembling an army, individuals are brought into association from all walks of life. They become soldiers only when the commander unites them. They have to create such powerful bonds that all come to share the same intentions. Drilling and training ensure the soldiers are solidly bonded into what we call sections or squads, respond to commands, are fully cognisant of their duties to each other and their commander, and are capable of executing manoeuvres and engaging the enemy without panicking in the chaos and stress of combat, and chaos, we might add prophetically, is the worst thing that can happen in the field. Good armies rely on alchemy to turn their raw metal into gold, the bonds of comradeship set rock-hard to link soldiers together in battleground households.

Bonding into squads (i.e. messes) of 15 men remained the concrete foundation of Spartan military organisation. In this way, the Spartans lived in close proximity, cooked their meals in groups of 15 and ate together,

---

on behalf of his father in 410 BCE, when he informs the law court that his father's demesmen could testify to the number of occasions he had served on campaign without shirking military service. The second (31.15–16), a certain Philon stands accused of not aiding the democrats in person and of failing to contribute funds to arm his fellow demesmen. The third (16.14), Mantitheos, when his fellow demesmen assembled to march to the relief of Haliartos in 395 BCE, donates 30 Attic *drakhmae* each to two of his fellow demesmen so that they could buy provisions for the campaign. The fourth, during the following campaign season, Mantitheos is with the Athenian contingent at the Nemea River where, he recalls for the jurors, his 'tribe had the worse fortune, and suffered the heaviest losses amongst its own men' (16.15). The earliest piece of evidence of Athenian demesmen fighting alongside each other comes from a fragment of a Corinthian helmet found at Rhamnous, the remote northernmost deme of Attica (39km northeast of Athens), and bears the inscription: 'The Rhamnousians (who were) in Lemnos dedicated (me) to Nemesis'. The helmet is probably best associated with the booty taken during Miltiades' expedition to seize the island of Lemnos in 499 BCE (Hdt. 6.137–40), which was then dedicated at the temple of Nemesis on behalf of the demesmen of Rhamnous who fought and died together on this overseas campaign. For this inscription, *vide* B. Chr. Petrakos, 'Ῥαμούντα'. Τὸ ῎Εργον τούς Ἀρχαιολογικκούς Ἑταίρεια κατὰ τὸ 1984 (Ἀθήνα, 1984), no.706, pl. 122b.

61   E.g. Thuc. 6.98.4, Xen. *Hell.* 4.2.19, Arist. [*Ath. pol.*] 42.1, Isaios 2.42, Lysias 13.79, 16.15, Diod. 18.10.2, Plut. *Arist.* 5, 19, Paus. 1.32.3, *IG* I² 929, 931, 943, 1085.

strengthening the sense of camaraderie. Moreover, the communal messes encouraged austerity by providing simple fare, precluding private indulgence, and bringing the conduct of each citizen under the scrutiny of his fellows. The institution of communal messes was not peculiar to Sparta, but the *Spartiātai* embraced the institution in a more thorough-going manner than did the citizens of other states, they having to eat the main meal of the day in their *sussítion* until they were 60, and between the ages of 20 to 30 had to spend the night with their messmates also.

The Spartan army was also evidently unique in being articulated down into manageable tactical units, the smallest of which, the *enōmotia* commanded by the *enōmotarchos*, had a campaigning strength of no more than 35 hoplites.[62] Contemporary western military theory, initially based on behavioural analysis of performance in the Second World War, recognises small groups of six, seven or eight soldiers as constituting the basic identifiable and motivational unit whose brutal atmosphere of comradeship was forged under fire – essentially validating the ancient insight. Being mutually responsible for each other, this is the foundation for combat, and 'small group cohesion', as this relationship is called, is a potent mélange of comradeship and firepower that steels the squad or section.

The 'buddy-buddy system', that is to say, a soldier fights for the soldier next to them, is the rawest form of this cohesion, whereby a soldier's natural fear of losing their reputation as a soldier among their immediate comrades armours them against the terrible experience of battle. It is a complex chemistry of individual and collective needs, loyalties and pressures that can urge soldiers to go forward or stand firm when even in the face of certain death. Consider those immortal words that Shakespeare put into the mouth of Henry V in the famous Saint Crispin's Day oratory: 'We few, we happy few, we band of brothers. / For he today that sheds his blood with me / Shall be my brother'.[63]

Experienced soldiers knew what it was like to submit themselves to the ordeal of battle again and again more or less willingly. To do otherwise was to disgrace themselves in the front of their fellow soldiers whose esteem was the foundation of their own self-respect. Physical courage could be motivated by the fear of shame, which for some could be an even greater fear than the fear of death. This is comparable to Sarpedon's pep talk to his comrade Glaukos, spoken by a hero entering the fray that is followed by his death:

> Ah my friend, if you and I [Glaukos and Sarpedon] could escape this fray / and live forever, never a trace of age, immortal, / I would never fight on the front lines again / or command you to the field where men win fame. / But now, as it is, the fates of death await us, / thousands poised to strike, and not a man alive / can flee them or escape – so in we go for the attack! / Give our enemy glory or win it for ourselves![64]

---

62   Thuc. 5.68.3, Xen. *Hell.* 6.4.12, 17, *Lak. pol.* 11.4.
63   Shakespeare, *Henry V*, 4.3.60–62.
64   Hom. *Il.* 12.374–81 Fagles.

Sarpedon, a son of Zeus and an ally of Troy, maintained that facing danger (and death) personally is a leader's duty. Besides, for our hero death is not as frightening if you know what you are dying for. In Sarpedon's case, the only way to win immortal glory, the only kind of immortality that mortals can aspire to, is to fight in the frontline.

Being committed to fighting and dying in battle would ensure the survival not only of the individual soldier but of the entire army. In other words, on the ground of battle – soon to become a burial ground – soldiers committed to fight to the death, they would hold on to life and gain victory, whereas if they sought to stay alive, they would suffer defeat and death. Xenophon had witnessed the self-same phenomenon:

> Those who are anxious in war to save their lives in any way they can, are the very men who usually meet with a base and shameful death; while those who have recognised that death is the common and inevitable portion of all mankind and therefore strive to meet death nobly, are precisely those who are somehow more likely to reach old age and who enjoy a happier existence while they do live.[65]

Still, it would seem to be easy to convince brave men that death comes more quickly and more surely to those who fly in disorder than to those who remain together and present a firm front to the enemy. In the grim words of an ancient Chinese proverb: 'The bodies of those who do not put their lives at stake will fertilise the fields and become carrion for the birds and beasts'.

Proverbs may be common sense, but the fundamental problem is simply that human beings fear danger and do not want to die, even for their native land. This is a normal human emotion. Of course, some will plunge recklessly on, as men do when determined to perform a thing they fear. Self-esteem is unquestionably one of the most powerful motives that moves soldiers in combat. Likewise, as well as their esteem and attachment for one another, the soldiers' devotion to their commander and combining the resultant positive motivation with their fear of harsh, certain punishment, a powerful well-disciplined army can be fashioned. If comradeship and leadership buttressed their resolve, then discipline coerced men. The key lay in ensuring that when the battlefield fears of death and of the enemy inevitably arose, they were insignificant compared with the soldiers' terror at the thought of the punishment they will certainly suffer for cowardice. When punishments were draconian, then soldiers would regard the enemy lightly.

Punishment, of course, always threatened the soldier who would not yield to reason: 'Pay well, command well, hang well' was Sir Ralph Hopton's brutal *précis* of the seventeenth-century general's art.[66] But no commander could afford to be too draconian, and the wise commander sought, on the contrary, to make his men obey not because he forces them to but because they so wished:

---

65 Xen. *Anab.* 3.1.43.
66 Attributed to Sir Ralph Hopton (1596–1652) by the biographer David Lloyd (1635–92) in his *Memories of Excellent Personages* (London, 1668), p.343. Lloyd personally knew the talented Royalist commander.

> Because such a general regards his men as infants they will march with him into the deepest valleys. He treats them as his own beloved sons and they will die with him.
>
> If a general indulges his troops but is unable to employ them; if he loves them but cannot enforce his commands; if the troops are disorderly and he is unable to control them, they may be compared to spoiled children, and are useless.[67]

United in profound comradeship with their commander, soldiers responded with uncompromising loyalty. They would obey every order; they would follow him anywhere, even into grave danger, into death. When Xenophon has, in his *Kúrou paideía*, Kŷros the Great thrown from his horse during a mêlée, the Persian king is saved by the love of his men, who eagerly rushed to the rescue,[68] a love that he has long cultivated.[69] Of course, by themselves, virtues such as kindness or love are ineffective means of leadership. They must be fully joined to discipline before they foster a natural hierarchy of things. The commander must be yielding and rigid, the iron hand under a silken glove.

Yet for most soldiers, almost despite themselves, the carrot of comradeship weighs heavier than the stick of coercion. And the most effective means of attaining this state of consent is fostering among them bonds of loyalty and regard for each other too strong for even the violent strains of battle to break. Thus, a good commander understands the difficulty of forcing soldiers to enter battle and engage in combat, of compelling them to kill other soldiers. They will consider ways to develop, manipulate, and ensure fighting spirit, what the ancient Chinese aptly called the *qi*, 'vital breath', of their soldiers and armies. This critical element is associated with will and intention; when soldiers are well trained, properly fed, clothed, and equipped, and if their spirits are aroused, they will fight vigorously. In short, taking care of soldiers binds them together as a cohesive unit, increases their faith and loyalty in the institution. Conversely, if physical or material conditions have blunted their spirit, if an imbalance exists in the relationship between the commander and their soldiers, or if for any reason the soldiers have lost their motivation, they will be defeated.

Another Day, Another Battle for the Spartans

According to Aristotle, the citizen peasant farmer was the backbone of the *polis* army.[70] That Sparta was an exception to this is the crux of an anecdote (perhaps apocryphal) told by Plutarch,[71] and repeated by Polyainos.[72] On one occasion,

---

67 Sun Tzu 10.20, 21 Griffith.

68 Xen. *Kúr.* 7.1.37, 38.

69 *Ibid.* 2.4.9–10, 3.1.42, cf. 8.2.1–9. According to Xenophon (*Ages.* 2.12), Agesilaos II of Sparta (r. 400–360 BCE) also cultivated his men's affections, while Plutarch records one of his many saying: 'He used to say that a *stratēgós* needs to show daring towards his opponents, goodwill towards his subordinates and a cool head in a crisis' (*Mor.* 213.66). Though he was described as a small man of unimpressive statue (and perhaps born lame but not exposed at birth), Agesilaos was a fierce warrior king.

70 Arist. *Pol.* 1291a.30.

71 Plut. *Ages.* 26.4, *Mor.* 214A.

72 Polyain. 2.17.

having received bitter complaints from Sparta's Peloponnesian allies about the comparative scarcity of the hoplites that it had fielded, Agesilaos ordered the whole army to sit down. The Spartan king then asked first the potters, then the smiths, then the carpenters, then the builders, and so on, to stand up, until almost all the allied hoplites were on their feet, but still not a single Spartan. The point, of course, was that the contingents of the allies were composed of essentially part-time soldiers who probably went years without dusting off the cobwebs from their panoply, the Spartans were full-time professionals – Spartan hoplites knew no other trade, as the above clearly illustrates.

Though war was not (and still is not) a normal human condition, the Spartan aggressive and warlike fighting spirit was a vital yet intangible quality whose roots lay in male bonding, which was fostered and preserved through a clear-cut group identity. A mutual trust of comradeship that was as plain as the devices on their shields, this was the complex chemistry that allowed the *Spartiātēs* to face death unflinchingly, battle after battle. But the personal bravery of a single individual does not decide the issue on the actual day of battle, but the bravery of the unit as a whole, and the latter rests on the good opinion and confidence that each individual places in the unit of which he is a member.

Remember those marauding freelance Thracians we mentioned earlier. Though born fighters, they were proud, fractious, and ungovernable. They could endure anything but tedium and would make any sacrifice save close cooperation with an ally. They were great fighters, but a bad army; their levels of unit discipline and military training were frankly sub-standard. For such headstrong warriors, given to irrational impulses and hastiness, fighting in an army was a novelty to be indulged before returning to their habitual round of low-level warfare upon one another.

In the ancient Greek world, specialised and continuous military training was the preserve of Sparta and, in some cases, of those states that kept small bodies of elite troops. It must be emphasised, however, that it was not the skill-at-arms of the individual *Spartiātēs* that was important, but his training as part of a coherent unit, for the simplicity of hoplite warfare left little scope for the display of personal skills. When, for example, Xerxes quizzes Demaratos about the martial nature of his fellow Spartans, the latter admits that the Spartans fighting as individuals are as good as the next man but fighting together are the 'best of all men'.[73] Thus, at Thermopylai, only troops trained to move as one and instantaneously execute the words of command could have carried out those series of feigned retreats in the face of the enemy described by Herodotos.[74] Or at Plataia the following year, Herodotos emphasises Persian courage, but they rushed out in ones, twos or tens, and fell upon the Spartans and were destroyed.[75] The Greeks were deeply imbued with the competitive spirit, and their word for competitiveness, *agōnia*, has given us our word 'agony', which surely tells us a lot about the nature of Greek competitiveness. Being adjudged 'the best' therefore meant a very great deal.

---

73   Hdt. 7.104.4.
74   *Ibid.* 7.211.3.
75   *Ibid.* 9.63.

The bedrock of military *esprit de corps*, comradeship in the Spartan army was extremely strong. According to Spartan tradition, the reforms of Lykourgos, the omni-provident lawgiver who brought about *eunomia*, 'good order', in Sparta,[76] had been most particular in fostering it. The *agōgē* initially fostered comradeship and belonging as one of its cornerstones. Young boys were drilled in packs. Having survived the *agōgē*, a young *Spartiátēs* sought membership to one of the communal messes. This *sussítion*, as it was sometimes called, comprised some 15 members who spent considerable time with one another, even when not in training. It was here, of course, that they dined communally and ate simple food, including a black broth that was infamous throughout Greece for its nastiness, and sipped much-diluted wines. It was not the sort of diet that would have made us smack our lips and belch with repletion, and even among their Greek contemporaries the aggressive and resilient Spartans were noted for their ability to fight well rather than to feed well – and the 'culinary horrors' of Spartan cuisine tested the toughest of guts.[77] Even the kings supped on black broth and barley bread,[78] and Plutarch notes that when the social reforming Kleomenes III

---

76 *Ibid.* 1.65.

77 The black broth of Sparta, μέλας ζωμός / *mélas zōmós* (Plut. *Mor.* 128C, *Lyk.* 12.7, *Kleom.* 13.5), was probably pork shank (including the trotters) cooked in its own blood, which gave it its dark colour, with salt and sour wine. It is thought the sour wine was used as an emulsifier to keep the blood from clotting during the cooking process.

78 Archilochos of Paros once sang that barley bread was the regular staple of his diet: 'In my spear is my daily bread, / In my spear my Ismaric wine, / On my spear I lean and drink' (fr. 2 author's translation). Ismaros was a *polis* on the Thracian coast not far from the island of Thasos. Its wines are referred to by Homer (*Od.* 9.39, 198). Any reader of Xenophon's *Anabasis* would find that food figured largely in soldiers' minds and he and his fellow mercenaries dined a great deal of the time on barley meal (ἄλφιτα / *álphita*: e.g. *Anab.* 4.5.26, 5.3.9, 6.1.15, 2.3, 5.1, 7.1.37, cf. Thuc. 8.100.2); barley meal was barley grain that had been roasted and milled, and the word *álphita* can denote the meal as either in the uncooked or cooked state. Humans can not readily digest barley in its raw form; it must be cooked. In fact, our soldier-cum-versifier is fairly specific and describes his daily bread as a 'kneaded thing of barley' (μᾶζα / *māza*: Arch. fr. 2, see also Thuc. 4.16.1, Ar. *Vesp.* 610, *Eq.* 55, *Ekkl.* 606, *Ran.* 1071–3, Antiphanes 266, [Homer] *Epigrammata* 15.6, Xen. *Kúr.* 6.2.28). Made for the occasion, Archilochos' bread had been made of barley grain that had been milled to produce barley meal, and soldiers (or their servants if they could afford to maintain one) had to convert their daily ration of grain into flour themselves. Hand mills were therefore to be found amongst the mundane equipment necessary for an army simply because they were, as Xenophon explains, 'the least heavy amongst implements used for grinding grain' (*ibid.* 6.2.31). This meant that the soldiers could carry un-milled grain and so reduce the risk of spoilage, as well as allowing them to take advantage of grain collected on the march. Most soldiers, if not all, were accustomed to seeing the daily supply of grain being milled by hand on the stone quern at home. So, a soldier's barley ration was ordinarily eaten in the form of *māza*, for having roasted and milled his barley grain, the soldier took his flour and kneaded it up with a little water, maybe olive oil and wine too, using a square of sheepskin as a kneading-trough, to produce a simple form of bread (*Ibid.* 6.2.28, Thuc. 3.49.3, Hermippos fr. 57 Kock). The fresh dough was rolled into wafer thin strips then baked quickly. The soldier would usually do this by twisting a strip around a stick and baking it the hot ashes of his campfire, which he then ate to comfort his stomach. Here we can cite the Attic comic poet Pherekrates who provides us with an idiot's guide for the making of *māza*: 'And now you must pile up your barley corns, / and hull 'em and parch 'em and boil. / Pound 'em, bolt 'em, water 'em, work 'em, / and serve at the end of your toil' (*Slave-trainer* 46a Edmonds). It would have been consumed hot, otherwise, being unleavened, it would have gone rock-hard. The quality of the bread itself tended to be poor, indeed, it would have contained substantial traces of abrasive mineral (feldspar, mica, sandstone, et cetera), introduced into the flour as it was laboriously

(r. 235–222 BCE) entertained foreign guests 'the servants brightened up the dinner a bit, not with any rich dishes or desserts, but by offering more generous portions and a more mellow wine'.[79] Even so, we should not expect boisterous celebrations and much good eating and drinking. Anyway, when in battle, the *sussítion* was the hoplite's 'tent', and was undoubtedly the basic building block for the formation of the *enōmotia*. In other words, the individual *Spartiātēs* ate, slept, and fought side by side with comrades he had probably known since his agonising boyhood days. His membership to a *sussítion* was decided by a collective ballot of its members, who were all called *homoioi*, dressed the same, made by-and-large identical mess contributions, and shared the same apparently unappetising food.

In the *Poroi*, a political pamphlet of his dotage, Xenophon advocates that Athenian citizens should once again serve together in the ranks of the phalanx and not be lumped in with 'Lydians, Phrygians, Syrians, and barbarians of all sorts'.[80] The whole premise of the *Poroi* is how to cure his native city's economic woes, and this is obviously a rhetorical point concerning Athens' strong reliance upon such 'riffraff', but the idea is clear all the same. As a former mercenary himself, Xenophon certainly appreciated the importance of small group cohesion. In the *Kúrou paideía*, for instance, the theme crops up time and time again. His fanciful quasi-fictional life of Kŷros the Great,[81] the founder of the Achaemenid Persian empire and the most successful conqueror who had lived up to that time (the mid-fourth century BCE), is busy organising and training his new model army. In the text, Xenophon makes the young Kŷros think of the professional army of Sparta as he does so, considering those who messed together would be less likely to desert each other, and that there could be no stronger phalanx than one composed of comrades.[82] Again, having trained his army to a peak of perfection and fostered the idea of comradeship within each unit (called *taxis* by Xenophon), the wise Persian king realises that the petty jealousies of his men will soon vanish like a summer mist once they are exposed to

---

ground on the coarse stone of a quern. Over a period of time this grit wore down the enamel of teeth, causing some discomfort and pain at best, and at worst, serious abscesses and infections, which could prove fatal.

79 Plut. *Kleom.* 13.4. Spartan kings customarily received double portions of food and drink (Hdt. 6.57.1, Xen. *Lak. pol.* 15.4, Ages. 5.1).

80 Xen. *Por.* 2.3, cf. Isok. 4.115.

81 For instance, Xenophon's account of Kŷros' victory over Kroesos of Lydia (*Kúr.* 6.4–7.1) bears little resemblance to that of Herodotos (1.75–85), which is closer to the original events of the mid-sixth century BCE.

82 Xen. *Kúr.* 2.1.28, 7.1.30, cf. Aineias *Taktikos* 27.13. Xenophon's *Kúrou paideía*, a political and philosophical romance, describes the boyhood and training of Kŷros II of Persia (†530 BCE), commonly known as Kŷros the Great. The work hardly answers to its name, being for the most part an account of the beginnings of the Persian empire – despite its moralising tone, it thus preserves useful Achaemenid information – and of the victorious career of Kŷros its founder. The *Kúrou paideía* contains the author's own ideas of training and education, as derived conjointly from the teachings of Sokrates and his favourite Spartan institutions. It is believed the work was written in opposition to the *Republic* of Plato, which, in turn, prompted a response from Plato in parts of *Laws*. Xenophon's expertise and passion shine throughout this work, and aspects of the *Kúrou paideía* would become a model for mediaeval writers of the educational literary genre mirrors for princes.

the harsh realities of the forthcoming campaign: 'For he knew that common dangers make comrades kindly disposed towards each other'.[83]

The campaign, an invasion of 'Assyria', culminated in the Battle of 'Thymbrara'. The king of Susa and steadfast ally of Kŷros, Abradatas, first charges the Lydian chariotry, putting them to flight, and then is killed in an attack on the Egyptian infantry stationed behind them. The king plunges recklessly into the fray and only his close comrades choose to follow him in death and glory. The moral of the tale is obvious as Xenophon is quick to point out:

> Now, it has been demonstrated on many occasions that there is no stronger phalanx than that which is composed of comrades that are close friends; and it was shown to be true on this occasion. For it was only the personal friends and messmates (hetaîroi… kaì homotrápezoi) of Abradatas who pressed home the charge with him, while the rest of the charioteers, when they saw that the Egyptians with their dense throng withstood them, turned aside after the fleeing chariots [of the enemy] and pursued them.[84]

Again, it must be stressed that Xenophon has clearly used the professional army of Sparta as the role model for Kŷros' invincible army, and not the typical polyglot army of disparate nationalities of the Persian empire, which he knew only too well. Furthermore, there is little doubt that he has drawn upon his own personal experiences as a mercenary captain to portray not only the tactics of Kŷros' army, but also the human dynamics of soldiering within the ranks. The argument for small units, however, cannot be pressed too far when dealing with Greek citizen armies, such as the aforementioned organisation of Athenian army. It is the Spartans alone who broke down their citizen army into manageable tactical units, the smallest of which, as we know, the enōmotia commanded by the enōmotarchos, probably had a campaigning strength of no more than 35 men. On the other hand, there is no evidence to suggest that the Athenian or Theban armies, for instance, contained units smaller than a lóchos, which, though the number varied from army to army and from time to time, almost always contained at least a couple of hundred men.

It can be argued, as is the case with Plato's *Republic*, that Xenophon's *Kúrou paideía* is based ultimately upon a simple military argument – Sparta is better at war than any other state, and therefore the best state must have a professional warrior elite of the Spartan type. In this regard, there was one truly professional unit (*not* army) outside Sparta that did exhibit this idea of small group cohesion, even to the extent that the 'buddy-buddy system' was very much in force within its ranks, the Sacred Band of Thebes. The 300 members of the Sacred Band first fought as a unit at the battle of Tegyra where they played a prominent part in the defeat of two Spartan *mórai*.[85] We shall return to this engagement in due course.

---

83   Xen. *Kúr.* 3.3.10, cf. 58.
84   *Ibid.* 7.1.30, cf. Onasandros *Stratēgikós* §24.
85   Plut. *Pel.* 17.2–4, 19.3, Diod. 15.81.2.

Here is worth commenting on that Greek word, *enōmotia*, which means, properly, a 'sworn band', it being derived from the noun *enōmotos*, 'a man bound by oath'. Apparently, at Plataia, the Spartans swore an oath, which probably ran as follows:

> I shall not desert my *taxiarchos* or *enōmotarchos*, whether he is alive or dead, and I shall not leave the battlefield unless our *hēgemōnes* [*viz*. his kings] lead us away, and I shall do whatever the *stratēgoi* may command, and I shall bury on the spot those of my fellow fighters who die, and I shall leave no one unburied.[86]

In the strictly hierarchic Spartan army, sworn loyalty to state-appointed officers thus took precedence over personal obligations and safety. Similarly, a new member of the Theban Sacred Band was expected to make an oath to Eros, vowing to die a glorious death in preference to a dishonourable and reprehensible life, or so says Athenaios of Naukratis.[87] We are told by Athenaios too, albeit using second-hand evidence, the Spartans would make preliminary sacrifice to Eros in front of the battle lines 'with the belief that safety and victory lies in the love (*philia*) of those ranged alongside each

---

86 Tod 204.25–31. An oath sworn by the Greeks before the Battle of Plataia is mentioned in several sources (e.g. Lykourgos *Against Leokrates* §80, Diod. 11.29.2), but this oath is recorded in a fourth century BCE inscription from Athens. However, as scholars argue, the lines quoted throw light upon the Spartans and not the Athenians in 479 BCE. The reference to *stratēgoi* is of course relevant to the Athenians, whose armies were led by such. However, the proceeding clause makes no sense in an Athenian context but a Spartan one, as *hēgemones* is what Spartans called their kings (e.g. Tyrt. fr. 19.11 West). The *enōmotarchos*, moreover, is a purely Spartan figure without Athenian parallel, and Herodotos (9.53.2) mentions *taxiárchoi* in the Spartan army, although the Athenian army also had *taxiárchoi*. As unchallenged leader of the ground forces, it seems probable that Sparta dictated the bulk of the oath, with the Athenians, perhaps, adding the addendum 'I shall do whatever the *stratēgoi* may command'. See van Wees 2004: pp.243–244.

87 Athen. 13.561f. Eros' most famous shrine was at Thespiai, where the Boiotians worshipped him during the Erōtídeai, festival of Eros, as 'an unwrought stone' (Paus. 9.27.1). Later Praxiteles of Athens, the most renowned of the Attic sculptors of the mid-fourth century BCE, made a large sculpture known as the Eros of Thespiai (lost by late antiquity), of which many Roman marble copies were made. It is generally thought to be cast in bronze, though Pausanias (9.27.3) says it was sculptured from Pentelic marble, a later bronze Eros being the work of Lysippos, the favourite sculptor of Alexander. Described by the Greek sophist Kallistratos at the turn of the fourth century CE, Praxiteles' Eros was 'a boy in the bloom of youth with wings and bow. Bronze gave expression to him… for though it was fixed solidly on a pedestal, it deceived one into thinking that it possessed the power to fly. It was filled with joy even to laughter…' (*Descriptions* 3). Pausanias (9.27.3) tells how this Praxitelean masterpiece was stolen from Thespiai by the wicked (and doomed) Caius Caligula, then returned by an obliging Claudius, but seized back by the wicked (but equally doomed) Nero. Hardly surprising when you consider that Praxiteles himself ranked it with his Faun as his best work and even the normally equable Cicero (*in Verrem* 4.2, 60) once raved about it. Strabo (9.2.25), likewise, says the only reason people choose to visit Thespiai was to view the Eros of Praxiteles. The celebrated courtesan Phryne (b. 371 BCE), Praxiteles' lover who modelled for him (the Aphrodite of Knidos, the original nude, was based on her), took the statue from him by a ruse and presented it to her native *polis* (Paus. 1.20.1, 2). Born into poverty, she moved to Athens and became one of the wealthiest self-made women in Greece. According to Kallistratos (*apud* Athen. 13.60), after Alexander razed Thebes in 335 BCE, Phryne offered to pay to rebuild the walls on condition that the words 'destroyed by Alexander, restored by Phryne the courtesan' were inscribed upon them (unsurprisingly, the offer was refused). Riches and lovers apart, Phryne was renowned for her beauty and her wit.

other'.[88] Eros is a deity not normally associated with the hard-bitten Spartans; we have a tendency to regard 'violet-eyed' Eros as a wanton wild chubby child who is only intermittently under the control of his mother Aphrodite.[89]

Still, whether or not we are prepared to accept the real possibility that sometimes the feelings of Spartans for their comrades were homosexual, though the Greeks themselves did not have a notion of a 'homosexual nature', the fact remains that the basic male bonding process is built upon mutual self-respect and a special kind of love that has nothing to do with sex, or even idealism. Besides, unlike the Sacred Band of Thebes, homosexual couples were not customarily stationed next to each other in the phalanx. If Athenaios is correct, and there is no real reason to doubt him here, it seems Spartan comrades were bound together by an obligation under Eros to stand by one another in weal or in woe regardless of their own lives. And so, if they had any choice in the matter at all, they invariably chose to die for each other and for their own vision of themselves. But why did they do it? The Spartans would argue that they did it for love. Love of one another.

To recap. When on campaign, the *sussítion* was the 'military cloak and camp bed' of the *Spartiātēs*, and was undoubtedly the basic building block for the formation of the *enōmotia*, the smallest unit in the Spartan army with a nominal strength of 40 men. Compare the Athenian army, for instance, where the *taxis*, the tribal contingent of around a thousand men, was only divided into a number of sub-tribal units, the *lóchoi*, each of which almost always contained at least several hundred men. In other words, an individual *Spartiātēs* ate, slept and fought side by side with comrades he had in all probability known since his boyhood days, and it was these comrades' good opinion that counted more strongly with him than the mortal fear of the enemy. Honour is a notion that seems distinctly antediluvian to most moderns, yet it is the value of a person in his own eyes, but also in the eyes of his society, an estimation of his own worth. A sense of honour is one thing valued more than life by the majority of tribal warriors.

---

88   Athen. 13.561e.
89   Eros was the Greek god of erotic, physical love in boy form, and an earlier equivalent of the Roman cherub-like Cupid (*putto*, 'plumb baby'). Some myths describe him as the disobedient but fiercely loyal son of Aphrodite, the goddess of love and beauty, and her lover Ares, the god of war (e.g. Stesikhoros fr. 575 Campbell: 'You cruel child of guileful Aphrodite, / whom she bore to Ares'). Other myths, however, claim Eros was the son of Iris, the personification of the rainbow and messenger of the gods (she was also sister of the Harpies and cousin of the Gorgons), and Zephyros, the god of the west wind (e.g. Alk. fr 327 West: 'most formidable god, / whom fair-shod Iris bore in love / with gold-haired Zephyros'). Yet again, he was an ancient primordial force created together with Gaia, Mother Earth, from chaos (e.g. Hes. *Th.* 116–20: '… fairest among the deathless gods…'). Whatever the strand of tradition about Eros one chooses to follow, his characteristic possession was his bow, a weapon that he deployed to 'make love, not war'. The bow was said to generate its own arrows or to shoot a single one that then returned to Eros. He was never considered a sufficiently responsible god to be counted among the ruling family, the Olympian Dozen.

Chapter 6

Boiotian Confederacy Army

> The Athenians are wont to call us Boiotians gross, senseless, and stupid fellows,
> for no other reason but our over-much eating; and Pindar calls us also swine
> (σύας),[1] for the same reason.
>
> Plutarch *De Esu Carnium* 1.6

The great biographer Plutarch was born in Chaironeia, Boiotia, and obviously
for him and his fellow Boiotians (Pindar notwithstanding)[2] the distinction
between the quick-witted Athenians and the dim-witted Boiotians was not
an accurate reflection of the truth.[3] Indeed, if we examine the sources of the
tradition, we find that the original verdict was popular and unreasoned,
receiving its literary support in Old Attic Comedy, which deliberately
appealed to vulgar prejudices. 'If you have any sense, avoid Boiotia,'[4] was
the acerbic advice of Pherekrates, the forerunner of Aristophanes. To the
comic poets that came after, Boiotian gluttony and Boiotian gaucherie
were a dependable resource to pleasure the fickle humours of the Athenian
masses within the Dionysiac theatre. Plutarch's ripe refinement is a late but
not solitary example of Boiotia having its own traditions of culture.[5] An
ever-loyal son of Boiotia, Plutarch assumed his share in the reproach of that
opprobrious epithet Βοιωτία ὗς, 'Boiotian swine'.

---

1   Pind. *Olymp*. 6.89 (468 BCE, probably).

2   Though born near Thebes, Pindar saw himself as a citizen of the whole of Greece, almost every
quarter of which he seemed to have visited. He certainly did not write in the Boiotian dialect;
any more than Erasmus wrote in the language of Burgundian Netherlands.

3   Cf. the proverbial 'sow and Athena' (Plut. *Mor*. 803D).

4   Pherekrates fr. 171 Storey.

5   At Khartoum, during the siege, General Charles Gordon wrote in his journal: 'Certainly I would
make *Plutarch's Lives* a handbook for our young officers; it is worth any number of 'Arts of War'
or 'Minor Tactics'' (*The Journals of Major-Gen. C. G. Gordon, C.B., at Khartoum* [Boston, 1885],
p.64).

The Land

Boiotia (Gk. Βοιωτία) was a large region in ancient central Greece, some 2,540km², within which some 15 *poleis* existed, each only a few kilometres apart from each other and each desiring to be completely independent of Thebes, the chief *polis* of Boiotia, and all other *poleis*.[6] Unlike Athens, which managed to subdue all communities in Attica (which was as large as Boiotia), Thebes was never able to achieve the same in its own backyard. One reason for this was the hard reality that Boiotia consisted of two natural basins separated by hills and surrounded by mountains, and this geographical duality manifested itself in the bitter rivalry of Thebes and Orkhomenos.

The flatness of the northern plain was unrelieved, and the rivers that flowed into it, like the Kephissos, found no outlets except by sinkholes (Gk. καταβόθρα / *katavóthra*), a common feature of karstic limestone terrain, which they forced for themselves under the north-eastern mountain chain of Ptoön (781m at its peak, Petalás), on whose slopes men once listened to Apollo Ptoiös.[7] From time to time these subterranean passages in Ptoön became choked with silt and debris, and in antiquity the stoppage of the sinkholes turned a large part of the northern plain into what was at that time Lake Kōpaïs. Before the rise of Thebes, Orkhomenos was the foremost community, not only of the northern plain but of the whole country.

The southern plain of Boiotia was smaller and also less homogenous and monotonous than its northern sister. Thebes, then the principal Boiotian community, occupied a plateau of its own on the northern side of a range of hills that divided it from the large part of the southern plain and overlooked the faulted basin watered by the river Asōpós. There were good harbours on the Gulf of Corinth,[8] which formed the southwest boundary of Boiotia, but these were not easily accessible due to the severe declivities of an almost continuous wall of mountains: Helikon, Korombili, and Kithairon.

Boiotia is isolated from marine influence by the mountains that surround it, and it is for this reason that the two basins are scorching in the summer and raw in the winter. As the poet Hesiod, in his authentic picture of a farmer's life in Boiotia at the close of the eighth century BCE, complains, 'a cursed place, cruel in winter, harsh in summer, never good'.[9] Even so, in antiquity Boiotia was noted for the fertility of its soil,[10] which produced excellent wheat,[11] and for the abundance of its horses and of its livestock. Even their sharp-tongued

---

6   Those that we know of are, from north to south, as follows: Orkhomenos, Chaironeia, Hyettos, Kopai, Anthedon, Akraiphnion, Lebadaia, Koroneia, Haliartos, Thebes, Thespiai, Tanagra, Thisbe, Eutresis, Plataia.

7   Herodotos (8.135.1) and Pausanias (9.23.3) record the sanctuary of Apollo Ptoiös as belonging to the Thebans.

8   Strab. 9.2.2.

9   Hes. *Op.* 640.

10   Thuc. 1.2.3–6, Strab. 9.2.1.

11   Theophrastos *On plants* 8.4.5. We are probably looking at einkorn and emmer here, the earliest varieties of wheat known to man, nourishment of the ancient world and progenitor of every grain we eat.

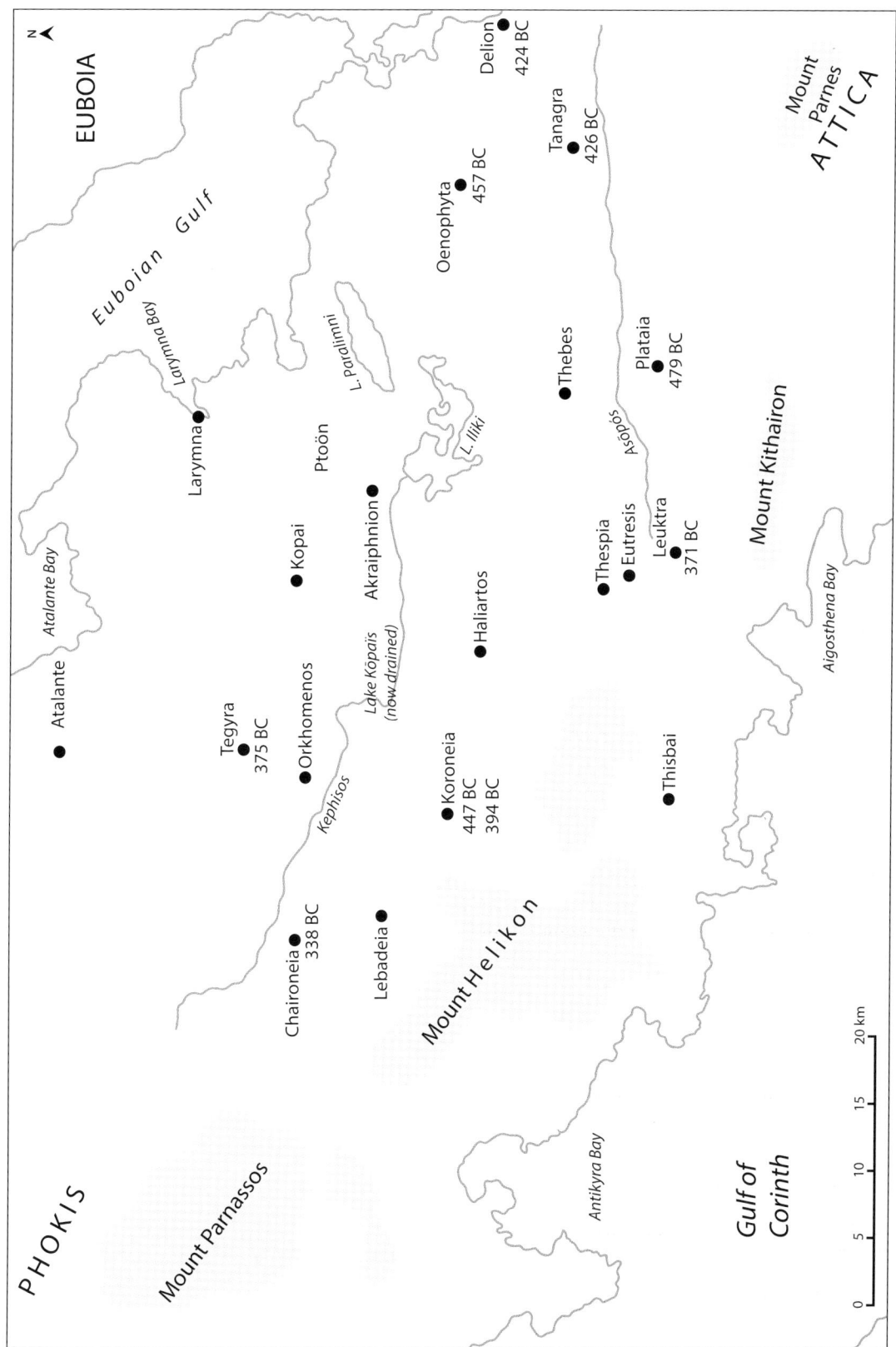

N

EUBOIA

Euboian Gulf

Larymna Bay

Atalante Bay

PHOKIS

Mount Parnassos

Atalante

Tegyra
375 BC

Orkhomenos

Kephisos

Chaironeia
338 BC

Lebadeia

Mount Helikon

Koroneia
447 BC
394 BC

Kopai

Lake Kōpaïs
(now drained)

Larymna

Ptoön

Akraiphnion

Haliartos

L. Paralimni

L. Iliki

Thisbai

Oenophyta
457 BC

Delion
424 BC

Tanagra
426 BC

Thebes

Thespia

Eutresis

Asōpós

Plataia
479 BC

Leuktra
371 BC

Mount Kithairon

Mount
Parnes
ATTICA

Aigosthena Bay

Antikyra Bay

Gulf of
Corinth

0 5 10 15 20 km

Boiotia, 'the dancing floor of Ares'.

neighbours, the Athenians, whose parched soil grudgingly offered the staff of life, longed for Boiotian produce. In Aristophanes, it is from Boiotia that good things for eating come, above all the famous eels fished from Lake Kōpaïs,[12] while the Boiotian trader with his oddities of dialect make an excellent target for comic tales.

The Confederacy

Although the Boiotian confederacy was founded during the last quarter of the sixth century BCE, the first detailed evidence of its existence comes from a fragment of papyrus found at the site of the Ptolemaic town of Oxyrhynchos, and known as the *Hellenika Oxyrhynchia*.[13] It was written by an anonymous chronicler who was writing in 395 BCE, the year of the Battle of Haliartos. He, who was perhaps a Boiotian, reports that in his day Boiotia was divided into 11 federal districts, each consisting of more than one *polis* and each supplying a *boiōtarchēs*, a federal official to serve as a *stratēgós* in the Boiotian confederacy army. Districts tended to combined so as to provide the *boiōtarchoi*: Thebes providing four (two on behalf of the *polis* itself and two on behalf of Plataia, which Sparta had conquered in 427 BCE),[14] Orkhomenos providing two, Thespiai along with Thisbai and Eutresis providing two, Tanagra providing one, Haliartos, Lebadaia, and Koroneia each taking turns to provide one, as was the case for Akraiphnion, Kopai, and Chaironeia.

The Army

For the army, each district was expected to raise a levy of 1,000 hoplites and 100 horsemen. This is a high horse owning total, implying plenty of suitable land for horse rearing. As mentioned earlier, Boiotia is essentially two sizeable plains surrounded by mountains and containing (in antiquity)[15] several large lakes but little high ground. Unlike Attica and the Peloponnese, it was excellent horse country, and the Boiotians in general seem to have had a long equestrian tradition.[16] Given the oligarchic nature of the constitution of the confederacy, it is certain that the cavalry was recruited from those who could supply their own horse and equipment – the wealthiest men in each *polis*. Contingents were supplied as follows: Thebes contributed 400 horsemen; Orkhomenos and Hysiai together sent 200; Thespiai, Eutresis, and Thisbai, jointly contributing 200; Tanagra sent 100; Haliartos, Lebadaia, and

---

12   Ar. *Ach*. 860–894, 962–963, 1043, *Pax* 1005–1015, *Lys*. 36, 700–703.

13   *Hell. Oxy*. 11.2–4 = Harding 15.

14   Thuc. 3.68.3, *Hell. Oxy*. 11.3 = Harding 15.11–12.

15   Lake Kōpaïs, for instance, is now drained; it was the largest lake in Greece, measuring 24km by 13km. Strabo (9.2.18) says it had a circuit of 380 *stadia* (68km).

16   For example, Homer calls the Thebans the 'horse-racing Kadmeians' (*Il*. 4.391 Lattimore), while Herodotos (9.68, 69) reports the Boiotian cavalry serving under Mardonios did sterling service during the aftermath of Plataia while the Persian army was on the run.

Boiotian marble grave stele (Cleveland, OH, Cleveland Museum of Art, inv. 1970.82), dated *c.* 390 BCE, with what is commonly referred to as a depiction of a Boiotian hoplite at the time of the Corinthian War. He wears a *pīlos* helmet, a model light in weight and providing all-round vision that was most likely first adopted by the Spartans. Additionally, he is armed with the signature short sword of a Spartan hoplite. Question: is this actually a representation of a Spartan hoplite, or a Boiotian equipped like a Spartan? More than likely the latter (note the short hair and lack of beard), suggesting that those pro-Spartan Boiotians, such as the Orkhomenians, were furnished with Spartan equipment. Though it must be said that the *pīlos* helmet was now a common item of kit throughout the Greek world. (Cleveland Museum of Art/Wikimedia Commons/CC0 1.0 Universal Public Domain Dedication)

Koroneia, jointly contributed 100; and Akraiphnion, Kopai, and Chaironeia, jointly contributed 100.[17] This was a large cavalry force by Greek standards, and Thucydides confirms that the confederacy could deploy around 1,000 horsemen during the Peloponnesian War.[18]

This army of 11,000 hoplites and 1,100 horsemen probably represented an estimate of the able-bodied landowners, from wealthy to moderate means, who were the enfranchised citizens of the *poleis* of Boiotia. A larger population of un-enfranchised but free Boiotians undoubtedly provided the lightly armed troops for the army. Some of these acted as *hamippoi*, men detailed to operate with the horsemen. Not for the timorous, they ran into battle grasping the tails or manes of the cavalry,[19] and then disengaged to disable the horses of the enemy. Presumably drawn from younger, fitter, and nimbler men, the *hamippoi* are attested as early as 418 BCE and were seemingly deployed on the basis of one *hamippos* per horseman.[20] At Second Mantineia in 362 BCE, as well as *hamippoi*,[21] the Boiotian horsemen also operated in tandem with Thessalian lightly armed troops.[22] All things considered, a united Boiotian confederacy army was certainly a match for the Athenians,[23] and such an army in central Greece was an essential ally to Sparta in their war against Athens.

The Federal Council

The federal council was organised in a complicated fashion, being divided into four units, each unit holding office in rotation – acting as a probouleutic council. The anonymous author of the *Hellenika Oxyrhynchia* infers 'four councils in each of the *poleis*', membership being restricted according to property class.[24] Thucydides also mentions 'the four councils of Boiotia',[25] but there is no reference in our primary sources to a primary federal council, although Thucydides does say that the councils formed 'the supreme authority of the state',[26] namely this quadripartite federal body held absolute sovereignty. Although this an incidental remark of Thucydides, we have no reason to doubt his statement on the Boiotian constitution and, therefore, what we have here is a good example of representative government.

Each district, according to the admirable account of the *Hellenika Oxyrhynchia*, provided 60 councillors for the federal council of 660 seats,

17   *Hell. Oxy.* 11.3–4 = Harding 15.12–13.
18   Thuc. 4.93.3, cf. Diod. 12.69.3–4, 13.72.4.
19   A fourth century BCE Attic grave relief (Paris, musée du Louvre, inv. 744) depicts a *hamippos* wearing a *pilos* helmet and wearing a *chlamýs* charging into battle holding on to the tail of a horse.
20   Thuc. 5.57.2, cf. Xen. *Hipp.* 5.13, 9.7. They are attested in Sicily as early as 480 BCE (Hdt. 7.158, *hippodromoi psiloi*).
21   Xen. *Hell.* 7.5.24–25.
22   Diod. 15.85.4–5.
23   Thuc. 4.94.1, Xen. *Mem.* 3.5.2–4, *Hipp.* 7.1.
24   *Hell. Oxy.* 11.2, 3–4 = Harding 15.
25   Thuc. 5.38.2.
26   Loc. cit.

and it was these men who would make decisions on behalf of the citizen that they represented. So, Tanagra provided, along with one *boiōtarchēs*, 60 councillors, Orkhomenos, along with two *boiōtarchoi*, 120 councillors. After Thebes swallowed up Plataia (courtesy of Sparta), it controlled four *boiōtarchoi* and 240 councillors.

Boiotia, of course, was oligarchic in outlook and so citizenship was restricted, almost certainly to those of hoplite status.[27] Nonetheless, the lasting legacy of the Boiotian constitution was dual citizenship: a man could be a citizen of both his *polis* and the greater political unit of the Boiotian confederacy. Dual citizenship was to become a common feature of the Hellenistic period.

The *Boiōtarchoi*

First mentioned by Herodotos in his narrative covering the events leading up to the Battle of Plataia in the summer of 479 BCE,[28] the 11 *boiōtarchoi* were the chief officials of Boiotia. Elected annually and taking up office at the winter solstice, constitutionally the *boiōtarchoi* were answerable to the councils,[29] yet commanded the confederacy's army and formed its council of war. Two or three *boiōtarchoi* could be detached to act independently, but, by 424 BCE, it appears that Theban *boiōtarchoi* exercised some form of constitutional authority over the others.[30]

Xenophon makes it quite clear that the same constitution prevailed down to 386 BCE, a time when Thebes, the largest and strongest *polis* in Boiotia, dominated the confederacy. During the initial peace talks between the Greeks and the Persians, held at Sardis in 392 BCE, the Thebans were worried by the proposal made by the Spartan delegates that all the Boiotian *poleis* were to have αὐτονμία, autonomy, since it entailed the break-up of the Boiotian confederacy which was the source of their strength.[31] Five years later, as Xenophon gleefully points out, the ratification of the King's Peace (or Peace of Antalkidas) of 387/386 BCE, a reconciliation between the Persian empire and the Greek states, forced the Thebans into granting independence to the Boiotian *poleis*, and so the confederacy came to an end.[32] The main aim of Spartan policy at the time was the break-up of the quadruple alliance (i.e. Thebes, Athens, Corinth, and Argos), which was threatening their hegemony of Greece.

The main beneficiary of the King's Peace were the Spartans, who had bargained away the Greeks in Anatolia, whom they longer had the means to control anyway, in return for the crippling of their enemies on the Greek mainland. So, the Thebans were once again allied to Sparta, dutifully serving in 385 BCE when the Spartans suppressed a resurgent Mantineia to impose a

---

27 For example, Arist. *Pol.* 1278a.25.
28 Hdt. 9.15.1.
29 Thuc. 5.38.2.
30 Ibid. 4.91.
31 Xen. *Hell.* 4.8.15.
32 Ibid. 5.1.31–3, cf. Diod. 14.110.3, Paus. 9.13.2.

narrow pro-Spartan oligarchy.[33] It was at Mantineia that Epameinondas and Pelopidas fought side by side as rank-and-file hoplites, 'where they served in a contingent sent by Thebes to support the Spartans'.[34]

Confederacy *Redux*

Regardless of Sparta's brazen meddling, six years later the Theban patriots, Pelopidas and his associates, liberated their *polis* from the pro-Spartan oligarchy.[35] This recovery led to the complete restoration of the old Boiotian confederacy under the banner of κοινόν, the commonwealth. The confederacy reborn only had seven *boiōtarchoi*,[36] which suggests there were only seven federal districts now, and as Orkhomenos and Thespiai were still held by Spartan garrisons they were probably abolished. However, its decision-making body was a federal assembly and not the federal council of 660 as before. Though more democratic in nature, the new federal assembly convened in Thebes and, as of old, the Thebans still retained the right to provide four *boiōtarchoi*.

Similarly, as the army numbered 7,000 hoplites and 700 horsemen, the old levy of 1,000 and 100 from each district was still in place. However, many of the powers of the former federal council were handed over to the *boiōtarchoi*. It is conceivable that these district levies were organised into *lóchoi* of around 300 hoplites. Xenophon, writing up the events in the Peloponnese leading up to the campaign of Second Mantineia (362 BCE), mentions a unit of 300 Boiotian hoplites billeted in Tegea.[37]

Band of Lovers

At this time Thebes also raised the famous Sacred Band, an elite hoplite unit created by Gorgidas, who was a *boiōtarchēs* in 378 BCE,[38] immediately after the liberation of Thebes from Spartan occupation in 379/378 BCE, and

---

33 Xen. *Hell*. 5.2.1–7, Isok. 14.27–28, Plut. *Pel*. 4.4–5, Paus. 9.13.1. When Mantineia lost its fortification walls after Agesipolis' successful siege, the Spartan terms of surrender included the reversal of the *synoikismós*, or concentration of population, through a *dioikismós* (literally 'breaking apart'), which scattered the citizens once again to their village settlements. Xenophon reports on the reactions of the Mantineians to this: 'They did not like it at first, since they had to demolish their existing houses and build others. But since those who had property were both living nearer to the plots of land that they had around the villages and were enjoying aristocratic government [i.e. oligarchy], being freed from the burdensome demagogues, they were rather pleased at what had happened' (*Hell*. 5.2.7). Sparta was more than happy too, for the Mantineians now readily supplied troops to the Peloponnesian League army, which it controlled. *Synoikismós* favoured democracy, and 15 years later, the Mantineians seized the chance offered by the decisive defeat of the Spartans at Leūktra to re-*synoikise* their *polis* and, as a consequence, installed a democratic government naturally hostile to Sparta (ibid. 6.5.3–5).

34 Plut. *Pel*. 4.4.

35 Xen. *Hell*. 5.4.1–14, cf. Nep. *Epam*. 10.3, *Pel*. 2.5.

36 *Hell. Oxy*. 19.3.

37 Xen. *Hell*. 7.4.36.

38 Cf. Plut. *Pel*. 14.

Remains of the splendid castle of Nicolas II de Saint-Omer, *seigneur de la moitié des terres des Thèbes* (r. 1258–94) during the *Frankokratía*, the Frankish occupation of Greece. Built from 1258 to 1274 only to be largely torn down after 1311 by the mercenary *Gran Companyia Catalana* following their victory against all odds over the *crème de la crème* of northern French and Burgundian chivalry on the Halmyros plain (15 March 1311), its ruins sit on the site of the Kadmeia, the akropolis of ancient Thebes (Θήβα). In its original form, the *donjon* was three-stories high and suitable to host an emperor and his court according to the *Chronicle of the Morea*; only the ground floor remains today and part of the first floor. Thíva (Θίνα), as it is called today, is one of the oldest continuous inhabited cities in the world, and the third oldest in Europe. It certainly inextricably bound up with Greek myth, being the birthplace or home of Kadmos, Pentheus, Oidipous, Antigone, Teiresias, Dionysos, Herakles, and others. (Chabe 01/Wikimedia Commons/ CC-BY-SA-4.0)

comprising 150 pairs of male lovers maintained at state expense and lodged in a barracks on the Kadmeia.[39] The original plan was to deploy them as a unit only in limited operations, usually forming 'the front ranks of the whole [Theban] phalanx',[40] but it was Pelopidas' victory at Tegyra in 375 BCE over the Spartan forces stationed at Orkhomenos that heralded the glory days of the Sacred Band.[41] As Plutarch wrote: 'A band that is held together by the

---

39   Polyain. 2.5.1, Plut. *Pel.* 18.1, cf. 18.5: 'band of lovers and beloved', each pair consisting of an older *erastēs*, 'lover', and a younger *erōmenos*, 'beloved' (Athen. 13.561e). The first literary reference to the Sacred Band dates to 324 BCE in a speech of the orator Deinarchos (361–291 BCE): 'When Pelopidas led the Sacred Band; when Epameinondas and his colleagues commanded the army. Then did the Thebans gain the victory at Leūktra' (1.72–3).

40   Plut. *Pel.* 19.3.

41   Xenophon, unsurprisingly despite his avid soldierly interest in all things military, makes no mention of the Sacred Band's glorious moment at Tegyra, likewise at Leūktra: his sole reference

friendship between lovers is indissoluble and not to be broken, since the lovers are ashamed to play the coward before their beloved, and the beloved before their lovers, and both stand firm in danger to protect the other.'[42]

Here a narrow route between the swampy margins of Lake Kōpaïs and hills to the north opened onto a small plain suitable for hoplite battle. The two Spartan *polémarchoi*, Gorgoleon and Theopompos, hastily deployed their *mórai* and advanced on the Thebans. Plutarch, in the only detailed extant account of the battle and pictures Tegyra as a prelude to Leūktra, has this to say:

> As soon as the Thebans caught sight of the Spartans emerging from the narrow defiles in the hills, one of them ran to Pelopidas and cried out, 'We have fallen into our enemy's hands!' 'Why not the enemy into our hands?' retorted Pelopidas. He immediately ordered his whole cavalry force to ride up from the rear and to prepare for a charge, and he drew up his infantry, who numbered three hundred [i.e. the Sacred Band], in close formation: his hope was that wherever the cavalry charged, this point would offer him the best chance to break through the enemy who outnumbered him. There were two *mórai* of Spartans, each consisting of five hundred men according to Ephoros,[43] although Kallisthenes gives their strength at seven hundred, and other writers, Polybios among them, put it at nine hundred.[44]

Note here that Plutarch highlights the problem concerning the actual strength of a Spartan *móra*. Pelopidas must have expected his horsemen, 200 in number, to harass the front and flanks of the Spartans and so prevent them from using their superior strength to surround the Sacred Band. Plutarch continues:

> There was a furious clash as the two lines met, the fighting being fiercest at the point in the line where the two commanders were stationed, and it was there that the Spartan *polémarchoi* engaged Pelopidas and were both killed. Then when the Spartans around them were also cut down, panic began to spread through the army, and they parted their ranks to make a passage for the Thebans, supposing they wanted to force their way to the rear and escape. However, Pelopidas used the corridor which was thus opened to attack the formations which were still holding their ground, and he cut his way through them with great slaughter, until finally the entire Spartan force turned and fled.[45]

There was no pursuit by the Thebans, wary that the Orkhomenians would sally forth and intervene, but they did set up a trophy and stripped the Spartan dead. As Diodoros Sikoulos points out, the battle marked the first occasion

---

(*Hell.* 7.1.19, cf. Plut. *Apophth.* 71.19) to this elite unit is its action outside Corinth in the summer of 369 BCE, a rare reverse for the Sacred Band which the author could have witnessed if he had been watching from the Akrocorinth.
42 Plut. *Pel.* 18.2, cf. Pl. *Symp.* 179e.
43 Source: Ephoros fr. 210 Jacoby, cf. Arist. fr. 540 Rose.
44 Plut. *Pel.* 17.1–2.
45 Ibid. 17.3–4.

The Lion Monument, Chaironeia, Boiotia. It was discovered on 3 June 1818 in the fields east of the ancient *polis* of Chaironeia by a passing party of British tourists; they were using Pausanias' *Description of Greece* as a guidebook. A common tale is that it was dynamited by the *kléphtēs* Odysseus Androutsos (1788–1825), the Greek military and political commander of eastern mainland Greece during the Greek War of Independence (1821–9), seeking buried treasure. The tale had been strongly refuted. Excavations in 1880 of the quadrangular enclosure brought to light the hastily buried, tightly packed skeletons of 254 men laid out in seven rows, possibly the final resting place of the members of the Theban Sacred Band. As Pausanias reports, though there is no inscription the gigantic grey stone lion marked the site (*viz.* a *polyándrion*) of 'the Thebans who were killed in the struggle against Philip' (9.40.10, cf. Strab. 9.2.37). It was at Chaironeia that the battle-tried Sacred Band (ιερός λόχος / *hierós lochós*) fought it out to the last with the indomitable spirit of the unit. Assailed by enemies on all sides, they were virtually annihilated. Many of the skeletons exhibit horrendous wounds. (©Nic Fields)

in which a Spartan force had been defeated by a numerically inferior enemy in a pitched battle.[46]

Thereafter, the Sacred Band was always deployed as a proper unit in its own right on all occasions thereafter,[47] and it was in this function that it truly became a crack force. As we shall hear, this would make for a crucial role at Leŭktra.

Unsurprisingly, it was the Spartans that were commonly satirised and caricatured outside Sparta by allegations that they were all hopelessly addicted to homosexual sex. Any sweeping judgement, good or bad, is unwise in the case of an individual; it is still more unwise in the case of a people. Such a description was somewhat exaggerated and was just a way of being offensive to the Spartans. Of more significance is the fact that the number of the Sacred Band was the same as that of the *hippeīs*, the royal bodyguard of Sparta and of the selected force that went to Thermopylai with Leonidas, so probably this was a deliberate echo of a Spartan idea, a Theban

---

46   Diod. 15.81.2.
47   Plut. *Pel.* 19.3.

clone. The Sacred Band was to remain unbeaten until its virtual annihilation on the fields of Chaironeia in 338 BCE when the leading forces of Greece united against Philip II of Macedon. Even during this tragic final act, the unit stubbornly stood its ground because all 300 members had decided to fight to the death.[48] Their burial en masse beneath the Lion Monument at Chaironeia is hotly disputed, but this illustrious Theban unit certainly never reformed, having raised one last memorial to their great leader Pelopidas, and offering one last atonement for the cowardice of Thebes in the Persian Wars.

Prime Movers

Although there was now a titular head of the confederacy, the eponymous *árchōn*,[49] still, as he is not known to have exercised real political clout, the most important executive office remained that of *boiōtarchēs*. In civilian life, the seven *boiōtarcho* served as members of a *probouloi*, the body that discussed the matters to be presented before the federal assembly. As members of the *probouloi* they were also responsible for initiating the proceedings of the assembly.[50] The seven likewise served as ambassadors.[51] Yet it was in the military sphere that their chief importance rested, and here all seven held equal authority. Before the Battle of Leūktra, as you shall hear in due time, the six *boiōtarchoi* present voted whether to fight and the outcome was a split three for and three against. It was not until the seventh *boiōtarchēs* arrived that the vote was decided in favour of battle.[52] Unity of command is the most important principle of war and, interestingly, Plutarch tells us that during the next campaigning season, when the Boiotians invaded Lakonia, Epameinondas' five colleagues surrendered their powers to him and Pelopidas.[53] However, it was winter and their commands were soon to lapse, so it is possible that the five could have got cold feet in more ways than one as Plutarch does in fact imply.

The military duties of the *boiōtarchoi* gave them virtual control of Boiotian foreign policy. For example, Epameinondas signed the terms of the treaty between the confederacy and Sikyon, and in 366 BCE between the confederacy and the Achaian League. Pelopidas behaved in a similar manner when campaigning in Thessaly and Macedonia. It appears therefore, that the man on the spot decided policy. However, the federal assembly could overturn a *boiōtarchēs*' decision. The assembly also elected him to office and failure to lay down the command at the end of the year was a capital offence. Moreover, incompetence was also punishable by death or a heavy fine depending on

---

48   Plut. *Pel.* 18.5, cf. *Alex.* 9.2, Diod. 16.86.3. Beneath the Lion of Chaironeia, a Macedonian monument, which stands at the western end of the battle site, were later discovered 254 skeletons laid out in seven rows. Was this the final resting place for these do or die professionals of Thebes? I would like to think so. See Pritchett 1958: 310–311.
49   Harding 48.4.
50   Diod. 15.79.5.
51   Xen. *Hell.* 7.4.40, Plut. *Pel.* 26, Nep. *Epam.* 6.4.
52   Diod. 15.33.3, Paus. 9.13.6–7.
53   Plut. *Pel.* 24.2.

the circumstances.[54] Thus, even though the *boiōtarchoi* held wide ranging powers, they were still controlled by the federal assembly, which was able to control and double check the power of the *boiōtarchoi*. This ability is best exemplified by a political trial that took place in 369 BCE. Epameinondas and Pelopidas returned from a military campaign in the Peloponnese and were indicted for extending their office of *boiōtarchēs* beyond the legal term of one year, specifically, to be in Thebes before the winter solstice.[55]

The most important difference between the reborn confederacy and its predecessor was indeed the federal assembly: theoretically, all free adult males were eligible to vote. Polybios, a dyed-in-the-wool oligarch and consequently no friend of democracy in any shape or form, imagined in Thebes that 'a mob manages everything on its own unfettered impulse… trained in long habits of violence and ferocity',[56] whereas the similarly anti-democratic Xenophon believed the confederacy had been re-established on the new basis of a democracy centred on Thebes.[57]

The new Boiotian constitution was probably modelled on that of Athens; many of the patriots had spent their years of exile in Athens, the home of radical democracy. In addition, during the liberation of Thebes the Athenians had stationed an army on the Attic-Boiotian border to support the patriots. Nevertheless, the plain fact that the federal assembly met in Thebes meant that the *polis* clearly dominated it and its policy making for the simple reason that participation of citizens from other Boiotian *poleis* was limited.

Nonetheless, as with the case of Epameinondas and Pelopidas, the federal assembly was one of the means by which the citizens in Thebes controlled *boiōtarchoi* who, as *stratēgoi*, were seen to overtly control the line of action of foreign policy for the confederacy as a whole. And herein lies the paradox of Boiotian autonomy in the fourth century BCE.

By asserting their autonomy from Thebes, Boiotian *poleis* were made more susceptible not only to foreign influence, but also domination. Only by ceding power to Thebes could Boiotia be autonomous from foreign powers. So, as for Sparta, its action regarding the Boiotian confederacy was clearly dictated by its attitude towards Thebes. When friendly to Thebes, Sparta helped it to maintain the confederacy against seceding members supported by Athens; when hostile, Sparta followed the policy that came more naturally to it, that of encouraging segregation. Yet it was precisely the lack of consensus among the Boiotians themselves about Thebes' leadership that led to federalism of so unusual and developed a kind, which in turn gave Boiotia the cohesion and the manpower to defeat Sparta at Leūktra.

In truth, the confederacy was one of convenience rather than genuine friendship, and the flowering time of Thebes had arrived too late, for the

---

54 Plut. *Pel.* 29, Nep. *Epam.* 7.5.
55 Cic. *Inv. rhet.* 1.33 (55–6), 38 (69), Nep. *Epam.* 7.3–8.5, Plut. *Pel.* 24.1–25.2, *Mor.* 194A-B, 540D-E, 799E-F, 817E-F, Paus. 9.14.2–4. According to Diodoros Sikoulos (15.72.1–2) Epameinondas was tried again after the second Peloponnesian campaign. This time he was charged with treason for allegedly having favoured the Spartans by granting a truce in a difficult moment. This is probably the truce mentioned by Xenophon (*Hell.* 7.1.17)
56 Polyb. 6.44.9.
57 Xen. *Hell.* 5.4.46.

halcyon days of Greece were on the wane. Removed to Rome for indefinite detention on political grounds, the Achaian statesman Polybios best sums up the ultimate decline of Thebes:

> Since fortune quickly made it evident that it was not the peculiarity of their constitution, but the valour of their leaders, which gave the Thebans their success. For the great power of Thebes notoriously took its rise, attained its zenith, and fell to the ground with the lives of Epameinondas and Pelopidas. We must therefore conclude that it was not its constitution, but its men, that caused the high fortune which it then enjoyed.[58]

Of course, it is hard to say what Thebes might not still have achieved if Epameinondas had not been cut down in the prime of maturity at Second Mantineia, with his friend Pelopidas dead two years before, likewise fallen in battle.

---

58   Polyb. 6.43.5–7.

Chapter 7

Opening Moves, Spring–Summer 371 BCE

Epameinondas speaks of the plain of Boiotia as 'a dancing floor of Ares'.

Plutarch *Marcellus* 21.2

Epameinondas justly told his fellow Boiotians that their country, 'which was flat and exposed',[1] was the amphitheatre of Ares. This was the awesome Greek god of war, the fully armoured, brazen warrior who was accompanied in his war chariot by his sons Phóbos (fear) and Deimós (fright). Unlike his Roman counterpart Mars, who was also an agricultural guardian, the short-tempered and combative Ares had no time for farming. He was an overwhelming, insatiable battlefield deity, totally destructive, destabilising, and man-slaughtering.[2] Epameinondas also advised them 'that they could not hold their power over it if they did not keep a grip on the handles (πόρακος, armbands) of their shields'.[3]

Though Ares had laid a curse on the house of Kadmos, the founder king of Thebes, the force of nature had played a greater part in the woes of Boiotia. Its great landlocked double basin, with its narrow entries and exits and major arteries north and south, had always been an area of antagonism, a constellation of rival *poleis*, great and small. Perikles, for instance, claimed that the Boiotians could be compared 'to Holm oaks, because they were ruining one another by civil wars just as one oak causes another oak to fall'.[4] Another example of this perception comes from a Theban himself. In his pre-battle harangue to his soldiers at Delion, the Theban *boiōtarchēs* Pagondas warns of the dangers of division: 'We have experience of this ourselves in dealing with these Athenians. By our victory over them at [First] Koroneia, in the days when, because of our internal quarrels, they were occupying Boiotia, we made our country secure right up to the present day.'[5]

---

1   Plut. *Apophth.* 71.18.
2   For example, Hom. *Il.* 4.439–41, 15.119–21, 17.210-12, 18.309 Lattimore.
3   Plut. *Apophth.* 71.18.
4   Arist. *Rh.* 3.4.1407a.
5   Thuc. 4.92.6.

Chapter 8

Leūktra, Summer 371 BCE

> The victory of the Thebans was the most famous of all those won by Greeks over Greeks.
>
> Pausanias 9.13.4

Before we begin our narrative of the battle, lets us look at the principal sources available to us. There are effectively three historical accounts, each with their virtues and vices. Though Xenophon was contemporaneous, his grudging account of Leūktra is rather wanting; being blinded by his attachment to Agesilaos and Sparta, Epameinondas and Pelopidas are not named and their plans and actions not explored.[1] However, despite the claim by Paul Cartledge that 'the precise details are as ever unrecoverable,[2] Xenophon does provide sufficient tactical detail to explain what happened when the two sides faced each other on the narrow plain of Leūktra. Some additional help is provided by those later writers, Diodoros Sikoulos and Plutarch,[3] though much does remain uncertain. In his account of the battle, Diodoros fails to give any hint of the cavalry action that opened the day's events, an important phase of the battle as it was probably coordinated with the rapid advance of the Theban phalanx. Plutarch, naturally, is more concerned with the doings of his fellow Boiotian whom he obviously admired, Pelopidas, while his biography of Epameinondas, torn from us by the shortfall of time, is a serious loss. Yet for all his faults, it has to be remembered that Xenophon, unlike Diodoros and Plutarch, lived through the war he describes.

These sources disagree about numbers beyond the fact that the Spartans and their mercenaries and allies outnumbered the Boiotians. Xenophon says nothing except that there were four Spartan *mórai*,[4] and that the *enōmotiai* were formed up in three files of not more than 12 men each.[5] Xenophon

---

1   Xen. *Hell.* 6.4.1–26. Epameinondas is named for the first time by Xenophon (*Hell.* 7.1.41) during the campaign in the north of the Peloponnese in 367 BCE, *four years after* Leūktra. Note, unlike his good comrade-in-arms Epameinondas, Pelopidas did not hold the rank of *boiōtarchēs* at Leūktra (Plut. *Pel.* 23.4).
2   Cartledge 1987: 238.
3   Diod. 15.51–6, Plut. *Pel.* 20.1–23.4, *Ages.* 28.3–6.
4   Xen. *Hell.* 6.4.17.
5   Ibid. 6.4.12.

mentions other troops, such as mercenary hoplites and Phokian peltasts.[6] Pausanias says Arkadians fought at the battle (mercenaries in all probability),[7] and there were probably hoplites from Phleious and Herakleia Trachinia too.[8] In any case, neither army will have exceeded 10,000 men, of whom the vast majority were hoplites, and perhaps 1,000 horsemen on either side. The figures generally accepted would give the Spartan army a total of 9,000 to 10,000 hoplites and between 800 and 1,000 horsemen.[9] The Lakedaimonians supplied between a quarter and half of the hoplites. The Boiotian confederacy army, which included no allied contingents, was composed of about 6,000 to 7,000 hoplites, 4,000 of whom were Thebans, and 700 horsemen.[10]

The Overture

According to Xenophon, the companions of Kleombrotos reminded the king of the suspicions he had incurred by his former lacklustre performances against the Thebans (as we have related), and warned him of the danger of repeating such conduct today.[11] Xenophon continues, saying: 'All this talk had the effect of making Kleombrotos eager to join battle'.[12]

Even if there was as much hesitation on the other side, Xenophon says the *boiōtarchoi* had no choice but to engage, 'since many of them had been in exile before, they estimated that it was better to die fighting than to be in exile again'.[13] On the other hand, Diodoros Sikoulos stresses the fact that the Boiotians were reluctant to join battle as they felt that a fight on a level plain would give the advantage to the Spartans because of their superior

---

6   Ibid. 6.4.9.

7   Like the Swiss of more recent times, the Arkadians were tough mountaineers from an impoverished region, and like the Swiss, they constantly served abroad as mercenaries. Lykomedes of Mantineia, the first leader of the Arcadians after the establishment of the Arkadian League by Epameinondas, is reputed to have boasted: 'When anyone wants mercenaries, they choose Arkadians second to none' (Xen. *Hell.* 7.1.23). The simple mannered delights of 'Arcady' are of course the creation of late and sophisticated folk seeking to retreat from the pressures and complexities of urban life (e.g. in art there is Poussin's *Et in Arcadia ego* and Cole's *Dream of Arcadia*), but Arkadia has always been, and still is, a pastoral country. Arkadia's stock epithet in ancient literature was 'of the many sheep' (e.g. Hom. *Il.* 2.605 Lattimore, Bacch. 38.94–5, Pind. *Olymp.* 6.100), while Arkadians were traditionally portrayed as 'acorn-eaters' (e.g. Hdt. 1.66, Paus. 8.1.6, 42.6, cf. Hom. *Od.* 3.242 Lattimore). *Vide* Fields 2001.

8   Paus. 8.6.2.

9   Plutarch (*Pel.* 20.1) gives the figure of 10,000 hoplites and 1,000 horsemen for the Spartan army, the latter being made up of Herakleots, Phleiousians and Lakedaimonians according to Xenophon (*Hell.* 6.4.9, 10). Plutarch's figures for the Spartan army are far more realistic than Frontinus' 24,000 infantry and 1,600 cavalry (4.2.6), or Polyainos' overall total of 40,000 men (2.3.8).

10   Diodoros (15.53.2, 3) and Pausanias (9.13.3) provide the figures of 4,000 and 3,000 for the Theban and Boiotian hoplites respectively, while Frontinus (4.2.6) says there were only 3,600 Theban hoplites, the other 400 being horsemen. Plutarch (*Pel.* 23.1) mentions the 300-strong Sacred Band. As for the horsemen, we are assuming of course that each of the seven federal divisions that made up the Boiotian confederacy provided one hundred horsemen, which meant 400 of them would have been the Thebans mentioned by Frontinus (loc. cit.).

11   Xen. *Hell.* 6.4.5.

12   Ibid. 6.4.6.

13   Loc. cit.

numbers.[14] All the sources agree, however, about the various omens of victory and disaster that were manifested to either side, some even going so far as to suggest that some or all were deliberately manufactured by Epameinondas and Pelopidas.[15] The most amusing, and perhaps the most likely to be authentic because it is the most unusual, is the anecdote told by Frontinus: 'When… Epameinondas was about to open battle against the Spartans, the chair on which he had sat down gave way beneath him, whereat all the soldiers, greatly troubled, interpreted this as an unlucky omen. But Epameinondas exclaimed: "Not at all; we are simply forbidden to sit."'[16]

It is a lovely line that, puncturing what must have been a doom-laden atmosphere with a feather-light touch. While this may seem a rather fanciful story, as you can see, it is nevertheless too singular to be omitted.

Xenophon has an interesting tale to tell too. Pointing out that in the coming battle the Boiotians had all the luck, while for the Spartans everything turned out for the worse: 'For it was after the morning meal that Kleombrotos held his last council over the battle, and drinking a little, as they did, at the middle of the day, it was said that the wine helped somewhat to excite them.'[17]

This rather cavalier behaviour is certainly at odds with the normal sober atmosphere of the Spartan scene when you pause for a second and think of their military messes. So, if Xenophon is correct in his analysis and not just searching around for a suitable excuse for the looming disaster, then it is possible that the Spartans were more than slightly sottish prior to the clash. Because of this Dionysiac strangeness, instead of stealing their nerves for the upcoming head-to-head with the Thebans, the (neat?)[18] wine had probably endangered their chances of success due to alcohol induced recklessness. Xenophon does give the impression that there was some initial Spartan confusion in the battle, which began an entire succession of fatal blunders.

While the Spartans were apparently enjoying a pre-battle swig, the sober Epameinondas was crowning a local tomb with wreaths. This was the tomb of the two virgin daughters of a local man by the name of Skedasos. Having been violated by two Spartan ambassadors and unable to bear the shame, the sisters, variously named as Molpia (or Miletia) and Hippō or Theano and Euxippe, hung themselves. The father sought justice in Sparta, but to no avail; he too committed suicide, doing so over his daughters' tomb while uttering a curse upon Sparta. An oracle had predicted that the Spartans would be defeated at the scene of this crime.[19]

---

14 Diod. 15.53.3–4

15 Ibid. 15.53.4–6, Plut. *Pel.* 20.3–4, Frontin. 1.11.16, Polyain. 2.3.8, 12.

16 Frontin. 1.12.7.

17 Xen. *Hell.* 6.4.8.

18 *Vide* Appendix 5.

19 Xen. *Hell.* 6.4.7, Plut. *Pel.* 20.3–4, Paus. 13.3.5, cf. Diod. 15.54.3, who has two sets of maidens, the daughters of Skedasos and the daughters of Leūktros (the eponym of Leūktra). The name Hippo, literary 'horse', appears in many Amazon names (e.g. Hippolytē, Hippomache, Hippothoë, et cetera). The most famous was the Amazon queen Hippo who helped found the cities of Ephesos, Smyrna, Kyrene, and Myrina (Diod. 2.45–6, Strab. 11.5.4, Just. 2.4). Her sister was Molpia ('melody'), a priestess of Artemis the Hanged One: jointed clay dolls representing the virgin goddess of fertility were hung from trees to ensure good crops. Artemis the Hanged One had a sacred grove and temple at Kondylea in Arkadia (Paus. 8.23.6).

Before going to war, the Spartans would have consulted Delphic Apollo, each king having within his personal entourage two of four *Pythioi* – envoys dispatched to the oracle on their behalf.[20] Once having reached the decision to go to war, the king who was to lead the expedition sacrificed in his house to Zeus Agetor ('Who leads out') and other gods associated with him. If the signs were favourable, the fire-bearer, *pōsphóros*, carried fire from the altar to the frontier of Lakonia where the king sacrificed to Zeus and Athena and, if the signs once again permitted, crossed the frontier with the army.[21] According to Pausanias: 'When Spartan kings marched to war, sheep went with them for sacrifice to the gods and omens before battle. The leaders of these flocks on the march were goats that the shepherd called sheep-leaders.'[22] Pausanias continues, saying that at some point prior to the battle (he is not specific as to exactly when), 'wolves attacked the flock and did no harm to the sheep but killed these sheep-leaders.'[23]

On reaching the battlefield, according to Plutarch, the king made another sacrifice, this time 'to the Muses, thereby apparently reminding his men of their training and their trials, so that they should be ready to face the dangers ahead, and should perform memorable feats in the fighting'.[24] All this was important, for as Xenophon has Sokrates say: 'You see men engaged in war try to propitiate the gods before taking action; and with sacrifices and omens seek to know what they ought to do and what they ought not to do'.[25]

For the Greeks in general, war involved spiritual values, a question of sacred as well as strategic considerations. Evidently the rigidity of the Spartans in such affairs was beyond doubt. Like all fighting people, the Spartans were incredibly superstitious and invariably self-dramatic. Yet for victory in open battle their austere offering was just a single cockerel to Ares, worth less than an *obolós*, not because they were mean or disrespected the war god, but because they held him in awe and deemed it dishonourable to over express their mortal joy in a god-given triumph.[26] Today, at Leūktra, Ares would be denied his cockerel.

The Deployment

The disposition of the contending armies was to some extent similar on both sides, with the horsemen posted opposite each other in front of their respective battle lines, right wing for the Spartans and left wing for the Boiotians. The terrain was a level, small valley between low, gentle hills. In other words, between the armies stretched level ground, upon which the Boiotian cavalry could be deployed to great advantage.

---

20 Hdt. 6.57.2, Xen. *Lak. pol.* 15.5, Cic. *Div.* 1.43.
21 Xen. *Lak. pol.* 13.2–3, cf. *Hell.* 3.4.3, 6.4.19.
22 Paus. 9.13.2.
23 Loc. cit.
24 Plut. *Lyk.* 21.3.
25 Xen. Oik. 5.19.
26 Plut. *Mor.* 25.

At Leūktra, not only were Spartan casualties heavy, but also politically the effects of the Boiotian victory were immense. Sparta lost much prestige by simply showing that its army could be beaten on the field of battle. Xenophon, in his description of the Spartan catastrophe, implies (*Hell.* 6.4.8) Kleombrotos and his men were more than a little tipsy on the wine they had drunk at high noon, perhaps strong and undiluted. Panoramic view of the battle site looking northeast towards the site of the Boiotian encampment. Having marched *post haste* to intercept Kleombrotos, Epameinondas and his fellow *boiōtarchoi* reached the low hills that rim the northern edge of the plain of Leūktra and encamped opposite the Spartans. In this photograph, the Spartans would have been arrayed on the right, the Boiotians on the left, while the narrow strip of ground between was where the two armies clashed. (©Nic Fields)

The Spartan battleline was 12 shields deep, Xenophon being very precise with his details here tells us that the Spartans had 'led each *enōmotia* three files abreast, and that this resulted in the phalanx being not more than twelve deep',[27] which also tells us that each *enōmotia* on this occasion was some 36 hoplites strong. Xenophon implies that Kleombrotos and the *hippeīs* were on the Spartan right,[28] and presumably the right wing of the Spartan array was composed of the four *mórai*, the king and his bodyguard perhaps stationed between the second and third *mórai* counting from the right.[29] The centre and the left wing would have been composed of the mercenaries and allies.

On the other side, it is clear that the Thebans were on the left wing of the Boiotian array, and 'were not less than fifty shields deep',[30] following their preference for the deep phalanx, though to a lesser degree, in other battles over the last five decades or so.[31] What appears to be a new departure

---

27 Xen. *Hell.* 6.4.12. Why Stylianou (1997: 401–403) suggests the Thebans formed only a 25-deep phalanx (as they certainly did at Delion) is somewhat bizarre. Xenophon, after all a contemporary observer, clearly says the Thebans *were* 'not less than fifty shields deep'.

28 Xen. *Hell.* 6.4.14.

29 *Contra* Buckler 1980B: 63.

30 Xen. *Hell.* 6.4.12.

31 At Delion in 424 BCE the Thebans on the Boiotian right had been massed 25 shields (Thuc. 4.93.4); at the Nemea in 394 BCE, the Boiotians had 'made their phalanx really deep' (Xen. *Hell.*

General view of battlefield as seen from the Spartan right flank a little west of the Theban Victory Monument. This would have been the position of the four *móra* along with the *hippeîs* protecting the Spartan king, Kleombrotos. Immediately opposite them would have been the heavily stacked Theban phalanx spearheaded by Pelopidas and the Sacred Band. It was at this particular spot that the battle was won and lost. The Spartans had entered Boiotia expecting their invasion to be crowned with victory. However, on the field of Leūktra the Theban attack was irresistible. The perspective of hindsight should not deceive us: at the time the Theban' victory seemed like, and indeed was, a stupefying reversal of certainties. In one afternoon, the Thebans had shattered the Spartan myth of invincibility. Note Mount Helikon in the far distance. (© Nic Fields)

is that the remainder of the Boiotian battleline was echeloned away so that the main clash of the Theban phalanx under Epameinondas would occur before the other Boiotians got stuck in. In fact, as to his centre and right wing Epameinondas' mind might be easy: by refusing these they were virtually out of the battle and were destined to play simply the role of spectators.

Epameinondas, as a *stratēgós*, was something new. His capacity for careful thought went hand-in-hand with courage and passion, and with the ability to take risks. He intended that the mass on the left would meet the Spartans at the point where Kleombrotos was and break the Spartan battleline before it had a chance to encircle his left flank. If we can believe Plutarch, and there is no real reason to doubt him here, the elite Sacred Band formed the cutting edge of the heavily stacked Theban phalanx,[32] perhaps its first three or four ranks. Their current commander was of course Epameinondas' very good friend, Pelopidas.[33] So, with 4,000 Theban hoplites massed 50-shields deep, this phalanx would only have had a narrow frontage of 80 shields. Epameinondas' tactic was simple, ingenious, and terribly risky. Yet, as is often the case, the audacious course can prove to be the best.

4.2.18), and certainly deeper than 16-shields deep.

32 Plut. *Pel.* 23.2.

33 Ibid. 20.2, cf. 23.4.

Epameinondas clearly understood the outcome of the battle depended on the result of the contest between the Thebans and the Spartans. In previous engagements, the Thebans and the Spartans had opposed each other on the right wing of their respective battle lines, the traditional position of honour in hoplite warfare. When the armies had fought, as in the dual engagements of the Nemea and Second Koroneia in 394 BCE, both right wings had won, but each time the Spartans had gone on to win the second phase of battle, when the victorious wings subsequently engaged.[34] Now Theban and Spartan phalanxes would engage immediately. Moreover, Epameinondas anticipated Kleombrotos would employ the traditional Spartan manoeuvre of wheeling his overlapping *mórai* so as to turn the Theban left flank. But Epameinondas, with his heavy phalanx spearheaded by the Sacred Band, which was in the very capable hands of Pelopidas, planned to strike the Spartans, and strike them hard, before they completed this battle-winning flanking manoeuvre.

The Advance

Plutarch gives the date as the fifth of the Hekatombaion,[35] which corresponds roughly to 8 July. The battle opened around midday that day, after Kleombrotos and his men perhaps had one or two too many (as has been before hinted). Nonetheless, with the battle about to commence, the Spartan king would have been in his element.

Just as Epameinondas anticipated, the initiative lay with the Spartans: Kleombrotos moved to attack, extending his battleline and wheeling his right flank. As he did so, according to Plutarch, he would have 'sacrificed the customary she-goat, commanded all warriors to set garlands upon their heads, and ordered the pipers to pipe the strains of the hymn to Kastor; then himself led off in a marching *paiān*'.[36] These garlands were the sanctifying signs of the Spartans' conviction and their fighting solidarity. As for the blood sacrifice, this would have been the second, the first that being made as the Spartans deployed for battle, as mentioned earlier. Xenophon says that this *sphagia*,[37] a propitiatory blood sacrifice, was performed in plain view of the enemy, though for him it was a year-old male goat that has its throat pierced, and done so in honour of Artemis Agrotéra, the Huntress,[38] 'as is their custom'.[39] With regards to the gender of the beast given up to Artemis, Xenophon is certainly to be favoured in this context. Not only would he have witnessed firsthand a Spartan *sphagia*, but solely for reasons of a practical nature, it was commonly males that were slaughtered, females being far too

---

34 Xen. *Hell*. 4.2.16–23, Diod. 14.83.2, 84.1–2.

35 Plut. *Ages*. 28.5.

36 Plut. *Lyk*. 22.2–3.

37 From the verb σφάζειν, 'to piece the throat'. Pottery iconography usually depicts a warrior holding the animal firm between his legs to keep it from struggling, and at the same time pulling back the head with one hand and stabbing it in the throat with the other. Note, in a battle context, the animal was not cooked and eaten after having been killed.

38 Hom. *Il*. 5.51–2, 21.470, 511 Lattimore, Xen. *Kyn*. 6.13, Bacch. 11.37–42.

39 Xen. *Hell*. 4.2.20, cf. 3.1.17, *Lak. pol*. 13.8, Plut. *Lyk*. 22.4, Hdt. 9.61.3–62.1.

Marble relief (Chalkis, Archaeological Museum of Chalkis, inv. 7) from the ancient Boiotian port of Larymna situated on the Euboian Gulf, dating to the fifth century BCE. Though broken, the relief clearly depicts a *sphagia*, the battleline sacrifice of a ram. No Greek army went into battle without a strong sense of the gods as onlookers and guides – the killing of the animal is immediately followed by the killing of men. Having forced the ram to its knees, the sacrificer firmly straddles the sacrificial victim and he pulls back its head so as to pierce its throat with his short sword. The noun *sphagia* is cognate with the verb *spházein*, 'to pierce the throat'. Signs were probably obtained from the observation of the flow of blood – Euripides speaks of *sphagia* as 'streams of blood-loving earth' (*Supp*. 174). In contrast with the more leisurely *hiera* ('rites') of customary sacrifice, when the victim was cut open and the innards were inspected and then burnt, for *sphagia* a sacrificial fire was irrelevant, and so no altar was required. Furthermore, the flesh of the victim was not eaten.
(C messier/Wikimedia Commons/CC-BY-SA-4.0)

useful to 'waste'. Besides, since battles tended to be the affairs of men, male animals (billy-goats, rams) were picked for the *sphagia*.[40]

As for the goddess Artemis, 'daughter of sovereign Zeus', she was one of the most esteemed of the Olympus-dwelling divinities. Much more than just the divinity of the hunt and the bow, Artemis was the goddess of chastity, childbirth, and the moon too. Both in poetry and in painting she was celebrated above all as the wild-willed mistress of wild animals, a virgin huntress armed with a bow, quiver, and arrows (she also carried a pair of hunting spears), who tracked her prey in lonely places, outside the bounds of

40 For the evidence, *vide* Pritchett 1971: 114, table 2.

what was considered civilised. Inviolate and vigorous, she typified both the vivifying and the destructive aspects of untamed nature: she presided over the crucial transition from girlhood and virginity to marriage and motherhood but, like her twin brother Phoibos Far Darter,[41] Apollo himself, she also slew men and beasts by means of her keen arrows, usually the victims of revenge. Sudden deaths were described as the effects of her arrows.[42] Presumably, therefore, this pre-battle sacrifice was a form of sympathetic magic designed to ensure that the same fate overtook their enemies on the field of battle which, after all, was traditionally a place on the periphery of what the Greeks considered civilisation, the sphere of human enterprise, which was represented by the *polis*. Chasing down their foes as if they were prey in the wilderness. Such was the Spartan way.

The Clash

The Boiotian horsemen were greatly superior to the Lakedaimonian, little surprise there, the latter being recruited from nominees provided by wealthy *Spartiātai* who supplied the mounts and the equipment. Since the best Lakedaimonians wished to keep their feet firmly planted on *terra firma* and so serve as hoplites, and since the nominee first encountered his horse and tack on mobilisation, standards were not good to say the least. As Xenophon says, these nominees were the least strong of body and the least ambitious too.[43]

The result was that the cavalry clash, which had taken place while the armies were still drawing up, was swiftly over, with the Lakedaimonian horsemen being driven back in disarray. Xenophon, himself a noted horseman, praises the Boiotian riders for being well trained and battle ready,[44] and here we witness Xenophon the professional soldier as opposed to Xenophon the pro-Spartan historian. Indeed, as mentioned earlier, the Boiotians appear to have had a long tradition as horsemen, consciously maintained by constant riding and mounted training. In contrast to his assessment of the Boiotian cavalry, Xenophon heavily criticises the pitiable quality of the Lakedaimonians, pointing out they were 'in very poor shape'.[45] Lacking in training and experience, they were quickly overridden and hunted back.

The victorious Boiotian cavalry were rapidly followed up by Epameinondas, and the result was the fleeing Lakedaimonian riders shoved their way through their own phalanx,[46] disorganised it, and it was still

---

41 Phoibos, φοῖβος, means 'shining', 'bright', or 'pure', while Far Darter ('the one who strikes from afar', Anon. *Homeric Hymn* 3.1) obviously refers to his use of the bow by which he makes his fatal influence felt from afar, particularly as a spreader of the plague.

42 E.g. Hom. *Il.* 6.205, 427–428, 19.59, 21.483–484, *Od.* 11.172, 324, 15.478, 18.202, 20.61 Lattimore.

43 Xen. *Hell.* 6.4.11. A force of 400 horsemen had first been instituted by Sparta after the Athenian occupation of the Lakonian island of Kythera in 424 BCE (Thuc. 4.55.2).

44 Xen. *Hell.* 6.4.10.

45 Loc. cit. Outside Lechaion 19 years previously, the Lakedaimonian horsemen put up an extremely dismal showing (ibid. 4.5.16).

46 Ibid. 6.4.13.

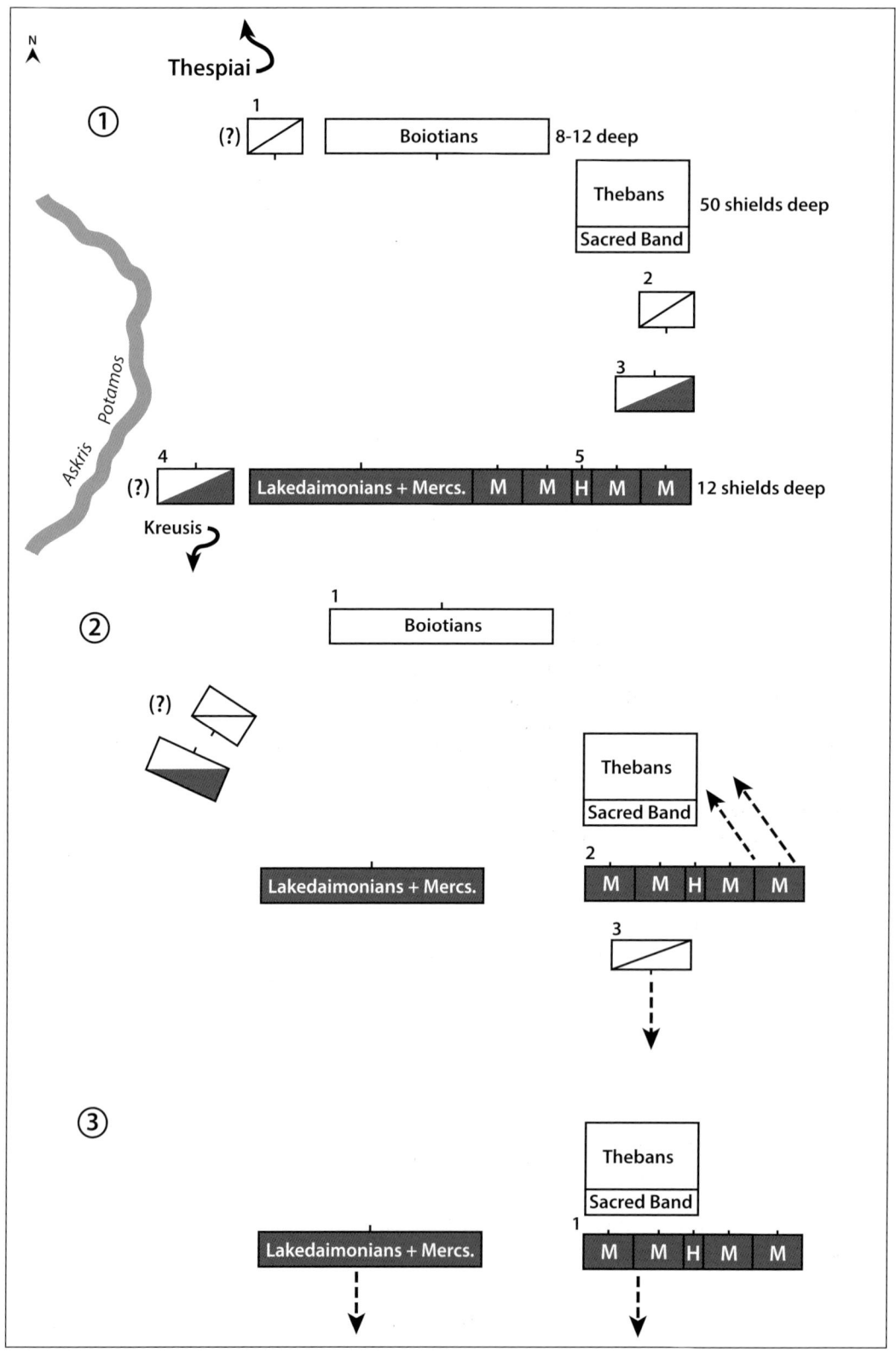

Map 3: Leūktra, summer 371 BCE.

Key to Map

1   300 Boiotian horsemen
2   400 Theban horsemen (cf. Frontin. 4.2.6, Polyb. 2.3.8, 12)
    Mmóra (x4) each under a *polémarchos* (Xen. *Hell.* 6.4.17)
    H 300 strong *hippeīs* around Kleombrotos (ibid. 6.4.14)
3 & 4   1,000 horsemen from Lakedaimon, Phleious & Herakleia Trachinia (ibid. 6.4.9, 10, Plut. *Pel.* 20.1)
5   Kleombrotos and his 'tent companions'

Phases (as indicated on the map)

Phase 1
The Theban horsemen screening the Theban phalanx advance against the Lakedaimonian horsemen. A brisk skirmish ensues.

Phase 2
(a) The Boiotians right and centre hold fast, i.e. refuse to offer battle, while on the left wing the heavily weighted Theban phalanx under Epameinondas advances to contact.
(b) As he moves to attack, Kleombrotos attempts to increase the depth of his phalanx (*viz.* from 12- to 16-shields deep) and shift to his right *at the same time.*
(c) The Lakedaimonian horsemen, having been sorely compromised, burst through the Spartan battleline with the Theban horsemen in hot pursuit.

Phase 3
(a)   The unusually deep Theban phalanx, spearheaded by the elite Sacred Band under Pelopidas, ploughs through the disorganised Spartan battleline and annihilates the *hippeīs* and those Spartans to either side of them.
(b)   Witnessing the demise of the Spartan phalanx, the Lakedaimonians, mercenaries, et cetera, on the centre and left wilt and vanish from the field. The Thebans have carried the day and are now in possession of the battlefield and the tokens of victory – the bodies of the dead.
Frontages (following Lazenby 1985: 155–6, and assuming 1m frontage per hoplite)

Spartan Army
(a) x 4 *mórai*, *viz.* 4,480 hoplites, + 300 *hippeīs* @ 12-shields deep   400m
(b) Lakedaimonians, mercenaries, et cetera, *viz.* 5,000 hoplites @
        10-shields deep   500m
Total frontage   900m

Boiotian Army
(a) 4,000 Thebans + 300 Sacred Band (front four ranks) @ 50-shields deep   80m
(b) 3,000 other Boiotian hoplites (minus the Thespians?) @ 10-shields deep   300m
Total frontage   380m

Boiotian helmet (Oxford, Ashmolean Museum, AN1977.256), late fourth century BCE, discovered June 1854 in the Tigris: it is believed to been lost by one of Alexander's horsemen. Xenophon (*Hell.* 7.5.20) mentions that at the Second Mantineia the Boiotian horseman whitened their helmets, perhaps to differentiate them from the opposing Athenian horseman who would have been using the same style of helmet. The helmet itself can best be described as a bronze riding hat with a down-turned brim that has been bent into elaborate folds. For cavalry use it had the advantage that the face was open and the wearer could hear battlefield commands without difficulty, and so proved a very popular type with horsemen as it 'affords the best protection … without obstructing the sight' (Xen. *PH* 12.3). The Boiotian helmet was usually hammered out from one piece of sheet bronze. (Gts-tg/Wikimedia Commons/CC-BY-SA-4.0)

disorganised when the Theban phalanx, in effect a human battering-ram, hit it square on and eventually broke it. Driving forward, fallen Spartans were suffocated, trampled to death, or dispatched with Theban butt spikes.

At the forefront of course was the Sacred Band under Pelopidas, which was 'the first to break the Lakedaimonian phalanx'.[47] If Plutarch is right, it was Pelopidas' initiative for his 300 men to come into contact 'at the run'.[48] As was expected of a commander in this period, Epameinondas was there in person (next to Pelopidas?) and was prompt to take advantage of the Spartan confusion. In the words of Diodoros Sikoulos:

> Now as long as king Kleombrotos of the Lakedaimonians was alive and had with him many comrades-in-arms who were quite ready to die in his defence, it was uncertain which way the scales of victory inclined; but when, though he shrank from no danger, he proved unable to bear down his opponents, and perished in an heroic resistance after sustaining many wounds, then, as masses of men thronged about his body, there was piled up a great mound of corpses. There being no one in command of the wing, the heavy phalanx led by Epameinondas bore down upon the Lakedaimonians, and at first by sheer force (τῇ βίᾳ βαχὺ) caused the line of the enemy to buckle somewhat; then, however, the Lakedaimonians, fighting gallantly about their king, got possession of his body, but were not strong enough to achieve victory. For as the *corps d'elite* [*viz.* Sacred Band] out did them in feats of courage, and the valour exhortations of Epameinondas contributed greatly to its prowess, the Lakedaimonians were in great difficulty forced back. [49]

---

47 Nep. *Pel.* 4.2.
48 Plut. *Pel.* 23.2.
49 Diod. 15.55.5–56.1.

Supposedly, it was at this crucial point of the *ōthismos* that Epameinondas asked his Thebans 'to give him one step more, and he would ensure victory',[50] which if true is much to the credit of Epameinondas' coolness and generalship.

The Collapse

All in all, the Theban's irresistible charge caught the Spartans in disorder, caused partly by their horsemen, partly by whatever tactical evolution they were attempting at the time – either a transfer of men from the left-hand *móra* to the right-hand *móra* to increase the depth of their phalanx there, or a turn to the right and so overlap the enemy battleline. Perhaps here Plutarch gives us a hint when he says Pelopidas, advancing at the head of the Theban phalanx 'with his band of three hundred men at the run', managed to catch the Spartans 'before Kleombrotos had either extended his wing or brought it back again into its old position and closed up his line of battle'.[51] Plutarch actually uses the term 'stretched out' (ἀνέπτυσσον), which does suggest Kleombrotos was attempting to overlap the Theban battleline. To make matters worse, Kleombrotos began to advance 'at first before the army with him so much realised that he was advancing': a fateful miscalculation.[52]

If true, it demonstrates how badly the Spartans had been caught napping. In came the Thebans and in the fierce fighting that followed down went Kleombrotos, mortally wounded – the first Spartan king to fall in battle since Leonidas. Though Diodoros Sikoulos above implies Kleombrotos had died under 'a great mound of corpses',[53] Xenophon says the surviving *hippeīs* were able 'to take him up and carry him off still living',[54] in other words, he was not quite dead at that point. Pausanias likewise implies Kleombrotos had fallen in the mêlée, adding that 'among the Lakedaimonians it was considered the greatest disgrace to allow the body of a king to come into the hands of the enemies'.[55]

Despite the fall of their mortally wounded king and the pandemonium around them, Plutarch at this juncture stresses that the Spartans:

> [W]ere the most skilled and experienced soldiers in the world, and in their training, they paid special attention to the problems of changing formation without falling into disorder or confusion; each man was accustomed to take any one of his comrades as his right-hand or rear-rank man, and whatever danger might threaten, to concentrate on that point, knit their ranks, and fight as effectively as ever.[56]

---

50 Polyain. 2.3.2, cf. 3.9.27 (Iphikrates), 4.3.8 (Alexander).
51 Plut. *Pel.* 23.2.
52 Xen. *Hell.* 6.4.13.
53 Diod. 15.55.5, cf. Hom. *Il.* 16.661–2 Lattimore: Sarpedon lying almost hidden among the dead, 'since many others had / above him'.
54 Xen. *Hell.* 6.4.13.
55 Paus. 9.13.4.
56 Plut. *Pel.* 23.3, cf. Xen. *Lak. Pol.* 11.7: 'To be sure the secret of carrying on in battle with any troops at hand when the line gets into confusion is not so easy to grasp, except for soldiers

Which brings us back to Xenophon, who unmistakably argues the Spartans must 'at first having the better of things in the fighting,'[57] since otherwise they would not have been able to carry their king, *still* living, from the field. Yet the fall of Kleombrotos and the death of many of those around him, including the *polémarchos* Deinon, one of the king's tent companions, Sphodrias, along with the latter's son, Kleonymos (who fell three times, before finally being dispatched),[58] must have added to the confusion and eventual collapse.

It goes without saying that in the push and shove of hoplite battle indescribable confusion reigned. Thus, in his account of the Athenian night attack on the rocky heights of Epipolai overlooking Syracuse (413 BCE), Thucydides says with no uncertain authority that: 'In daylight those who take part in an action have a clearer idea of it, though even then they cannot see everything, and in fact no one knows much more than what is going on around himself.'[59]

Euripides, Thucydides' contemporary, makes a good point when he has Theseus declare the one question he will not ask, in case he is openly mocked, is who met whom in the battle.[60] This is a justified concern, even for a semi-divine hero. Regarding the confusion of battle, it is significant that there was obviously no clear tradition about how Epameinondas met his end at Second Mantineia.[61]

Anyway, let us return to Epameinondas' triumph: the turning point on the field of Leūktra. Xenophon claims that even then discipline was maintained, the surviving Spartans 'fell back under the pressure from the Theban mass', and having crossed 'the trench that chanced to be in front of their camp they grounded their arms at the spot from which they had set forth.'[62] So, for Xenophon, the Spartans fought like the Spartans; when that is said, there is no more to say. On the other hand, Diodoros Sikoulos and Plutarch paint the final events in a less stoic light, suggesting a larger element of everyman for themselves.[63]

Unable to reorganise, it does appear that the Spartans had fallen back to their hillside encampment, and at this point both sides broke off the engagement. The Thebans had carried the day and were masters of the battlefield and the dead and dying strewn across it. Some diehard Spartans, having recovered their spirits and refusing to recognise defeat, were keen for a rematch. This was almost certainly an instance of fighting was what

---

trained under the laws of Lykourgos'.

57 Xen. *Hell.* 6.4.13.
58 Ibid. 5.4.33.
59 Thuc. 7.44.1.
60 Eur. *Supp.* 846–847.
61 Plut. *Ages.* 35.1, Paus. 8.11.5–6. Likewise, there is a contradiction of the literary sources concerning the death of Epameinondas' close friend, Pelopidas. He was killed in battle at Kynoskephalai (364 BCE): in Plutarch's account (*Pel.* 32.5–7) he falls while leading an infantry charge, while Nepos (*Pel.* 5.4) records it was during a cavalry charge, and then again Diodoros Sikoulos (15.80.5) is rather vague on the matter. One modern commentator, Terry Buckler (1980: 176–180), has seen fit to homogenise the contradiction by having Pelopidas first led a cavalry charge, then dismounting only to fall at the head of an infantry assault.
62 Xen. *Hell.* 6.4.14.
63 Diod. 15.56.2, Plut. *Pel.* 23.4.

Site of the Spartan encampment as seen from the west with the ancient track from Kreūsis to Thespiai running below the hill. Kleombrotos encamped 'in the territory of Thespiai' (Xen. *Hell*. 6.4.4) 'on the slope of a hill' (*ibid*. 6.4.14) on the southern edge of the plain of Leūktra. The low hill itself is a fairly steep convex type, and according to Xenophon (loc. cite) happened to have a 'trench' on its north side. Unlike the Romans, the Greeks did not normally fortify their overnight encampments, so the existing trench and steepness of the hill would have provided a modicum of defence to Kleombrotos' camp at Leūktra. Generally speaking, a Greek camp was a rather jerry-built affair, a mixture of tents, improvised bivouacs, and men huddle together sleeping in the open air. Life in camp was anarchic by modern military standards, with soldiers going to bed, rising, and breakfasting pretty much as they pleased. Xenophon (*Hell*. 2.4.6) describes such a camp scene – the young Xenophon himself was likely present at the time – involving the cavalry of Athens. Even with the enemy close at hand, some horsemen were still slumbering in their beds while their comrades were already taking up their battle stations and the grooms were up and about currying the horses. Conceivably, a Spartan camp was touch more orderly than this. (©Nic Fields)

they had done all their lives, and they did not know what else to do. Yet the surviving *polémarchoi*, being more even-tempered, thought otherwise, mainly because the allies and mercenaries were unwilling to take the field again. At this point the sound of battle would have faded, only to be replaced with the inevitable aftermath, the smell of blood and death, screams and groans of wounded and dying. There is a human dimension to warfare that is too easily overlooked.

The Aftermath

The following day the Spartans sent a herald to petition the Thebans for permission to collect their dead, an admission of defeat. After erecting a trophy from the arms of the fallen Spartans, Epameinondas granted permission. The Battle of Leūktra was over, though it was to be several days before both sides recognised that there would be no further fighting.

Messengers from both sides summoned reinforcements. The *éphoroi* mobilised the rest of the army under Archidamos (son of Agesilaos and future king) and sent it north towards Boiotia. The well-informed Xenophon says this relief army was made up of the following contingents:

[T]he two remaining *mórai*, bringing in men who were forty years above the minimum age for service [*viz*. those 56 to 60 years old]; and they also sent out all men up to the same age who belonged to the *mórai* now serving abroad. For in the original expedition to Phokis only the age groups up to thirty-five from the minimum had been serving [*viz*. those 20 to 55 years old]. In addition, they ordered [*viz*. the *éphoroi*] ordered out those who at the time of the first expedition had been left behind because of official duties. Since Agesilaos had still not recovered from his illness, the state ordered his son, Archidamos, to take command.[64]

Desperate times call for desperate measures, and so the *éphoroi* had mustered, apart from the 'cooks and bottle washers', all those Spartans of fighting age that had been left in Sparta.

Predictably, a Theban request for Athenian aid was met with stony silence. Their ally Iason of Pherai, however, responded immediately, marching south at the head of 1,500 well-trained mercenaries and 500 horsemen, passing so quickly through the land of the Phokians, whom he was at war, that they had no time to muster an army to oppose him – a feat the fellow professional Xenophon says was 'a good example of how speed often counts for more than force when it comes to getting things done'.[65] When the *tagos* of Thessaly arrived at Leūktra, Epameinondas proposed a joint attack so as to destroy the Spartans once and for all. Iason, a man who primarily looked to his interests and probably did not welcome a too-powerful Thebes as a near neighbour, persuaded Epameinondas and his colleagues that victory was already theirs, and it would be wiser to avoid further risks and allow the Spartans to withdraw from Boiotia.[66]

The Spartans did so. They broke up their camp, retiring under the cover of darkness,[67] meeting their relieving force under Archidamos a day's march away 'at Aigosthena in the territory of Megara'.[68] This was the same route Kleombrotos had taken back in 379 BCE when he withdrew from Thespiai, leaving a garrison there under the *harmostēs* Sphodrias, to Kreūsis. Kleombrotos then quit Kreūsis and crossed Mount Kithairon where he and his men experienced a violent tempest, the force of which wrested the shields from their hands and blew many of the pack animals over the precipices into the sea, before descending down to Aigosthena.[69] The surviving *polémarchoi* used the same difficult route, probably having gone that way themselves back in 379 BCE, 'relying so much on the truce as on keeping their intentions secret'.[70]

Having started the campaign believing they would return home to bask in the glory of their victory, with the gloom of defeat haunting them, they

---

64 Xen. *Hell*. 6.4.17.
65 Ibid. 6.4.21. Iason, a great 'might-have-been' of Greek history, was considered by Xenophon to be 'the greatest man of his times' (ibid. 6.4.28).
66 Ibid. 6.4.22–24.
67 Ibid. 6.4.25.
68 Ibid. 6.4.26.
69 Ibid. 5.4.15–18.
70 Ibid. 6.4.26.

all returned to the Peloponnese and disbanded. Naturally there was great jubilation among the victors. Not only had they won a decisive battle, but for the first time they had beaten the Spartans in a fair fight.

The Butcher's Bill

The losses of the Spartans were unusually heavy in this, the first defeat in the memory of their army in a pitched hoplite battle. According to Xenophon's figures, of 700 *Spartiātai* present, 400 fell, along with 'almost a thousand' other Lakedaimonians,[71] while Plutarch says 'the Lakedaimonian dead numbered over a thousand'.[72] On the other hand, Diodoros Sikoulos reckons 'More than 4,000 Lakedaimonians fell in battle but only about three hundred Boiotians' (all Thebans, probably),[73] which is surely better than Pausanias' paltry 47 Boiotian dead,[74] although it could be argued that this was the figure for those of the Sacred Band who fell. Diodoros' figure for the Spartan army probably includes the allies and mercenaries too.

Returning to Xenophon's figures, if correct, we can presume of the 400 *Spartiātai* who fell, the majority of these were the *hippeīs* who naturally formed the king's immediate entourage, virtually wiped out during the furious struggle to save the mortally wounded Kleombrotos. However, battlefield casualties are difficult for third parties to estimate, but the figure given by Xenophon, who after all was intimate with the affairs of Sparta, gives a broad indication of the intensity of the fighting around the king at the height of the battle.

The Reason Why

Many things lie behind the Spartans' defeat at Leūktra. Certainly, the two commanders were well matched in physical and moral courage, even if a pungent whiff of cowardice hung about Kleombrotos, but the victory rested with Epameinondas. The trophy made up of the arms of the defeated was remembered not long afterward in an epigram inscribed on the limestone base of a monument dedicated to Zeus at Thebes. It read in part: 'When the Spartan spear held sway, then it fell to Xenokrates' lot to carry the trophy in honour of Zeus, fearing neither the army from Eurotas nor the Lakonian shield. "Thebans (are) superior in battle" proclaims the trophy at Leūktra that announces the victory won by the spear, nor did we run second to Epameinondas.'[75]

---

71 Ibid. 6.4.15.
72 Plut. *Apophth.* 71.12, cf. Paus. 9.13.4.
73 Diod. 15.56.4.
74 Paus. 9.13.4.
75 Tod 130.92–4 = Harding 46.5–11.

Xenokrates was one of the seven *boiōtarchoi* at Leūktra,[76] and he had been chosen by lot before the battle to carry some armour to serve as a trophy indicating that Zeus had already given victory to Thebes. He was assisted in this task by Theopompos and Mnasilaos.[77] The last line reflects that the trophy bearer and his assistants marched in the forefront of the Theban army.

Victory foretold or not, what was unprecedented about Leūktra was that Epameinondas had formed an irresistible Theban phalanx with which he won the battle before the other Boiotian and the mercenary hoplites of the centre and right wing could lose it. The traditional Spartan tactic of rolling up the line from their right to left had been countered at a single stroke, which was delivered sharply, swiftly, and surprisingly. Xenophon may have written, 'wise generalship consists in attacking where the enemy is weakest, even if the point be some way distant',[78] but Epameinondas is an instance of the exception not the rule, for he had come to believe that if you defeated one part of an army, the rest would give way. The best illustration of this notion is the story Polyainos recounts of how Epameinondas caught a snake, and by crushing its head, showed his men how useless the rest of it was,[79] and even Xenophon hints as much when he says the Thebans 'calculated that, if they proved superior in that part of the field where the [Spartan] king was, all the rest would be easy'.[80] In other words, by 'decapitating the head of the snake', Epameinondas would profit from the consequential confusion, and so it proved. Nonetheless, his defeat of the Spartan army was not, however, a bold ruse.

Arguably, Epameinondas' success was largely due to his adversary's mistakes; but there remains the matter of the oblique order of battle.[81] Did Epameinondas deliberately use the oblique order of battle, which would be used to tremendous effect by that once-in-a-generation military genius, Alexander III of Macedon, or was he simply hoping to achieve a local superiority on the left wing? Whichever the case, Epameinondas' tactic was perfect for the moment as it allowed him with a weaker – and non-professional – army to achieve that superior concentration of force on one wing. In this manner the Spartans were beaten not through superior training or weaponry, but through superior tactics. Consider the evidence:

> *First*, Epameinondas enlarged upon and developed certain features that were traditional elements in hoplite warfare in combination with a peculiarity of Theban hoplite tactics, namely their habit to array their hoplites in an unusually deep phalanx. After the initial clash, hoplite battle was determined by the 'pushing power' of the phalanx: at Leūktra the Theban phalanx was four times more powerful than the Spartan phalanx.

---

76 Paus. 9.13.3.
77 Tod 130.92–4 = Harding 46.4. Mnasilaos is also mentioned in Plut. *Pel.* 8.2.
78 Xen. *Hipp.* 4.14.
79 Polyain. 2.3.15.
80 Xen. *Hell.* 6.4.12.
81 The Greek writer and philosopher Asklepiodotos Taktikos (*fl.* first century BCE) mentions the 'oblique front' (Gk. λοξὴ φάλαγξ) in his *Taktiká* (10.1, cf. 11.1), while Diodoros Sikoulos goes for the rather clunky 'oblique formation phalanx' (Gk. λοξὴν ποήσας τὴν φάλαγγα) in his account (15.55.2) of the battle, and similarly Plutarch 'phalanx obliquely towards the left' (Gk. τὴν φάλαγγα λοξὴν ἐπὶ τὸ εὐώνυμον ἕλκοντας) in his *Pelopidas* (23.1).

Second, Epameinondas made use of, in a purposeful manner, a normal characteristic of hoplite warfare, namely the decision on one wing, habitually the right wing. The Theban phalanx, spearheaded by the Sacred Band, was positioned on the left of the Boiotian battleline, *not* the right.

Third, Epameinondas' tactics were purposely contrived to overcome the Spartans themselves on their right wing, where they had been accustomed to winning their battles (having rigged the system to their advantage), as at First Mantineia, the Nemea, and Second Koroneia, and by refusing his right wing and centre to deny the enemy any chance of retrieving the situation there. As Xenophon explains in his account of Second Mantineia, Epameinondas' 'plan was to fight the battle with the strongest part of his army, and he had left the weakest part far in the rear, since he knew that if it were defeated, this would discourage the troops that were with him and give heart to the enemy'.[82] In other words, as before at Leūktra, Epameinondas deployed the deep Theban phalanx on his left and refused his weaker centre and right. Once more Epameinondas personally led this phalanx, and Xenophon describes it 'like the ram of a trireme'.[83]

Fourth, Epameinondas assumed the offensive and so gained the initiative from the outset. This was an unexpected event for the Spartans, who were used to seeing their enemies flinch because they were facing Spartans. Epameinondas had elevated into a principle the idea that if you could defeat one part of an army, the rest would give way, believing, as Xenophon explains once again in his account of Second Mantineia: 'it is very difficult to find men who will stand their ground when they see any of their own side in flight… By overwhelming the force against which he [Epameinondas] struck, he caused the whole enemy army to turn and fly'.[84] As previously discussed, at Leūktra the allies and mercenaries on the Spartan left gave way when they witnessed the right 'was being pushed back'.[85]

Ought we to judge battles by the numbers killed and the ruin meted out? Or ought we to not rather judge them by the results that flowed from them? Truly, one will say that a battle is only truly great or small according to its results. Judging by results, Leūktra was more than great, it was epoch making. Many empires have been lost through a series of battles, a process of battles, a weary tale of wasting conflicts stretching over years, but Sparta reached that point in a single afternoon and by a single pitched battle. For Sparta there was to be no phoney comfort of small but significant signs of imperial decline. The dramatic defeat at Leūktra meant Epameinondas had 'Sparta shorn of her glory',[86] an apposite metaphor in tune with the uncommonly length and archaic style of Spartan hair.[87] I leave the reader to judge what glee there was

---

82   Xen. *Hell.* 7.5.23.
83   Loc. cit.
84   Xen. *Hell.* 7.5.24.
85   Ibid. 6.4.14.
86   Paus. 9.15.6. This was actually one of the verse lines of the epitaph inscribed upon the statue of Epameinondas at Thebes. Fitting words, for he was of course the chief architect of Sparta's downfall and Thebes' ascendancy. For Spartan hairstyles, *vide* Appendix 2.
87   *Vide* Appendix 3.

among the enemies of Sparta. For them, especially in the Peloponnese, it was the end of empire show. As Henry Kissinger once properly said, 'the Gods are offended by *hubris*',[88] which, after all, is in line with the story of fair Troy, in which the Trojans were not saved, but the Greeks were punished collectively while sailing for home.[89] Much the same can be said of that afternoon's events on the narrow plain of Leūktra. You had *hubris*. You had tragedy. You had death.

---

88   Source: Hal Brands, *What Good is Grand Strategy? Power and Purpose in American Statecraft from Harry S. Truman to George W. Bush* (Ithaca, NY, 2014), p.100.

89   Everyone knows the myth of origin. Trojan prince Paris abducts Helen, divine wife of Spartan king Menalaos. The Greeks lay siege to Troy in revenge. A decade of bitter war ends only when Odysseus comes up with the ruse of the gigantic wooden horse, filled with warriors, which the Trojans foolishly drag within their 'peerless walls' only to be massacred by night. Dark blood runs in torrents, drenching the earth, and Troy is left a ruin. And so Troy and the Trojans paid for Helen's sin. Love and war had long been linked. But this is a subject for a monograph, not a note.

Chapter 9

After Leūktra

The Thebans, having beaten the Lakedaimonians at Leūktra, marched to the river Eurotas itself, where one of them boasting said, 'Where are the Spartans now?

Plutarch *Moralia* 233C

No matter how much we care to dress it up, Leūktra was a complete and utter disaster for Sparta. Let us generously say it was an absolute shamble. The statistics alone confirm this.

All full citizens, *Spartiātai*, from 20 to 60 years of age were liable for military service. At Plataia (479 BCE) Sparta put 10,000 hoplites into the field of which 5,000 were *Spartiātai*.[1] We are assuming here that those were *Spartiātai* in the prime of life (between 39 and 55 years of age) and that during a national crisis such as this, the main strength of Spartan manhood would have been mobilised. If these assumptions are correct, and if about 3,000 are added for the reserve and for citizens past military age, we might consider the total number of *Spartiātai* at that time to have been roughly 8,000. This is a figure that Herodotos offers for all the adult males for the year 480 BCE,[2] and it corresponds fairly well with Plutarch's 9,000 *klēroi*, the equal allotments traditionally assigned to the *Spartiātai* by the state.[3]

From the first quarter of the fifth century BCE, we now shift to the last quarter. Thucydides informs us that only 120 of the 292 Lakedaimonians captured on the island of Sphakteria (425 BCE) were *Spartiātai*,[4] and as these, he adds, were chosen by lot from the 12 *lóchoi*,[5] it can be calculated that there were some 3,500 *Spartiātai* in total at that time. This figure, if correct, indicates a dramatic 64 percent decline since Plataia, though at First Mantineia (418 BCE) it can be argued that the number mustered for battle was some 4,000,[6] thereby readjusting the decline to 50 percent. Still, by

1   Hdt. 9.10.1, 11.3, 28.2.
2   Ibid. 7.234.2.
3   Plut. *Lyk*. 8.3, cf. 16.1.
4   Thuc. 4.38.3.
5   Ibid. 4.8.9.
6   Ibid. 5.68.3.

Leūktra (371 BCE) the battle strength stood at only 700 of which 400 fell that fateful day,[7] so, we assume there were only 1,100 or 1,200 *Spartiātai* in total. So, we have yet another dramatic decline since Sphakteria.

In a crucial passage highlighting the defects of the Spartan system, the philosophic Aristotle, contrasting the theory underlying the 'Lykourgan' distribution of equal allotments with the actual practice of his day, has this to say: 'Although the country could support 1,500 horsemen and 30,000 hoplites, they do not even number 1,000. The defects of Spartan arrangements in this respect have been clearly displayed by their own experience; for the *polis* was not able to withstand a single stroke but perished on account of its small population.'[8]

The 'single stroke' to which Aristotle refers is the Theban attack, which led to the demolition of the Spartan army at Leūktra. Yet, as Aristotle makes abundantly clear, the inescapable truth that the architect of Sparta's downfall was Sparta.

Evidently, the total number of *Spartiātai* available to Sparta declined throughout the classical period, a demographic process Aristotle calls *oliganthrōpia* (fewness of men), and attributes Sparta's ruin to it.[9] Even before Leūktra, the Spartans had been forced to reject an appeal for help from Polydamas of Pharsalos for lack of manpower.[10] There is enough evidence to indicate that Aristotle was spot-on with his analysis. There are three main reasons.

First, many *Spartiātai* simply got themselves killed either in battle or through mishaps of one sort or another. Certainly, over time this would have ground down their fighting capability, but most modern demographic studies demonstrate that losses in war are speedily replaced.

Second, there is the economic cause, that is to say, as Aristotle makes clear, the population declined through the Spartan habit of encouraging *Spartiātai* to rear as many children as possible, 'hence the law which exempts fathers of three sons from military service, and fathers of four from tax'.[11] This state benefice had the negative effect of family land being parcelled out amongst an increasing number of progeny. This would have included daughters too, as Aristotle bluntly points out when he reports that no less than 40 percent of the land was held by Spartan women, 'partly because so many women inherit it as heiresses and partly because of the practice of giving large dowries'.[12] Certainly, Spartan women, unlike their Athenian counterparts, enjoyed full legal capacity. They were free to marry late, and to marry whom they liked, 'heiresses' in particular being free from property restrictions. Of course, we must not forget the intimate connection between land tenure and citizenship.

---

7   Xen. *Hell.* 6.4.15, 17.
8   Arist. *Pol.* 1270a.29–34.
9   Ibid. 1270a.33.
10   Xen. *Hell.* 6.1.17. For the decline in the number of *Spartiātai* see especially Cartledge 1987: 38 fig. 4.2.
11   Arist. *Pol.* 1270b.3–4.
12   Ibid. 1270a.15.

Third, this Aristotelian thesis may well be the answer to *oliganthrōpia*, but into this economic pot Paul Cartledge throws in 'the greed of the wealthy'. Be that as it may, this idea can be sharpened up slightly if we consider the following: a point was surely reached in the fifth century BCE when the full horrors of *oliganthrōpia* suddenly hit home. At the time, the majority of *Spartiātai* probably owned an estate that enabled them to live quite comfortably and fulfil one of the two qualifying conditions for full Spartan citizenship, namely to produce the surplus required to pay their 'mess bills': the other of course being successful in *agōgē*. However, at the time they surely knew that as their tidy piece of family land would be divided through the generations until a point of no return was reached. It would be wise of us to remember that there are two antagonistic ideals at work here: the self-sufficient citizen 'farmer' versus the prolific citizen 'soldier'. Ergo, in the hundred or so years between Plataia and Leūktra there came a point of no return.

Naturally warfare was a constant event in those hundred or so years, but if modern demographics are anything to go by, this should not have been the cause of *oliganthrōpia*. All the same, if we consider that each campaigning *Spartiātēs* was attended by at least one helot, and there were at least 5,000 of them at Plataia.[13] So for that summer alone 5,000 helots were in Boiotia on campaign and not in Lakedaimon or Messenia working the land for their masters. The following decade saw a helot revolt when large tracts of Messenia around Mount Ithome were in the rebel hands. Therefore, those *Spartiātai* whose estates were to be found in this area would have remained unproductive for them, and this situation lasted for at least five years if not longer. When the rebellion was brought to heel, Sparta allowed the rebel helots to go free. As a result, some *Spartiātai* in Messenia lost out economically and probably never recovered from this, even losing their citizen status.

The Spartans next experienced 14 years of intermittent warfare with Athens, the first Peloponnesian War, followed by 15 years of relative peace until the next conflict between Athens and Sparta, the great Peloponnesian War. During this protracted conflict, the Spartans were forced into freeing and arming helots for service abroad in their ever-diminishing army. Needless to say, this self-destructive practice was to continue during Sparta's overseas campaigns in Anatolia and during the Corinthian and Boiotian wars that followed soon after: Xenophon says that after Leūktra 6,000 helots were enrolled in the army with a promise of freedom.[14] All things considered, and given the luxury of hindsight, the helot system was the weak link in Sparta's social system. Despite that, they had never changed their antiquated system and they never would. A historical blip, like the Latin emperors of Byzantium or Vichy France: Sparta's end was in its beginning.

---

13   Herodotos' claim (9.29) for 35,000 helots at Plataia may in fact be the figure for the total helot population of Lakonia and Messenia.

14   Xen. *Hell*. 6.5.28–9.

Yesterday's Warriors

How we understand the Spartans today is very much shaped by myths, and it is worth remembering that the most notable myth of Spartan invincibility is based on Thermopylai, a three-day battle that they resoundingly lost. It was in this furious fight that the legend of Spartan invincibility was born. Suspended in time, Sparta's focus on maintaining tradition allowed their enemies to continually out innovate them, and tradition, in any event, is nothing but an innovation that was once successful. A moment arrived when the horizon closed, and the Spartans started only looking back towards the past and engaging in a tactical system that was almost past its expiration date. The problem with myths, of course, is that they stand to become demythologised by unsavoury fact. It gets in the way.

Myth also relies on belief. Often suspended. As a Theban ambassador said to the Athenians in 395 BCE on the eve of the Corinthian War:

> This too, is a point that should be understood: this greedy and arrogant dominion of Sparta is much easier to destroy than was the empire which you had. You had a navy while your subjects did not; the Spartans, few in number themselves, are greedily dominating people who are many times as numerous as they and also just as well armed.[15]

The finest hoplites in the Greek world did little for them by the end of the Peloponnesian War; Athens was the greatest maritime empire that the Mediterranean had ever known, and the Spartans had to create a navy from scratch to win. Then Epameinondas outsmarted them by developing better hoplite tactics. Myths do not die overnight. But the truth about the Spartan myth was put in the Theban epigram commemorating their victory at Leūktra: 'Thebans (are) superior in battle'.[16] This was clearly inscribed using the precise, measured language of Lakonian minimalism, leavened with a sense of the absurd that was focused on one particular howling irony: the fact that part-time soldiers had soundly beaten professional soldiers at their own game.

A lost battle does not mean a lost war. Thermopylai is an apposite example of this, Leūktra not so. If the myth of Spartan invincibility on the red field of battle was forged at Thermopylai, when a handful of Spartans (forgetting the Thespians of course) withstood to the last man thousands of on-rushing Persians, then it was shattered at Leūktra where Kleombrotos – the first Spartan king to die in battle since Leonidas, he of immortal memory – several of his highborn companions, and the *Spartiātai* element in his army were obliterated by Theban hoplites, which in the end was decisive. This was not so much because the Spartan army had been destroyed, or even because this defeat put an end to its victories – there were Spartan victories to come – but because it revealed that Sparta's position as the great hegemonic

---

15   Ibid. 3.5.15.
16   Tod 130.92–4 = Harding 46.8.

superpower of the Aegean Greek world had long rested on what amounted to a big bluff, since its manpower resources, in terms of actual citizen soldiers who enjoyed full constitutional rights, the *Spartiātai*, had never really been sufficient to sustain that position.

Yet behind that bluff there had always remained, in the last resort, the hard reality of the Spartan army, and its defeat at Leūktra was a symbol of the passing of a great power: it would have been a mere bagatelle, a flea bite, if Sparta had had manpower fitted to its hegemonic policy. But you cannot resist reality forever: Sparta was beggared. As the Athenian pamphleteer Isokrates made clear in his address to Philip II of Macedon, which was delivered around 346 BCE:

> The Lakedaimonians were leaders of the Hellenes, not long ago, on both land and sea, and yet they suffered so great a reversal of fortune when they met defeat at Leūktra that they were deprived of their power over the Hellenes, and lost such of their warriors [i.e. *Spartiātai*] as chose to die rather than survive defeat at the hands of those over whom they had once been masters.[17]

Isokrates' orations had a propensity to contain darker, apocalyptic undercurrents, but the truth is that Sparta was at the nadir of its strength post-Leūktra. Still, as is always the case in hegemonic wars, the enemy's weakness is only significant if you have the capacity to capitalise upon it. And this is exactly what Epameinondas did.

The conflicts of the following years are too complex for justice to be done to them here. Suffice to say that Epameinondas' victory was followed by a number of invasions of the Peloponnese, and his successes there were as swift as they were sure. He overran the country north of Sparta on four occasions: Spartan power over the peninsula came to an end. The *poleis* of the Peloponnese were now banded together in federal leagues, the prime example being that of the Arkadian League established in 370 BCE, to guarantee their independence.

On the first occasion, during the winter of 370/369 BCE, Epameinondas and Pelopidas invaded the heartland of Sparta, threatening the un-walled *polis* itself and ravaging much of its hinterland.[18] The Spartans, although aided by Corinth, Epidauros, and a few other faithful Peloponnesian League states, could do little to prevent this humiliation, and 'the very sight of smoke seemed unendurable to the women, who had never seen an enemy in their lives'.[19] It is doubtful that Epameinondas aimed at the total destruction of Sparta, since its existence would be a constant source of disunity in the Peloponnese. This would be very convenient for the security of Boiotia and its current ascendancy in Greece. It should be noted at this point that the lack of manpower and financial resources prevented Thebes from gaining

---

17   Isok. 5.47.
18   Xen. *Hell.* 6.5.27–32, cf. Dein. 1.73: 'they invaded the Spartans' territory which, it was thought, could not be ravaged'.
19   Xen. *Hell.* 6.5.28.

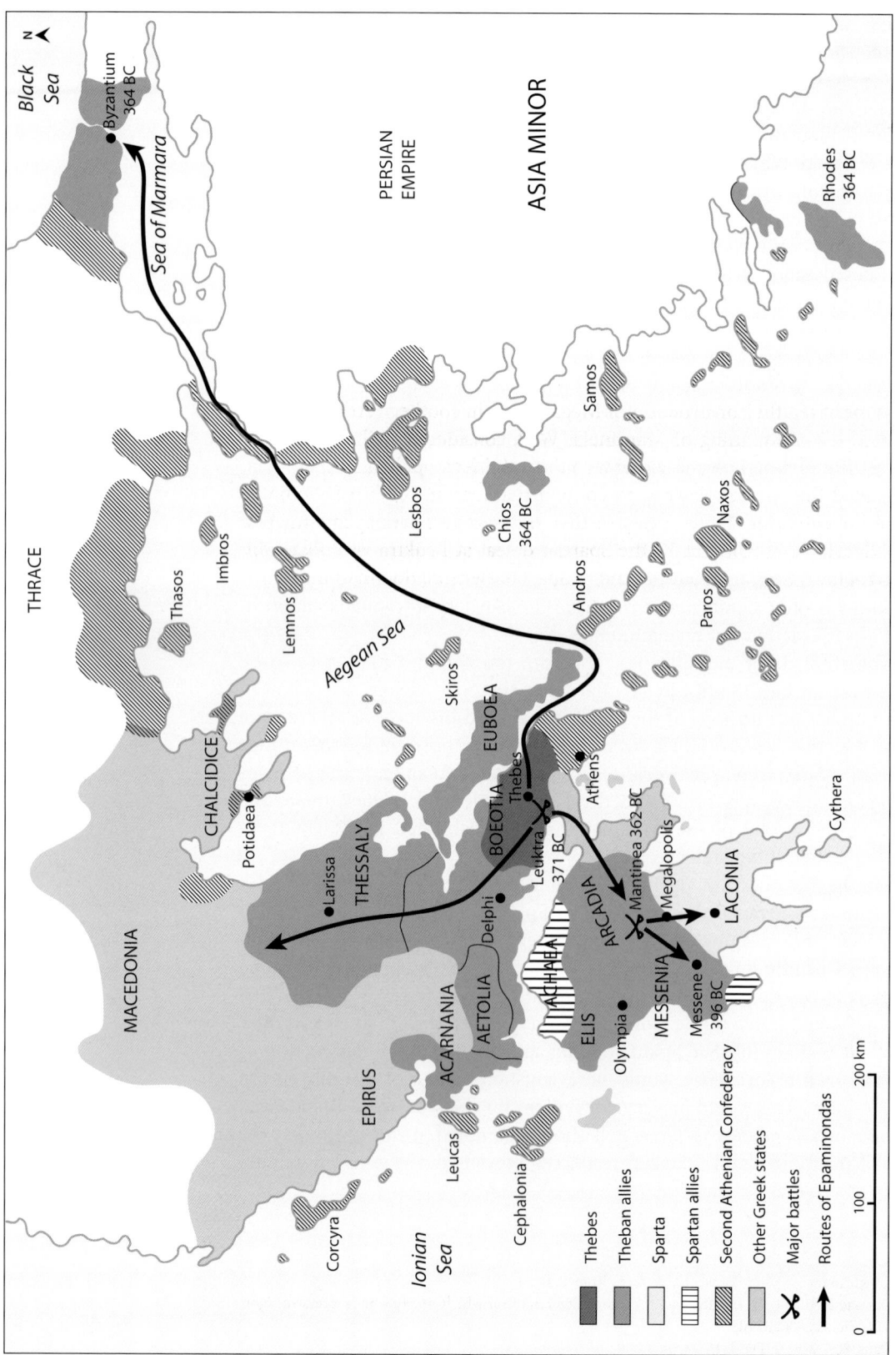

Theban dominance following Leŭktra.

the hegemony of Greece, and Epameinondas made no attempt to create an empire by conquest, nor to impose governors and garrisons, nor levy tribute.

It was the Spartans, not the Thebans, who were essentially the architects of their own demise. After three centuries of enslavement by the Spartans, the Messenians were liberated by Epameinondas and reacquired their own *polis*; the foundation of Messene would be the outward and very visible sign of Sparta's humiliation.[20] The massive circuit of Messene went up in the winter of 369 BCE after Epameinondas invaded Lakonia for a second time and then proceeded over Mount Taïygettos to liberate Messenia. Built with incredible rapidity by the combined Theban and Argive armies and the exiled Messenians who had been invited to return and establish an independent *polis*, the fortifications of Messene, which included towers to accommodate artillery that shot from shuttered windows, were considered the finest example of fourth century BCE Greek military architecture.[21] Epameinondas also supervised the construction of Megalopolis in southern Arkadia,[22] and initiated the re-founding of Mantineia. Well, considered civil engineering, the fortifications of Messene, along with those of Megalopolis and Mantineia, completed the strategic barrier to contain the Spartans within Lakonia. It was a policy driven by the premise that war should never again emanate from Spartan soil. Ultimately, the Spartan defeat at Leūktra was politically catastrophic, bringing about the end of Sparta's Hellenic domination.

---

20 Diod. 15.66.1, 6, 67.1, Paus. 4.27.5–7, cf. Strab. 8.4.1.
21 For the fortifications of Messene, the enormous circuit of which remains an impressive sight, *vide* Fields 2006: 33–8.
22 Paus. 8.27.2, 8, cf. Diod. 15.72.4.

Chapter 10

The Battlefield Today

There is always a difficulty when it comes to conjuring up the grunting armour-clad men and bloody close-quarter combat of hoplite battle. It is more so, which is often the case with prominent battle sites of such ancient date, when we turn to the real physical setting of the events we have been discussing at great length: the field of Leūktra is remarkably unimpressive. It is slightly rolling countryside, with no dramatic features, and that is about all that can be said of it. Close by is the modern village of Lévktra (before 1915 Parapoúngia), a collection of three hamlets which have been identified with ancient Leūktra. Ancient blocks can be seen in the village, but the site of Eutresis,[1] a couple of kilometres distant to the northeast, may have supplied building stone for the hamlets. The ridge of Parapoúngia was examined for sherds by W.K. Pritchett.[2]

The battlefield sits between the fork in an ancient track that ran from Kreūsis to Thespiai and the location of the Theban Victory Monument, and between the Áskris Potamós flowing roughly west and the Asōpós Potamós flowing roughly east.[3] On the tinder-dry plain during summer months the Áskris is little more than a parched riverbed. Likewise, the Asōpós, which at that time formed the boundary between the *poleis* of Thebes and Plataia.[4] This river was well known for the Battle of Plataia (479 BCE) being fought close to its southern banks.

The Spartan encampment overlooked the practically level plain of Leūktra, probably just south of the level ground between the fork in the modern Livadóstro–Thespiai road and the Theban Victory Monument. A line of low rounded hills, running roughly east-west, squat either side of the plain. Livadóstro on the Gulf of Corinth is the site of ancient Kreūsis, which in all probability served as the seaport of Thespiai,[5] was where Kleombrotos captured a dozen Theban *triērēis* (triremes) before the battle.[6] A pathway from Kreūsis runs across the eastern shoulder of Mount Korombili before

---

1   Strab. 9.2.28, cf. 39.
2   Pritchett 1965: 49–52.
3   *Vide* ibid. 57.
4   Paus. 9.4.4.
5   Liv. 36.21.5, Strab. 9.2.25, Paus. 9.32.1.
6   Xen. *Hell.* 6.4.3, cf. Diod. 15.53.1, who puts the number at 10.

General view of the plain of Leūktra looking north from the foot of the hill where the Spartans encamped, close to the fork in the ancient track that ran from Kreūsis to Thespiai. The ancient track bearing for Thespiai can be seen running north alongside the parched bed of the Áskris Potamós (clearly discernible by the tree line). The Spartan left flank (Lakedaimonians, mercenaries, et cetera) would have been anchored by this river, which even if dry at the time would have still presented an obstacle. In the far distance of the photograph is the line of low rounded hills that runs roughly east-west along the northern edge of the narrow plain: the site of the Boiotian encampment would have been approximately in the vicinity of the higher hill to the left. (©Nic Fields)

The Theban Victory Monument looking southwest towards the hills lining the southern edge of the plain of Leūktra. Permanent monuments had been erected to mark Greek victories over Persians, as at Marathon (Paus. 1.32.5), but according to Cicero (*Inv. rhet*. 2.23) this was the first such battlefield memorial to a Greek victory over Greeks. Reconstructed is the cylindrical plinth (diameter: 3.38m), trapezoidal masonry (*viz*. vertical joints are skewed) in regular courses, erected on three steps. This is crowned by the original Doric frieze of triglyphs and metopes (height: 0.68m). Further on top, series of nine stone *aspídes* (diameter: 0.97m) sculptured in relief: all are original bar one, which was to be found later and sits to the left of the monument. The circular balustrade almost certainly supported a *trópaion* in bronze. The monument was probably erected as the fourth century BCE turned into the third century BCE (*IG* VII 2462). Another missing part of the monument, found on 7 August 1991 by the Cambridge/Bradford Boeotia Project lying in a cotton field south of the site of ancient Thespiai some 4km away to the northeast), sits to the right of the monument. This is a large worked block of marble, which was identified as originating from the monument's circular Doric frieze of triglyphs and metopes. (©Nic Fields)

traversing the plain of Leūktra, coming down the slope of the southern hills through the village of Lévktra, and ascends the northern line of hills.

The Boiotians, for their part, probably had their encampment directly opposite to the north on what is indicated on decent topographical maps as Hill 371.[7] The plain itself is about one kilometre in breadth and slopes gently towards the south. It is for the most part featureless, and little could have happened in the plain without it being observed from either encampment.

The Theban Victory Monument (locally Μάρμαρα) sits to the east of the battle site and has been heavily reconstructed. It is a modern interpretation mixed with original fragments, the first of which German classicist Heinrich Nicolaus Ulrichs discovered in 1839.[8] The restoration work was done by the Greek architect-turned-archaeologist Anastasios Orlandos in the early 1960s. The sculptured shields are originals, bar one – this was later found and left at the foot of the monument – and are full-size stone replicas of the *aspís*. On 7 August 1991, the Boeotia Project Survey Team B (Cambridge University) located a large worked block of marble, which was soon identified as one of the circular triglyphs and metopes belonging to the monument. The find was some four kilometres from the battlefield, sitting in a cotton field just south of the site of ancient Thespiai.

As reconstructed, the monument is a circular marble plinth erected on three steps and crowned with a Doric frieze of triglyphs and metopes supporting a dome shaped roof of nine hoplite shields sculptured full-size in high relief. According to numismatic evidence, a series of base metal coins of the Boiotian κοινόν feature on their reverse the legend ΒΟΙΩΤΩΝ and a trophy of arms, *trópaion*, in the form of hoplite *panopliā* suspended from a wooden stake.[9] On the circular balustrade crowning the dome most likely sat a comparable *trópaion* in bronze.[10]

Diodoros notes that it was customary for victorious Greek armies to erect temporary battle monuments.[11] In other words, a *trópaion* was meant to be ephemeral, erected immediately after the battle on the battlefield by hanging or nailing enemy arms and armour to a wooden stake or tree trunk. Cicero on the Leūktra Monument is worth quoting in full:

> The Thebans, having defeated the Lakedaimonians in battle, set up a trophy in bronze. They were accused before the Amphiktyons, that is, before the common council of Greece. The charge is: 'It was not right'. The reply is: 'It was right'. The question is: 'Was it right?' The defendant's reason is: 'By our valour we won such glory in war that we wished to have a perpetual memorial of it to our descendants'. The counter-argument is: 'Still it is not right for Greeks to set up a permanent monument of their quarrels with Greeks'.[12]

---

7   *Vide* Pritchett 1965, pp.57–59.
8   Pritchett 1965, p.51.
9   BMC 8, p.39, pp.64–65 = Sear Greek 2410. The coin's obverse carries a bust of the goddess Athena wearing a crested Corinthian helmet in the 'at ease' position.
10 A *trópaion* (τρόπαιον), from which the English word 'trophy' is derived, was set up at the site of the 'turning point' (Gk. τροπη) at which the enemy broke, turned, and ran.
11 Diod. 13.24.5.
12 Cic. *Inv. rhet.* 2.23.69–70.

Boiotian κοινὸν base metal coin (Thíva, Archaeological Museum of Thebes), issued between 288 BCE and 244 BCE. The reverse, seen here, bears the legend ΒΟΙΩΤΩΝ and a battlefield trophy of arms, *trópaion*, in the form of hoplite *panopliā* suspended from a wooden stake. It is most likely that this motif actually represents the permanent *trópaion* executed in bronze that adorned the circular balustrade crowning the dome of the Theban Victory Monument at Leūktra (O. Mustafin/Wikimedia Commons/CC0 1.0 Public Domain Dedication)

Or, to put it more simply, the testimony of Cicero suggests that this was a moral guideline not written law.

Of interest and nearby are the tumbled remains of a mid-fourth century BCE circular watchtower. This ruin can be found some 100 metres southwest of the church of Áyios Mámas, which is southwest of the hamlets of Lévktra, and close to the ancient track from Kreūsis to Thespiai. Possibly built by the Thebans post-Leūktra, the watchtower would have offered sweeping views of the port of Kreūsis and the Gulf of Corinth. Many of its marble blocks now form part of the fabric of Áyios Mámas (rebuilt around 1973). According to Vitruvius, a Roman architect and engineer, circular towers were more resistant to battering rams.[13] They also, as here, provided better fields of vision and, of course, fire.

---

13   Vitruvius 1.5.5.

Colour Plate Commentaries

Plate A: A Noontime Nip

It was commonly said in antiquity that wine was the mirror of each man, and Xenophon has a rather strange tale to tell, namely that it was likely that the Spartans were more than slightly sottish prior to their clash with the Thebans. His words are: 'It was after the morning meal that Kleombrotos held his last council over the battle. They had been drinking a bit at midday, and it was said that the wine had a certain stimulating effect on them.'[1]

Xenophon sees the cause of Sparta's defeat that day in part on too much alcohol. Aristotle felt, in a more philosophical vein, that the inebriated can never count as brave because they become optimistic about their chances of victory.[2]

Gathered around Kleombrotos, the members of the king's council of war are about to drink neat wine, the king's helot attendant having filled their drinking cups, κώθωνος, *kōthōnos*, from a wineskin. Helots, if not armed as hoplites by the state in lieu of their promised freedom,[3] served the army on campaign as baggage carriers and camp servants, normally one per *Spartiātēs*.[4] Armed with a bundle of javelins or alternatively a couple of slings, helots fought as lightly armed troops in battle.[5]

A κώθων, *kōthōn*, a small-handled terracotta drinking vessel, was convenient for stowing away and therefore widely used by campaigning soldiers. It is believed to have originated from Sparta,[6] whose soldiers, after all, were professionals. While shallow and lidless, the *kōthōn* was designed with an inward curving rim that prevented the liquids inside from sloshing out. This rim also trapped any dirt or particles that might be floating in water taken from a stream, so making the water less unpleasant to drink.

Much like his forefathers at Thermopylai, hairstyle of a *Spartiātēs* continues to be dressed (and oiled) in four locks falling to the front, two on

---

1   Xen. *Hell.* 6.4.8.
2   Arist. *Nik. Eth.* 1117a.14–15.
3   Thuc.4.78.1, 80.5, 5.34.1, 7.19.3, 58.3, Xen. *Hell.* 3.1.4, 4.2, 6.5.29, Diod. 12.67.1, 3, 5.
4   Thuc. 4.16.1
5   Hdt. 8.25.1, 9.28.
6   Archil. fr. 4 Swift, Ar. *Eq.* 600, *Ach.* 549, Xen. *Kúr.* 1.2.8, Plut. *Lyk.* 9.4, Krit. fr. 34D Diels-Kranz, Alex. fr. 181 Kassel-Austin, *Soûda* s.v. κώθων, *IG* II² 47.6, cf. Ar. *Pax* 1094, Athen. 11.483b.

either shoulder, and four to the back. The upper lip continues to be shaved, but his beard is now generally longer than before. Formerly the universal custom among Greek aristocrats *per se*, the wearing of long hair is nowadays exclusive to *Spartiātai*. They are wearing fresh garlands, which show the *Spartiātai* as warriors and as worshippers.

Crimson was a colour that appeared to embody the power of the Spartan army. It was the semi-legendary lawgiver Lykourgos, it is said by Xenophon, who had ordered the *Spartiātai* to wear crimson cloaks and tunics, since these garments were 'least effeminate and most warlike', and to carry bronze-faced shields, since bronze was 'quickest to polish and slow to tarnish'.[7] The Spartan military cloak, known as a *tribōn*, literally 'worn cloak', is habitually described as being 'mean', *phaūlos*, that is to say, thin as opposed to short.[8] Certainly, austerity was the keynote to the Spartan lifestyle, and a *Spartiātēs* would visually emphasise his masculine toughness by making use of a single woollen cloak, summer and winter, and allow it to wear thin and never be washed. This particular article of his uniform was treasured above all else, so much so, if we are to believe Plutarch,[9] he would be buried without grave goods, but wrapped in his crimson cloak and crowned with an olive wreath. Obviously for purely practical reasons, the *tribōn* was discarded before battle commenced and left behind in camp. Even so, as Plutarch observes, the crimson-coloured tunic alone would have aroused terror in the inexperienced opponent and helped to disguise battle wounds.[10]

No less than a uniform and no less of a distinctly Spartan trait, particularly abroad where it came to represent the symbol of the supposed solemnity of Sparta' *hegemonia*, was the 'crooked' walking stick, the βακτηριων, *baktēriōn*. It has a T-shaped crosspiece at the top, which allows the bearer to lean on it when standing. Spartan violence off the battlefield often took the form of the threat or actual use of a *baktēriōn*, such as in the case of the 'madness' of king Kleomenes.[11] As we can see, Kleombrotos is leaning on his *baktēriōn* as he tosses back his *kōthōn*.

We do not know the king's thoughts. We do not know whether he or any of his senior officers and tent companions, now under the influence of alcohol, understood that they probably were making a grave mistake.

Plate B: Arming for Battle

The panoply of helmet, body armour, greaves, shield, spear, and sword was an incredible burden to endure for a hoplite, who probably stood some 160cm tall and weighed no more than between 55 and 57kg. Cumbersome, uncomfortable, insufferably stifling, it was especially poorly suited for the fierce Mediterranean summer. Because of this and the fact they fought

---

7   Xen. *Lak. pol.* 11.3.
8   Plut. *Nik.* 19.4.
9   Plut. *Lyk.* 27.1.
10 Plut. *Mor.* 238F.
11 Hdt. 6.75.1.

their battles during the hottest months of the year, armed hoplites faced considerable discomfort: heatstroke must have been a very real risk. Understandably, therefore, hoplites adopted the habit of delaying arming for battle as long as it was feasible to do so. Nevertheless, we do hear of hoplites that are caught surprised without their panoply even if battle was imminent.[12]

In this reconstruction two brothers, members of the Theban phalanx, are arming before battle. The setting is the Boiotian camp at Leūktra. Because of the heavy, awkward nature of the panoply, there was a set sequence when it came to arming for battle. As it was difficult for the hoplite to bend forward while wearing body armour,[13] the greaves were snapped into place first.

Beautifully shaped, greaves were flexible bronze protections (between 0.5 and 2mm thick) that ran from the kneecap all the way down to the ankle. Ideally, they fitted perfectly to the morphology of the lower legs of their wearer and were held due to the elasticity of the metal that closed at the rear of the calf muscles.

As to the body armour of a hoplite, pottery iconography of the period commonly depicts a corselet know as a *linothōrax*. This had a U-shaped yoke that covered and protected the shoulders, each shoulder flap being tied down on the chest, a main body piece wrapping around the wearer and covering the chest from the waist up, and two overlapping rows of *ptéruges* or strips around the bottom, which covered the lower belly, hips, and groin. Attic red-figure vases occasionally show bronze or iron scales covering part of the armour (normally restricted to the chest and abdomen), which presumably gave its wearer added protection but at a cost in increased weight.

There is still much scholarly debate on the materials historically used in the manufacture of a *linothōrax*, whether of leather, glued or stitched layers of linen (10–15 layers has been suggested), or a combination of both. Still, though opinions differ, the term λινοθώραξ seems to bear out that it was made from linen; and so does the fact that it is represented in vase paintings by a relatively rare brilliant white.[14] Since it was made almost exclusively of organic material, which has of course perished completely, there are no surviving examples from the archaeological record.

When it came to arming, the *linothōrax* was wrapped around the trunk and the main body piece was tightly secured at the left side, which would be covered by the hoplite shield or *aspís*, by laces tied to two small bronze finials. At this stage the two flaps of the U-shaped yoke would stand erect. Having secured the body piece, these would be pulled down in turn to form wide shoulder guards and tied to one or two bronze finials on the chest. This would ensure that the brunt of the corselet's weight was borne by the shoulders. Between the shoulder guards, the *linothōrax* had a rudimentary neck guard. This stood erect and for that reason protected the back of the

---

12 Hdt. 7.218.1–2, Thuc. 6.69.2, Xen. *Hell.* 4.8.37–9, 7.5.22, cf. 6.1.6 (Polydamas brags that he always leads his men, mercenaries in truth, in full panoply).

13 *Vide* Hom. *Il.* 3.330–338, 11.17–44, 16.131–144, 19.369–391 (once body armour was on, stooping was a problem).

14 Λινοθώραξ: Hom. *Il.* 2.529–530, 828–833, Alk. fr. 140.10 Voigt. For the toughness of linen, *vide* Ael. *NA* 9.17, Plin. 19.2.11.

neck. An ill-fitting corselet, according to no less an authority than Xenophon, was next to useless.[15]

A straight double-edged sword, a *xíphos*, would be hung over the right shoulder by means of a baldric once the *linothōrax* was firmly in place and secure. The bronze helmet, in this case of the Boiotian pattern, would not be worn until the last possible minute.

As an open helmet, the Boiotian pattern provided good peripheral vision – as well as unimpaired hearing – recommended by Xenophon for this very reason: 'For the helmet we consider the Boiotian pattern (*Boiōtiourgés*) the most satisfactory: for this, again, affords the best protection to all the parts that project above the breastplate without obstructing the sight.'[16]

It had a domed skull surrounded by a wide, flaring, down-sloping brim. The brim came down at the rear to protect the back of the neck, projected forward over the forehead and was worked into flutes at the sides, with downward pointing folds affording some lateral protection to the face. It was beaten from a single sheet of bronze using a helmet-shaped former.

Herodotos tells us that every hoplite was followed on campaign by a servant who served as a σκευοφόρος, *skeuophóros*, baggage carrier.[17] The two baggage carriers have already loaded the brothers' shared mule with their campaigning equipment.[18] Xenophon, a man who certainly knew firsthand the campaigning life, provides a list of essential kit that should be taken on campaign.[19] He also recommends that a whittling knife should be carried so that replacement spear shafts can be smoothed down, and a file to sharpen spearheads. Whittling knives can be seen on the belts of the baggage carriers.

Plate C: Head-to-Head, Toe-to-Toe

War is a horrible trade, where men fight like beasts and hideous things are done. War, that devourer of men: 'To the inexperienced battle is pleasant, but he who has had experience of it, in his heart he sorely fears its approach', so wrote the Boiotian lyric poet Pindar.[20] In this reconstruction we are witnessing the clash phase of hoplite battle. This is not a sight for those who desire to paint battle in heroic colours.

Opposing front ranks were often crushed hard against each other by the press of those behind, jabbing with spears over the heads and shoulders of their comrades, searching furiously with the points of their weapons for a crippling strike – a thigh, a groin, a throat, an armpit exposed by an outstretched arm – while fending off the jabs of their adversaries. Though it was a pair of hoplites who stabbed at each other with spear before one or

---

15   Xen. *Mem.* 3.10.9–13.

16   Xen. *PH* 12.3.

17   Hdt. 9.29, cf. Xen. *Hell.* 4.8.39, 6.4.9.

18   Xen. *Anab.* 4.3.30, 6.4.22 (several hoplites sharing a mule).

19   Xen. *Kyr.* 6.2.26–33.

20   Pind. *Dance Songs* 110. According to Pindar (*Olymp.* 6.9), it was by facing the horrors of battle that an aristocrat proved his worth and courage. Born in Kynoskephalai near Thebes around 518 BCE, we can safely assume that Pindar himself would have known firsthand the horrors of battle.

the other went down, there was nothing personal in the exchange: we do not witness the choreographic encounters of bright shining Homeric heroes.

The closed Corinthian helmet we are all quite familiar with from Greek art has been replaced by, for example, the *pīlos* helmet, a simple bronze cap distinguished by its conical shape and narrow rim. Another open-faced pattern was the Boiotian helmet, also seen here. Note also Spartan swords had become shorter and straighter; so much so that by the Peloponnesian War they were exceedingly short, virtually dirks or even daggers – allegedly because Spartans preferred to fight at such close quarters.

By this date many hoplites had abandoned the bronze bell-shaped corselet, *thōrax*, commonly worn by their forbearers and wore instead the lighter more flexible linen corselet, *linothōrax*. This type of body armour is made up of numerous layers of linen glued or stitched together to form a stiff shirt, which can be reinforced with plates or scales made of iron or bronze. The body piece of this shirt has armholes cut out. Below the waist it is cut into strips, *pteruges*, for ease of movement, with a second layer of *pteruges* being fixed behind the first, thereby covering the gaps between them and forming a kind of kilt that protects the wearer's groin. The shirt wraps around the torso and is laced together on the left-hand side, where the join is protected by the hoplite shield, *aspís*. A U-shaped yoke, which bends forward over the shoulders and ties to the chest, completes the corselet.

In this adrenalin fuelled *tête-à-tête*, we witness how the shield provides vital protection. For the *aspís* covers the bearer from chin to knee, and because it partially protects the man to the left too, more than anything else it makes the phalanx possible. Observe too the distinctive convex shape of the *aspís* with its flat, offset rim, which provides rigidity to the bowl of the shield. At some point, certainly by 371 BCE and maybe as early as 422 BCE, Sparta began to use the letter Λ, *lá(m)bda*, most likely coloured in crimson, for Lakedaimonians as a state shield device. Similarly, at some point in their history, most probably after their liberation, the Thebans proudly take on the mighty club of Herakles as their *polis* blazon.

Plate D: The Death of a King

Kleombrotos, fighting alongside his men like a primordial warrior chieftain, was to fall in the ranks of the phalanx. Once fallen, a man was horribly vulnerable and likely to be trampled to death. Spartan military doctrine called upon Spartans to never abandon their king on the field of battle. After a struggle somewhat reminiscent of Homer, the Spartans gain control over the body of their mortally wounded king. As Xenophon says, the Spartans 'had been able to take him [Kleombrotos] up and carrying him off while still alive'.[21]

But something is happening to the Spartans that had never happened before: a battlefield reverse. Forced to fight in unfavourable conditions, the

---

21   Xen. *Hell.* 6.4.13.

Spartiātai are suffering heavy casualties. The fall of the king and the death of many of those around him, including the *polémarchos* Deinon, one of the king's tent companions, Sphodrias, along with the latter's son, Kleonymos, must have added to the initial confusion and eventual collapse. In this scene we see the Spartans, blinded by the dust kicked up by thousands of feet on all sides, fighting furiously in what seems a sea of Thebans. Helmets and shields dented and cut about, the 'long-haired Spartans' still fight on, conspicuous in their crimson tunics. Originally a garment typically worn by labourers to allow free movement of the right arm, the Spartans have adopted the versatile *exōmis* for warfare. This tunic is two-sleeved, but the right-hand sleeve can be let down to leave the right shoulder and arm free to handle weapons in combat providing, of course, the warrior lacked body armour.

With their spears snapped and their phalanx in a shambles, most of the Spartans have resorted to their short swords. When one Athenian politician foolishly mocked that Spartan swords were so lacking in the length department conjurors could swallow them, Agis III (r. 338–331 BCE) briskly replied: 'All the same, the Spartans do reach the enemy with their swords'.[22] Antalkidas (*fl.* 390–360 BCE), when asked why the Spartan swords were so short, is reputed to have said: 'Because we fight close to the enemy'.[23] Plutarch attributes a very similar statement to an unidentified Spartan, who says that they could get to close quarters thanks to their short swords.[24] Conversely, a Spartan mother, when her son complained that his sword was far too short, gave him the motherly advice to 'extend it by a stride'.[25] It is significant that in these passages the use of this extremely short sword is clearly regarded as a Spartan practice. It is also significant that in these same passages the Spartan short sword is called ἐγχειρίδιον, literally a 'dagger', as does Xenophon in his eyewitness account of the aftermath of Second Koroneia.[26]

---

22 Plut. *Lyk.* 19.2, *Mor.* 191E, 216E.1.
23 *Ibid.* 217E.8.
24 *Ibid.* 323E.
25 *Ibid.* 241F.18.
26 Xen. *Ages.* 2.14.

Appendix I

The Greek Language

Greek, ancient or modern, has an intimidating reputation for us Anglophones. Greek is frightful, Greek is alien. Did not Shakespeare feel obliged to vent his frustrations and penned that immortal (and oft misquoted) line in *Julius Caesar*, 'It was Greek to me'.[1] Some would throw up their hands and cry there is enough trauma in the world today without volunteering to witness great thundering quotations in the Greek language.

Ancient Greek is the language spoken by the ancient Greeks in Greece proper, and the various Greek colonies in Anatolia, Magna Graecia, North Africa and the Black Sea region. There are three principle dialects of Greek:

Aeolic: Divided into Lesbian Aeolic (e.g. Sappho) and Boiotian Aeolic (e.g. Pindar)

Doric: Spoken in the Peloponnese and colonies such as Syracuse

Ionic: Divided into Old Ionic (e.g. Homer) and New Ionic (e.g. Herodotos); the latter includes Attic, the ordinary dialect of Athenian writers (e.g. Thucydides, Xenophon)

Because Greek employs a totally different alphabet from ours, turning proper nouns into the English (Latin) alphabet is not always straightforward. Hence you will find names of ancient places and people cropping up in various forms in the books you read.

In a nutshell, there is either a more Greek-like system of transliteration (becoming increasingly popular, and the one that I prefer), or a more Latin-like system, which we inherited from the Greeks' *bête noir*, the Romans, and from mediaeval scholars who wrote in Latin. It should be remembered that Latin was the language of Rome, which quickly spread with the power of Rome until it became the language of most of Western Europe. Italian, French, Spanish, Portuguese, and also Romanian derive from it. Some typical things to watch out for are the following:

---

1   Servilius Casca to Cassius in Shakespeare, *Julius Caesar* (1599), 1.2.273. In origin, the phrase may have been a direct translation of the mediaeval Latin proverb: *Graecum est; non potest legi* ('It is Greek, [therefore] it cannot be read').

'k' in Greek becomes 'c' in Latin, e.g. Perikles becomes Pericles

'kh' in Greek becomes 'ch' in Latin, e.g. Khios becomes Chios

'ai' in Greek becomes 'ae' in Latin, e.g. Aigina become Aegina ('Egg-ina')

'oi' becomes 'oe', while the ending 'oi' becomes 'i' in Latin, e.g. Boiotia becomes Boeotia ('Bee-oh-sha'), whereas Delphoi becomes Delphi

The ending 'os' becomes 'us' in Latin, e.g. Aiskhylos thus becomes Aeschylus, whereas Diodoros Sikoulos becomes Diodorus Siculus

Of course there are limits. Though we try and use the Greek form if at all possible, however, when there is a commonly known alternative, we employ that. Thus, we opt for Polykrates rather than Polycrates, but Corinth, Athens, Attica, Thucydides, and Plutarch, as opposed to Korinthos, Athenai, Attika, Thoukydides, and Ploutarkhos.

Appendix II

The Literary Evidence for the Spartan Army

For those who wish to solve the enigma that is the Spartan army, particularly regarding its numerical size and unit organisation, not to mention that rather ticklish topic of *lóchoi* and *mórai*, the following table will be of some use in that quest. The evidence is presented in reverse order, *viz.* from Leūktra back to Thermopylai.

Xenophon *Hellenika*

6.1.1, 4.17	six *mórai* in total at the time of the Boiotian War
6.4.12, 17	strength of each *enōmotia* at Leūktra (i.e. three files by 12 deep), and at full strength (i.e. 40 age groups, 20- to 60-years of age)
4.5.12	strength of *móra* near Lechaion in 390 BCE (*c.* 600 men)
4.5.14	'ten from manhood' (i.e. 20- to 30-years of age) dash out against Iphikrates' peltasts
4.5.16	'the fifteen from manhood' (i.e. 20- to 35 years of age) dash out against Iphikrates' peltasts
5.4.13, 6.4.17	liability for military service up to 'forty years from manhood' (i.e. 60-years of age)
7.1.30, 4.20, 5.10	the only references to *lóchoi* in *Hellenika*
3.5.22, 4.5.7	*enōmotarchoi* and *pentekostēres* at councils of war
6.4.14	*hippeīs* (i.e. king's guard) who surround Kleombrotos at Leūktra

Xenophon *Lakedaimoniōn politeia*

11.4	six in number, each *móra* contains one *polémarchos*, four *lochagoí*, eight *pentekostēres*, 16 *enōmotarchoi*
4.3	selection process of the *hippeīs*

Thucydides

5.64.3, 66.2, 67.1, 68.3, 72.3	organisation of Spartan army at First Mantineia in 418 BCE
5.72.4	*hippeīs* who surround the king at First Mantineia in 418 BCE
4.8.9, 31.2, 38.5	organisation of Spartan army at the time of Sphakteria in 425 BCE

Herodotos

1.65.5, 7.173.2, 9.53.2, 57.1, 72, 85	organisation of Spartan army in his day
6.56, cf. 1.67.5, 8.124.3	*hippeīs* – note Herodotos says that when on a campaign the kings were attended by a bodyguard of one hundred picked men, but it is not known why he gives this number. He may be thinking of the strength of the contingent supplied by each of the three tribes of Sparta rather than the overall total, since he does give the correct figure elsewhere. We know from several allusions that the *hippeīs* was composed of 300 picked *Spartiātai* at full strength (e.g. Thuc. 5.72.4, Strab. 10.4.18). Originally, the *hippeīs* were probably mounted warriors – they may have been the horsemen that Pausanias (4.7.5, 8.12) records as participants in the First Messenian War – but hoplites in the wars of the fifth and fourth centuries BCE
7.203, cf. 1.82.3, 7.202, 205.2, 9.64.2	*hippeīs* is a force of 300 men, and the Spartans, according to Herodotos (8.123), used the term *hippeīs* for their king's guard. Moreover, even though the aristocracy generally owned horses, they did not normally act as the cavalry arm of a *polis'* army, mounts being ridden to and not in battle. Indeed, the ability to own and pasture horses was an outward sign of wealth

Appendix III

Spartan Hairstyles

Male hair is potently symbolic stuff. The Spartans signalled their virility and belligerence by growing theirs and went into battle with it all braided and be-wreathed with flowers. In this way, no less than a uniform and no less of a distinctly Spartan trait was the long hair grown specifically for its military function. As to the origins of this Spartan custom we can turn to Herodotos, who reckons the legislation enjoining the *Spartiātai* to grow their hair proudly and terrifyingly long, contrary to previous practice, had first been instituted after the victory over the Argives at the so-called 'Battle of the Champions', supposedly fought in about 546 BCE.[1] The reality of the 'Battle of the Champions' has been doubted by some scholars, and that is understandable, but it seems that at least in the fifth century BCE it was taken as historical not legend. Still, whether we chose to believe in the historical truth of this battle is irrelevant here. The point of Herodotos' story is that the Spartans, at some point in their history, adopted the idea of wearing the hair long as a symbol of militaristic pride and this is certainly the view later promoted by Xenophon.[2] According to Aristotle, on the other hand, the Spartans thought long hair noble because it was the mark of a free man, since it was difficult to perform servile tasks with long hair.[3]

It has been suggested, therefore, that the Spartans wore their hair long because in archaic times long hair was the mark of an aristocrat throughout the Greek world, what Homer constantly calls κᾰρηκομόωντες, 'long-haired'. In other words, the retention of this fashion was a symptom of the increasing conservatism of Spartan society from the middle of the sixth century BCE onwards. Certainly, in fifth century BCE democratic Athens, long hair became the sign of those holding Lakonian sympathies. Take, for instance, Plutarch's picture of the chameleon-like adaptation by Alkibiades, the adopted son of the Athenian *stratēgós* and statesman Perikles, to Spartan

---

1   Hdt. 1.82.8. Apparently, 300 men each of Argos and Sparta were picked to fight for Thyrea, a sliver of debatable land between the Argive and Lakonia. The whole thing went to pot when the two Argive survivors decamped, claiming victory, leaving the sole Spartan survivor to stake a rival claim as being left in possession of the battlefield. The dispute was resolved by a full-scale battle in which the Spartans carried the day.
2   Xen. *Lak. pol.* 13.8, cf. Plut. *Lys.* 1.1.
3   Arist. *Rh.* 1367a.28–33.

long hair, cold baths, and black broth, his bearing Spartan beyond Spartan.[4] However, this hypothesis only goes part way to answer the question why Spartans wore their hair long. More important, it was a symbolic reminder of belligerent arrogance, almost inverted snobbery. As Xenophon says, men who had just entered manhood were not only permitted to don the highly-prized crimson military cloak, *tribōn*,[5] but also, to wear their hair long in the belief that it made them look taller, more dignified, and of course more terrifying.[6] According to a later tradition, Plutarch to be precise, wearing the hair long made handsome *Spartiātai* more beautiful and uglier *Spartiātai* more terrible.[7] As adornment, of course, it was also free.

This argument is strengthened by a couple of anecdotes that are set in the arena of battle. One is that well-known story of Herodotos where the Spartans, calmly awaiting the arrival of the Persians at Thermopylai, are passing their

---

4 Plut. *Alk.* 23. Young Athenian aristocrats such as Xenophon were generally noted for their blatant pro-Spartan oligarchic leanings and anti-democratic views, an attitude that found a natural home in the very masculine atmosphere of the gymnasium. In one of his dialogues, *Gorgias,* Plato points to the connection of an addiction to contact-sport with Lakonian sympathies and distaste for Athenian democratic politics: the 'lads with the cauliflower ears' who maintained that Perikles had 'made the Athenians lazy and cowardly and garrulous and covetous by his introduction of payment for service to the State' (515e). For these pugnacious young gentlemen, the Sparta of their day was partly seen as a kind of replica-Athens from 'the good old days', an Athens where the Homeric and aristocratic virtues of κλέος, κῦδος, and τιμή were all important (cf. Ar. *Nub.* 961–83, Xen. *Mem.* 4.4.15–7). The Aristophanic character Bdelykleon undoubtedly represents this class of rich young Athenian: he stands accused by the geriatric chorus (the eponymous *Vespae*) of staunchly pro-democratic 'Marathon-fighters' of being 'a long-haired, tassel-fringed pro-Spartan, hand in glove with Brasidas' (Ar. *Vesp.* 473–6, cf. 1069–70). Thus, Bdelykleon attempts to convert his staunchly pro-democratic father, Philokleon, to his own political and moral worldview. This comic socio-political metamorphosis is to be achieved by getting Philokleon to adopt exotic and unpatriotic attire, instructing him how to parade himself in a homosexual fashion, and suggesting that he talks of nothing other than the pankration, boar hunting, hare-coursing, and the torch race when in polite circles (Ar. *Vesp.* 1168, 1196–1204). It is in the light of all this that we can begin to understand the young Xenophon's role during the short and bloody reign of the Thirty Tyrants. Note, *Vespae* was written and performed at a time when bellicose and anti-Spartan feelings were running high in Athens. Amphipolis had not long been captured by Brasidas, and recent news from the north informed the Athenians that the city of Skione had just revolted from the empire and promptly gone over to Brasidas (Thuc. 4.102–106, 120.1).

5 The best representation of the *tribōn* is the bronze statuette of a draped warrior (Hartford, CT, Wadsworth Atheneum Museum of Art, inv. 1917.815), dated 510/500 BCE. The distinctive hairstyle, which falls below his Corinthian helmet, indicates that this warrior is a Spartan, and the transverse crest suggests he is an officer. He wears his *tribōn* tightly wrapped around his body: this cloak was often described as 'mean' (Gk. φαῦλος / *phaûlos*), that is to say, thin as opposed to short (Plut. *Nik.* 19.4). When the prestigious Agesilaos landed in Egypt for what, would be the last campaign of his long career, the Egyptians flocked to see him with high expectations of Spartan splendour and spectacle. To their utter amusement they found instead 'nothing but a little old man with a deformed body wearing a cloak that was coarse and mean' (Plut. *Ages.* 36.5, cf. *Mor.* 214D.76). It was a habit of a (hard) lifetime. Spartan boys under training had to wear the same cloak in summer and winter to become accustomed to the cold (Xen. *Lak. Pol.* 2.4). Oddly enough, there is a parody of this draped Spartan warrior, namely a bronze statuette of Sokrates (Manchester, Manchester Museum, inv. 11083) from Egypt similarly wearing a *tribōn* tightly wrapped around his body. This is clearly an allegorical reference to those Athenians, young followers of the philosopher, who held Lakonian sympathies and distaste for Athenian democratic politics.

6 Xen. *Lak. pol.* 11.3.

7 Plut. *Lyk.* 22.1, *Mor.* 189E, 228F.

time in taking exercise and combing their hair.[8] Questioned about this, so Herodotos' tale continues, the deposed Spartan king, Demaratos, is said to have told Xerxes that combing their hair was a sign that the Spartans were preparing for battle.[9] Similarly, Xenophon reports young men would enter battle with their hair immaculately groomed and oiled, 'looking cheerful and impressive'.[10] If this was so, an indispensable piece of equipment for any self-respecting *Spartiātēs* was his comb. When Klearkhos, the Spartan *generalissimo* who commanded the Ten Thousand under Kŷros the Younger, was unexpectedly captured he was hastily shuffled off to the Persian court loaded with chains. There he begged a comb from the Greek court physician, Ktesias of Knidos in Caria; he was so pleased at being able to carefully dress his hair that he 'gave Ktesias his ring as a token of friendship which he might show to his kindred and friends in Sparta'.[11]

Despite the conservative nature of the Spartans, their coiffure did change somewhat over time. On warrior statuettes of the sixth century BCE all the locks are swept to the back under the helmet. In the early fifth century BCE, hair is normally dressed in four locks to the front, two falling on each shoulder, and four to the back. The beard is short and pointed and the upper lip is normally shaven. Plutarch, quoting Aristotle's lost *Lakedaimoniōn politeia*, informs us that every year upon entering office the *éphoroi* would order the *Spartiātai* to 'cut their moustaches and obey the law'.[12] In the late fifth century BCE, it seems that the hair continued to be dressed in four locks to the front, two falling on each shoulder, and the upper lip continued to be shaved, but the beard was generally longer. Plutarch appears to confirm this when he describes the statue of Lysandros in the treasury of the Akanthians at Delphi, where Apollo proclaimed human and divine justice to the Greeks, as having very long hair and beard 'in the old style'.[13] Again, Plutarch preserves a saying of a Spartan who, upon being asked why he wore his beard so very long, replied: 'So I can see my grey hairs and never do anything unworthy of them'.[14]

There is a fascinating parallel to this Spartan *coiffeur*. The archaic Gorgon is the most terrifying manifestation of Greek art; her large glaring eyes, flared nostrils, fangs bared, protruding tongue, and venomous snakes instead of hair, witnesses the belief in her petrifying power, described by the Boiotians Hesiod and Pindar, and later poets and playwrights.[15] The bronze

---

8   Hdt. 7.208.2–3.

9   Ibid. 7.209.

10 Xen. *Lak. pol.* 13.9, cf. Plut. *Lyk.* 22.1.

11 Ktesias *apud* Plut. *Artax.* 18.1. Klearkhos had become the most prominent of the Greek *stratēgoi* serving under Kŷrus (Xen. *Anab.* 1.6.5, 7.1, 8.4, 12) and represents the archetypal soldier of fortune who seeks not only wealth but power. He personally commanded one thousand hoplites from the Chersonese (ibid. 1.2.9). Previously, he had led an unsuccessful but colourful career as the tyrant of Byzantium (formerly its Spartan *harmostēs*) and hence his Chersonesian contingent (Diod. 14.12.2–9, Polyain. 2.2.7).

12 Plut. *Kleom.* 9.3.

13 Plut. *Lys.* 1.1.

14 Plut. *Mor.* 232E.

15 For example, Hes. *Th.* 274–9, 281, Pind. *Pyth.* 12.7–11, Aiskh. *PB* 793–9, Ov. *Met.* 4.794–803. The Homeric heroes knew only a single, nameless Gorgon, who was a shade in Tartarus (Hom.

volute *kratēr* (in effect a large bowl for mixing wine with water, a vessel most essential for the Greek symposium)[16] from the village of Vix, about 6km north of Châtillon-sur-Seine (*département* Côte-d' Or), was made in Sparta or a Lakonian workshop in southern Italy and is dated to the end of the sixth century BCE. This enormous *kratēr*,[17] the largest (and finest) ever found (height: 1.64m / diameter: 1.27m / weight: 208.6kg / capacity: 1,100 litres), is equipped with two elaborate curving volute-handles, the lower part being formed by the head and bust of a grimacing Gorgon from which, instead of legs, two snakes branch out, and a pair of snakes writhe upwards from behind her arms. Of particular interest to us is the fact that her hair (not the customary full head of serpentine tresses) is shown dressed with four locks to the front, two falling on each shoulder, and four to the back, precisely like the hairdo of our *Spartiātēs* warrior. For many a Greek, Gorgon freak or Spartan fighter, equally petrifying.

Od. 11.633–5 Lattimore), and whose hideous head, an object of terror to Odysseus (ibid. 634), 'grey-eyed' Athena put on her tasselled aegis, the divine goatskin she wore over her shoulders (Hom. *Il.* 5.738–42 Lattimore): little wonder, therefore, she came across as insufficiently charming for Paris to award her the Apple of Discord. By the Archaic period we witness three sisters, Stheino ('mighty'), Euryale ('wide roaming'), and of course Medusa ('guardian'), the one beheaded and bagged by the bold Perseus. Pausanias (5.10.4, 8.47.5, et cetera, et cetera) provides details of where and how Gorgons were represented in Greek art and architecture.

16   *Vide* Appendix 5.
17   Cratère de Vix, Musée du Pays Châtillonnais, Châtillon-sur-Seine.

Appendix IV

The *lá(m)bda* and the Club

Initially, in common with the rest of the Greek world, the shield of a Spartan hoplite was decorated with the owner's individual shield device. In a rather witty anecdote, as retold by Plutarch, we hear of a Spartan who had an image of a life-sized fly as a blazon on his shield. When taunted that he only wanted to escape notice, he replied that on the contrary he got so close to his enemies that his emblem was seen at its true size.[1] Also, we can surmise, the fly is the bravest of the brave because it keeps coming back however often it is shooed away by a man many times its size.

The *lá(m)bda*

At some point, possibly at the outbreak of the Peloponnesian War, Sparta began to use a uniform state shield device. In the lexicon of Photios, under the entry for the Greek letter *lá(m)bda* (λά(μ)βδα, Λ),[2] we are informed that the Spartans painted this letter (in the uppercase) on their shields. This letter, of course, stood for Λακεδαίμων, *Lakedaímōn*. Photios, a ninth-century Byzantine cleric and scholar, mentions as his source Eupolis, an Athenian comic poet born in 446 BCE, and the fiercest rival of the greatest poet of Old Attic Comedy, Aristophanes. His last known comedy drama was staged in 412 BCE, and he died on active service 'in a shipwreck in the Hellespont during the Peloponnesian War',[3] probably at the naval engagement off Kynossema of the following year. Therefore, it is certain that the *lá(m)bda* device was in use before 412 BCE, and it is generally thought that this fragment of Eupolis comes from a comedy that may well deal with Kleon's Amphipolis campaign of 422 BCE.[4] The use of the proud *lá(m)bda*, incidentally, continued into third century BCE, when we are told that Messenian soldiers managed to seize Elis by chicanery, having painted Spartan blazons onto their shields.[5]

---

1 Plut. *Mor.* 234C-D.
2 In classical Greek times, Λ was pronounced and written λάμβδα or λάβδα.
3 *Soûda* ε 3657.
4 E.g. Gomme 1956: 653.
5 Paus. 4.28.5.

The letter was presumably painted on the bronze face of the shield in the uniform crimson colour, and it soon became, like the cloak and coiffure of the Spartan, a weapon of terror. Eupolis crows about a fellow citizen (Kleon?), who seeing 'the flashing *lábdas* (τὰ λάβδα) he was terrified'.[6] But an incident recorded by Xenophon is especially revealing. A Spartan cavalry officer, seeing some hoplites from Sparta's ally, Sikyon, reeling back from an Argive attack, dismounted his men, ordering them to tie their horses to trees, and, taking the shields from the retreating Sikyonians, boldly advanced against the enemy. Meanwhile, the Argives, seeing the letter *sígma* (σίγμα, Σ) on each of the advancing shields, 'feared nothing from them as though they were Sikyonians'.[7] The implication is clear: the Argives would have felt very differently had the shields each borne the letter *lá(m)bda*. It had been a completely different story at First Mantineia in 418 BCE. For the centre of the allied line, which included the Argives as well as the Athenians, had hardly waited to cross spears with the Spartans, but had promptly broken in a desperate dash to escape the battlefield: 'most of them, in fact, did not even stand up to come to grips (ες χεῖρας), but gave way immediately when the Spartans charged, some being actually trampled underfoot in their anxiety to get away before the enemy reached them.'[8]

It would be a mistake to say that the resistance of the opposition collapsed; none was ever offered. The mere sight of an advancing phalanx of Spartan hoplites had been enough to break the nerve of their opponents, even before the shock of arms. Flinch turned to flight as their own fear of death had defeated them. Equally at the so-called 'Tearless Battle' in 367 BCE, 'only a few of the enemy waited till they came within range of the spears (εις δόρυ)'.[9] Once again in the face of the Spartans, and this was post-Leūktra, most of the opposition were no longer soldiers – only a panicking crowd, everyone driven only by the instinct for self-preservation. The Spartans had been properly frightening. Euripides might well say the test of a man's courage was 'to stand and look and outface the spear's swift stroke, / keeping the line firm',[10] but standing and outfacing the Spartan *lá[m]bdas* was an entirely different ballgame. As Archilochos once shrewdly sang, 'In that situation your legs are your best possession'.[11]

However, shield devices still remained a matter of personal preference – at times with disastrous results, as when the Athenians at Delion killed each

6   Eupolis fr. 394 Storey.

7   Xen. *Hell*. 4.4.10.

8   Thuc. 5.72.4, cf. Eur. *Bacch*. 303–4.

9   Xen. *Hell*. 7.1.31.

10   Eur. *HF* 163–4.

11   Archil. fr. 233 West. The Spartans considered his verses about fleeing from the battlefield and boasting about leaving his shield to the enemy (fr. 5 West) so dangerous that they ordered him to be banished from the *polis* lest his 'anti-heroic' views should corrupt their children (Plut. *Mor.* 239B). This anecdote implies that Archilochos was believed to have travelled to Sparta but, on the other hand, it is more plausible that the story was always understood as a prohibition against performing his stinging poetry, as is stated by Valerius Maximus (6.3), rather than physical banishment of the barbed-tongue poet. It seems that Archilochos was mostly believed to have wandered as a soldier rather than a performing poet.

other in the confusion of battle.[12] Still, the Spartans, with or without their dreaded *lá[m]bdas*, as Plutarch implies: 'possessed an invincible spirit and when they came to close quarters their mere reputation was enough to give them an ascendancy over their enemies, since other men could not believe that they were a match for the same number of Spartans.'[13]

Long before Napoléon, Xenophon had come to fully understand that morale counted for more than mere numbers.[14] Napoléon, nevertheless, maintained that: 'In war, three-quarters turns on personal character and relations; the balance of manpower and material counts only for the remaining quarter.'[15]

The Spartans would have agreed. In battle, morale gives victory, and theirs was markedly superior.

The Club

Xenophon tells us that at Second Mantineia (362 BCE) 'the hoplites of the Arkadians painted clubs upon their shields, as though they were Thebans'.[16] A contemporary of the battle, Xenophon's evidence clearly implies that the Thebans were using the club of Herakles as their state device. This Theban device was perhaps painted on the shields of all the Boiotian contingents. If this was the case, however, then it was conceivably a fairly recent development, one connected with the Theban domination of the Boiotian confederacy post 379/378 BCE. Some six years prior to the liberation of Thebes, Neokhoros of Haliartos, the hoplite who dispatched Lysandros – the *naúarchos* most responsible for defeating Athens in the Peloponnesian War and in turn its democracy – bore a device of a dragon on his *aspís*, or so says Plutarch.[17] True or not, the dragon motif is clearly a reference to the founder hero Kadmos and the sowing the teeth of Ares' *drákōn* (dragon) at the future site of Thebes.[18]

Kadmos was also the forebear of a much-cursed house. Predictably there was a well-established trope of Thebes as a tragic city incapable of breaking its cyclical fate described as early as Stesikhoros of Himera and popularised

---

12 Thuc. 4.96.5.

13 Plut. *Pel.* 17.6.

14 Xen. *Anab.* 3.1.42, *Kúr.* 3.3.19, cf. *Mem.* 3.3.7.

15 *Correspondance de Napoléon Ier* [Paris, 1857–70], vol. XVII, no.14276, 'Observations sur les affaires l'Espagne', Saint-Cloud, 27 août 1808. Variants: 'Moral force, rather than numbers, decides victory' (General Gaspard Gourgaud, *Journal de Sainte-Hélène 1815–1818* [Paris, 1899], vol. II, p.119); 'In war, moral power is to the physical as three parts out of four'.

16 Xen. *Hell.* 7.5.20.

17 Plut. *Lys.* 29.5–6.

18 Paus. 9.10.1, Apoll. 3.4.1. In an earlier passage Pausanias has this to say: 'On the grave [of Epameinondas] stands a pillar, and on it is a shield with a *drákōn* in relief. The *drákōn* means that Epameinondas belonged to the race of those called the *Spartoí*' (8.11.8).

in the Athenian tragedies of Aiskhylos,[19] Sophokles,[20] and Euripides.[21] This brings us to Herakles.

Few can say they have never heard of Herakles. The most awesome of all the chthonic heroes of Greek mythology, the heavily muscled, extremely strong and courageous Herakles was an extraordinarily popular character, about which many adventurous tales were told and who was portrayed prolifically in art (private and public) and literature (serious and satirical), habitually as a huge drinker and eater, very amorous (towards both sexes),[22] a superb wrestler, and generally kindly but prone to outbursts of brutal rage. Despite his thuggish voracity, Herakles was worshipped both as a hero and a god. He was the common property of all Greeks, but it is his close connection to Thebes that concerns us at this point.

'Seven-gated' Thebes was famous when Athens and Sparta were barely known. And yet it was at Athens, as mentioned above, that the great Theban legends more than any others, save those of Argos, were ennobled and immortalised by tragedy. At Thebes itself the locals would point out the actual spot where the *Spartoí* ('sown [men]') sprang fully grown and armed for battle from the soil, or where the blind prophet Teiresias listened to sharp cries and whirling wings of the prescient birds, or where the double cursed sons/brothers of Oidipous fell with mutual slaughter.[23] The events of Thebes' heroic age and their ineffaceable reality to historic Thebans may be illustrated by a tale current in antiquity. At a conference in Arkadia and Athenian ambassador taunted the Thebans and the Argives with having begotten the patricide Oidipous and the matricide Orestes. Our hero Epameinondas enters the tale at this point. In reply to the taunt, the Theban *boiōtarchēs* acknowledged their heinous crimes but noted that Thebes and Argos having exiled them, 'they had found asylum with the Athenians',[24] as the Athenian ambassador should have indubitably known. Yet it was the bright deeds – tanking up between monsters and missions to world's end – of the Olympian demigod Herakles during his earthly life that confirmed the belief that the mythological past of Thebes was greater than any of its historical periods.

The most tragic episode of Herakles' life occurred at Thebes, the much-cursed place of his birth. It was his victorious war against the kingdom of Orkhomenos on behalf of Kreon of Thebes that won the youthful Herakles the hand of the king's eldest daughter, Megara.[25] But he slew their children

---

19 *Seven Against Thebes* (467 BCE).

20 *Antigone* (441 BCE), *Oidipous Tyrannous* (429 BCE), *Oidipous at Kolonos* (401 BCE). The *Oidipous Tyrannous* was selected by Aristotle as the most perfect specimen, in technical construction, of Greek drama.

21 *Supplices* (423 BCE), *Herakles* (416 BCE), *Phoenissae* (408 BCE), *Bacchae* (405 BCE).

22 Herakles' legion of children, the *Herakleidai*, invaded the Peloponnese and divided it up between themselves.

23 The double curse: the curse of Ares on Kadmos for his slaying of the god's *drákōn*; the curse of Dionysos on the next generation for their snubbing of the god's mother, Semele.

24 Nep. *Epam.* 6.3, cf. Plut. *Apophth.* 71.15, who names the Athenian as Kallistratos, an orator and *stratēgós* who believed Thebes to be more dangerous to Athens than Sparta (Xen. *Hell.* 6.2.39, Diod. 15.30.7, 38.3).

25 Hom. *Od.* 11.269–70 Lattimore, Apoll. 2.4.11. Apparently, in a deliberate act of war, Herakles burns Orkhomenos to the ground and floods its land by damning up the river Kephissos (Paus.

(and in some versions Megara as well)²⁶ in a fit of homicidal madness sent by the vengeful Hera and consequently, was obliged to serve Eurytheos of Tiryns, his archenemy, for ten years (Twelve Labours of Herakles).²⁷ This household homicide notwithstanding, Herakles became the patron deity of Thebes. Though he was highly skilled with the bow (he was trained by Teutaros the Scythian), and his often depicted with a Scythian bow in the pottery iconography (Teutaros bequeathed his bow to him),²⁸ his most common weapon was the heavy knotted club. This was an untrimmed club he had cut in his youth from a wild olive tree which he had uprooted on Mount Helikon.²⁹ As befitting a legendary hero wielding his weapon of choice, Herakles would bludgeon through his enemies in true heroic fashion. Yet with his god-given gifts of strength and bravery, there is a clear tension in the character of Herakles: his legendary heroism struggles to manifest itself without tremendous violence. He even found the time to turn Troy into a pile of ashes and rubble. This was when Podarkes (the original name of Priam)³⁰ was but a young boy.

One final point regarding Herakles' intimate connection with Thebes and that is one concerning the homophilic Sacred Band. As Plutarch helpfully informs us:

> It is related too, that Iólaōs, who shared the labours of Herakles and fought by his side, was beloved of him. And Aristotle says [fr. 97 Rose] that even down to his day the tomb of Iólaōs was a place where lovers and beloved plighted mutual faith. It was natural, then, that the band should also be called sacred [viz. the Sacred Band], because even Plato [Symp. 179a] calls the lover a friend 'inspired of God'.³¹

Iólaōs often acted as Herakles' charioteer and companion. Herakles gave his wife, Megara, to Iólaōs – ostensibly because the sight of her reminded him

---

9.38.5, Diod. 4.18.7, Strab. 9.2.40). Kreon, of course, was the brother of Iokástē, the mother/wife of Oidipous (Apoll. 2.4.11, 7.8).

26 E.g. Seneca *Hercules Furens* 1024 (Herakles smashes Megara with his club).

27 Diod. 4.11.1, Apoll. 2.4.12. The canonical list of the labours, from hydra slaying and Kerberos taming to golden apple picking and industrial-scale stable cleaning, can be found in Apoll. 2.5.1–12. The name Herakles is ironic (his given name was Alkaios or Alkeidēs), as it literally means 'glory (κλέος / *kléos*) of Hera'. Her hostility is one of the themes that runs through many of Herakles' stories, starting with his delayed birth that made him subservient to his cousin Eurytheos: Herakles is the son of her brother-husband, Zeus, who had bribed (or raped) the mortal Alkmene. Still, if the goddess had not driven him mad in the first place, he would never had performed the labours and won immortal glory. In trying to break Herakles, she had only ensured his eventual apotheosis.

28 Lykophron *Alexandra* §31.

29 Cf. Apoll. 2.4.11, Paus. 2.31.10. A hard wood that wears well, it was also the appropriate wood of the club wielded by the Cyclops Polyphemos (Hom. *Od.* 9.322–3 Lattimore). The wild olive, *eláos*, in Greece, like the birch in Italy and North-western Europe, was used for the expulsion of evil spirits.

30 A captive of Herakles, Podakes was ransomed by Hesione, his sister: hence thereafter Podakes was called Priam, from the verb πρίαμαι, 'to buy' (Apoll. 2.6.4). Of course Priam, as king of the most marvellous kingdom in all the Mediterranean world, was to witness the second sack of Troy.

31 Plut. *Pel.* 18.4.

of the murder of their children.[32] Iólaōs was honoured annually in Thebes by the *Ioláeia*, an athletic festival consisting of gymnastics and equestrian events.[33] He was the son of Herakles' twin brother Iphikles: they had the same mother, Alkmene, but different fathers. Herakles' father, of course, was Zeus, the supreme god notorious for his many dalliances, while Iphikles' was Amphitryon, the exiled king of Tiryns and husband of Alkmene, the granddaughter of Perseus, who was also a son of Zeus. The Herakles family tree is unquestionably complicated, as befitting a Greek semi-divine hero.

To end with some soldierly blether. In the gossip in the Boiotian camp at Leūktra was that Herakles' *panopliā* had mysteriously disappeared from his temple in Thebes.[34] The buzz around the campfires was that the demigod was marching to join his fellow Thebans and fight the Spartan invaders alongside them, though Xenophon says there were those who reckoned that this story 'was fabricated by the Theban leaders'.[35]

---

32   Apoll. 2.6.1.
33   Pind. *Olymp.* 8.84.
34   Diod. 15.33.5, cf. Polyain. 2.3.8. The carvings depicting most of the Twelve Labours on the temple gables were executed by Praxiteles (Paus. 9.11.1).
35   Xen. *Hell.* 6.4.7.

Appendix V

In vino veritas

This is not the place to launch a grand disquisition on the virtues and the vices of wine, but a few words may be in order with specific regards to the Spartans. Wine for us is generally associated with mirth and merriment, but for the Greeks it was a deeply symbolic substance. For this reason, it was almost never taken neat, a vice to which the Greeks were strangers, or as they called it, 'to drink like a Scythian' (Σκυθίζειν / *Skythízein*),[1] a nomadic people from north of the Black Sea. As such it was normally cut with water and served from a mixing bowl, *kratēr*, the proportion of water to wine noted

---

1   Fore xample, Anakr. fr. 356b.2 West. Plato informs us that the Scythians (and the Thracians) 'take their wine neat and let it pour down their clothes' (*Leg.* 1.637e). Among the Greeks (and the Romans) there were exceptions to the rule, such as when the exiled poet Alkaios of Lesbos (fr. 332 West, cf. fr. 338.4 West: 'mix the sweet wine unstintingly'), on the death of Myrsilos, the tyrant of Mytilene, calls for straight wine, even as Horace (*Odes* 1.37) must have done when he heard of the death of Kleopatra. This reminds us of the sinister death of the Agiadai king Kleomenes I (r. *c.* 520–490 BCE), probably the most outstanding of all the 'Zeus-born' kings of Sparta. The official line was that Kleomenes, having turned stark raving mad, was put in chains where at last he took his own life by a nasty process of slicing himself into pieces from the feet up, or so Herodotos (6.75.2–3, 84.1) was told by the Spartans (he actually provides four different versions that circulated in Greece to explain Kleomenes' death). 'Look to the end' was a popular Greek wisdom expression meaning never judge the success of a man's life until you see how he meets his maker (e.g. Solon to Kroesos: Hdt. 1.32.9, cf. 1 Corinthians 15:26). Those whom the gods wish to destroy, they first make mad, or so a character in a play of Euripides is believed to have said (actually this is an anonymous ancient proverb, misattributed to Euripides). Most Greeks believed that it was for his various acts of sacrilege (against the Argives, the Athenians, the Delphic oracle, et cetera) that he was punished by his madness: regarding the celestial sphere with the eye of a diplomat, no one used or abused religion so much as Kleomenes. The Spartans disagreed – his sticky end was brought about because his brain had been befuddled by drinking great quantities of wine unmixed with water, a particularly nasty habit he had learned from Scythian envoys who came all the way from the northern shores of the Black Sea to propose a joint invasion of Anatolia after the misguided Persian expedition against them in 514 BCE. Their plan was rejected but the habit stuck and eventually went to his head. Kleomenes became a demented alcoholic and died, unpleasantly, his brain desiccated by kingly folly. So by regularly taking his wine in the 'Scythian fashion' if that is what he did, Kleomenes was no better than the most barbarous of barbarians at the furthest edge of the *oikouménē*, the known world. It was well known that the Scythians imbibed immoderately and when inebriated were capable of any excess (Ar. *Lys.* 184, *Thesm.* 1002, Anakr. fr. 356b West). The custom of drinking wine was adopted by the Scythians (mainly by the Scythian elite) from the Greeks who had colonised the northern coast of the Euxine (Black Sea).

by ancient authors being 3:1, 2:1, 5:3, and, at its strongest, 3:2.[2] Of course, drinking does have a tendency to promote aggressiveness, but this would strike us as an irresponsible alcoholic binge, even if the Greeks mixed in a ratio of three parts water to one part wine for ordinary use, a litter stronger for a good festivity.[3]

Yet the Spartans were notoriously abstemious and controlled wine drinkers, and the cult of Dionysos was certainly not ascribed to them, a staple of religious expression elsewhere in the Greek world, for both men and women. The Spartans knew the true nature of the ambiguous god of wine and death, and a verse fragment of Kritias preserves a contrast between Spartan drinking habits and others:

> Spartan young men drink enough to bring joyful hope to the mind of all, and friendship and restrained gaiety to their conversation. Such drinking is good for the body, good for the mind, and not harmful to the purse... The Spartan way brings food and drink enough for thinking and working, but no excess; they have no day set aside for overindulgence and drunkenness.[4]

There were many sayings in the ancient world that wine was the keyhole into the mind, and the one we are all familiar with of course is *in vino veritas* of the Romans.[5] But wine can also be seen as having hallucinogenic effects. The cult of Dionysos shows many traits that lead in this direction, perhaps best seen in the *Bacchae* of Euripides where feminine ecstasy culminates in ritually accelerated murder. The god of drunk, disorderly release was the very opposite of masculine Spartan control. Indeed, the only people in Sparta who were allowed – or rather were compelled – to really embrace wine and get rip-roaring drunk were helots, and this Dionysiac condition was forced on them as a deliberate demonstration by the adult Spartans to the upcoming generation of how a Spartan should not behave.

---

2   3:1(Anakr. fr. 383 West); 2:1 (Alk. fr. 346.4 West, Anakr. 356a.3–4 West); 5:3 (Anakr. 409 West).

3   The modern Greek word for wine, κρασί / *krasí*, is derived from the ancient Greek word, κρᾶσις / *krāsis*, 'mixing', 'blending'.

4   Krit. fr. 88B.11 Diels-Kranz.

5   Cf. Alk. fr. 333 West: 'For wine's the window to see through a man'.

Bibliography

Printed Sources, Books

Allinson, F. G., and Allinson, A. C. E., *Greek Letters and Lands* (Boston, MA: Houghton Mifflin Company, 1909)

Anderson, J. K., *Military Theory and Practice in the Age of Xenophon* (Berkeley & Los Angeles, CA: University of California Press, 1970)

Anderson, J. K., *Xenophon* (London: Duckworth, 1974)

Best, J. G. P., *Thracian Peltasts and their Influence on Greek Warfare* (Groningen: Wolters-Noordhoff, 1969)

Bintliff, J. L., Howard, P., and Snodgrass, A. (eds.), *Testing the hinterland: the work of the Boeotian Survey (1989-1991) in the southern approaches to the city of Thespiai.* (Cambridge: Cambridge University Press (Macdonald Institute Monographs), 2007)

Buck, R. J., *A History of Boeotia* (Edmonton: University of Alberta Press, 1979)

Buck, R. J., *Boeotia and the Boeotian League. 431-371 BCE* (Edmonton: University of Alberta Press, 1994)

Buckler, J., *The Theban Hegemony, 371-362 BCE* (Cambridge, MA: Harvard University Press, 1980)

Buckler, J., and Beck, H., *Central Greece and the Politics of Power in the Fourth Century BCE* (Cambridge: Cambridge University Press, 2008)

Buckley, T., *Aspects of Greek History 750-323 BC: A Source-Based Approach* (London: Routledge, 2010 2nd edition)

Campbell, D. B., *Spartan Warrior* (Oxford: Osprey Publishing, 2012), Warrior no.163

Cartledge, P. A., *Sparta and Lakonia: A Regional History, 1300-362 BCE.* (London: Duckworth, 1979)

Cartledge, P. A., *Agesilaos and the Crisis of Sparta* (London: Duckworth, 1987)

Cartledge, P. A., *Spartan Reflections* (London: Duckworth, 2001)

Cartledge, P. A., *The Spartans: An Epic History* (London: Channel 4 Books, 2003, 2nd edition)

Cartledge, P. A., *Thebes. The Forgotten City of Ancient Greece* (London: Pan Macmillan, 2020)

Ducat, J., Stafford, E. and Shaw, P-J., *Spartan Education; Youth and Society in the Classical Period* (Swansea: Classical Press of Wales, 2006)

Fields, N., 2006. *Ancient Greek Fortifications 500-300 BCE* (Oxford: Osprey Publishing, 2006), Fortress no.40

Fields, N., *Thermopylae 480 BC: Last Stand of the 300* (Oxford: Osprey Publishing, 2007), Campaign no.188

Fields, N., *Syracuse 415-413 BC: Destruction of the Athenian Imperial Fleet* Oxford: Osprey Publishing, 2008), Campaign no.195

Fields, N., *The Spartan Way* (Barnsley: Pen & Sword Military, 2013)

Forrest, W.G., *A History of Sparta* (Bristol: Bristol Classical Press, 1995 3rd edition)

Fortina, M., *Epaminonda* (Turin: Società Editrice Internazionale, 1958)

Gaebel, R. E., *Cavalry Operations in the Ancient Greek World* (Norman, OK: University of Oklahoma Press, 2002)

Gartland, S. D. (ed.), *Boiotia in the Fourth Century BCE* (Philadelphia, PA: University of Pennsylvania Press, 2016)

Gomme, A. W., *A Historical Commentary on Thucydides, III* (Oxford: Oxford University Press, 1956)

Gorgiadou, A., 1997. *Plutarch's* Pelopidas: *a Historical and Philosophical Commentary* (Stuttgart/Leipzig: B. G. Teubner, Beiträge zur Alterumskunde 105, 1997)

Griffith, G.T., *The Mercenaries of the Hellenistic World* (Chicago, IL, Ares Publishers, 1984)

Grundy, G. B., *The Topography of the Battle of Platæa: The City of Platæa. The Field of Leuctra*, Proceeding of the Royal Geographical Society (London: John Murray, 1894)

Hamilton, C. D., *Sparta's Bitter Victories* (Ithaca, NY: Cornell University Press, 1979)

Hanson V. D., *Warfare and Agriculture in Classical Greece* (Pisa: Giardini Editori, 1983)

Hanson, V. D., *The Western Way of War: Infantry Battle in Classical Greece* (London: Hodder & Stoughton, 1989)

Hanson, V. D. (ed.), *Hoplites: The Classical Greek Battle Experience* (London: Routledge, 1991)

Hanson, V. D., *The Wars of the Ancient Greeks* (London: Cassell, 1999)

Hodkinson, S., 2000. *Property and Wealth in Classical Sparta*. London: David Brown

Hodkinson, S., and Powell, A. (eds.), 1999. *Sparta: New Perspectives*. London: Duckworth

Holladay, A. J., 1982. 'Hoplites and heresies'. *JHS* 102: 94–104

Hooker, J. T., 1980. *The Ancient Spartans*. London: J.M. Dent & Sons

Hornblower, S., *A Commentary on Thucydides* (Oxford: Clarendon Press, 1991)

Hornblower, S., *The Greek World 479–323 BCE* (London: Routledge, 2002, 3rd edition)

Hornblower, S., 'Thucydides on Boiotia and Boiotians', in Hornblower, S. *Thucydidean Themes* (Oxford: Clarendon Press, 2010), pp.116–138

Jones, A. H. M., *Sparta* (New York: Barnes & Noble, 2008)

Kagan, D., *The Outbreak of the Peloponnesian War* (Ithaca, NY: Cornell University Press, 1969)

Kagan, D., *The Archidamian War* (Ithaca, NY: Cornell University Press, 1974)

Kagan, D., *The Peace of Nicias and the Sicilian Expedition* (Ithaca, NY: Cornell University Press, 1981)

Kagan, D., *Fall of the Athenian Empire* (Ithaca, NY: Cornell University Press, 1987)

Kagan, D., *The Peloponnesian War: Athens and Sparta in Savage Conflict 431–404 BCE* (London: Harper Collins, 2003)

Lazenby, J. F., *The Spartan Army* (Warminster: Aris & Phillips, 1985)

Lazenby, J. F., *The Peloponnesian War: A Military Study* (London: Routledge, 2004)

Lewis, D. M., *Sparta and Persia* (Leiden: E.J. Brill, 1977)

Luraghi, N., and Alcock, S. (eds.), *Helots and their Masters in Laconia and Messenia*. Cambridge, MA : Harvard University Press, Hellenic Studies 4, 2004)

MacDowell, D. M., *Spartan Law* (Edinburgh: Scottish Academic Press, 1986)

Manfred, C., *Sparta. Einführung in seine Geschichte und Zivilisation* (Munich: C.H. Beck, 1983)

Meiggs, R., *The Athenian Empire* (Oxford: Clarendon Press, 1972)

Moore, J. M., *Aristotle and Xenophon on Democracy and Oligarchy* (London: Chatto & Windus, 1983 2nd edition)

Pomeroy, S. B., *Spartan Women* (Oxford: Oxford University Press, 2002)

Powell, A. (ed.), *Classical Sparta: Techniques behind Her Success* (London: Routledge, 1989)

Powell, A., *Athens and Sparta: Constructing Greek Political and Social History to 323 BCE* (London: Routledge, 2001, 2nd edition)

Pritchett, W. K., *Studies in Ancient Greek Topography*, vol. 1 (Berkeley & Los Angeles, CA: University of California Press, 1965)

Pritchett, W. K., *Ancient Greek Military Practices* (Berkeley & Los Angeles, CA: University of California Press, 1971)

Rhys Roberts, W., *The Ancient Boeotians: their Character and Culture, and their Reputation* (Cambridge: Cambridge University Press, 1985)

Rusch, S. M., *Sparta at War: Strategy, Tactics, and Campaigns, 550–362 BCE.* (London: Frontline Books, 2011)

Schwartz, A., *Reinstating the Hoplite: Arms, Armour and Phalanx Fighting in Archaic and Classical Greece* (Stuttgart: Franz Steiner Verlag, Historia Einzelschriften 207, 2009)

Sekunda, N. V., *The Ancient Greeks: Armies of Classical Greece 5th and 4th Centuries BCE* (Oxford: Osprey Publishing, 1986), Man-at Arms Elite no.7

Sekunda, N. V., *The Spartans* (Oxford: Osprey Publishing, 1998), Man-at Arms Elite no.66

Sekunda, N. V., *Greek Hoplite, 480–323 BCE* (Oxford: Osprey Publishing, 2000) Warrior no.27

Snodgrass, A. M., 1967. *Arms and Armour of the Greeks*. London: Thames & Hudson

de Souza, P., 2003. *The Peloponnesian War, 431–404 BCE.* London: Routledge

Spence, I. G., *The Cavalry of Classical Greece: A Social and Military History* (Oxford: Clarendon Press, 1993)

Stylianou, P. J., *A Historical Commentary on Diodorus Siculus, Book 15* (Oxford: Oxford University Press, 1997)

Tritle, L. A. (ed.), *The Greek World in the Fourth Century: from the fall of Athens to the Successors of Alexander* (London: Routledge, 1997)

Tritle, L. A., *The Peloponnesian War* (Westport, CT: Greenwood Press, 2004)

Wallace, P. W., *Strabo's Description of Boiotia: a Commentary* (Heidelberg: Carl Winter Universitätsverlag, 1979)

van Wees, H., *Greek Warfare: Myths and Realities* (London: Duckworth, 2004)

Printed Sources, Journals and Chapters

Buckler, J., 'Plutarch on Leuktra' in *Symbolae Osloenses* 55, 1980, pp.75-93

Cartledge, P. A., 'Hoplites and heroes: Sparta's contribution to the technique of ancient warfare' in *JHS* 97, 1997, pp.11–27

Cooper, F. A., 'Epaminondas and Greek fortifications' in *AJA* 90, 1986, p.195

Cawkwell, G. L., 'Epaminondas and Thebes' in *CQ* 22/2, 1972, pp.254–78

Cawkwell, G. L., 'Orthodoxy and hoplites' in *CQ* 39, 1989, pp.375–89

Dillon, M. P. J., 2008. 'Xenophon sacrificed on account of an expedition»: divination and the *sphagia* before ancient Greek battles' in Mehl, V. & Brulé, P. (eds.) *Le sacrifice antique: Vestiges, procedures et strategies* (Rennes: Presses universitaires de Rennes, 2008), pp.235–251

Epps, P. H., 'Fear in Spartan character' in *Classical Philology* 28, 1933, pp.12–29

Fields, N., 'Apollo: God of War, protector of mercenaries' in Sheedy K. A. (ed.), *Archaeology in the Peloponnese: new excavations and research* (Oxford: Oxbow Books, 1994), pp.95–113

Fields, N. 'A soldier's diet' in *Ad Familiares* 8, 1995, pp.13–14

Fields, N., 'Et ex Arcadia ego' in *AHB* 15/3, 2001, pp.102–30

Goldsworthy, A. K., 'The *ôthismos*, myths and heresies: the nature of hoplite battle' in *War in History* 4, 1997, pp.1–26

Frazer, A. D., 'The myth of the phalanx scrimmage' in *CW* 36, 1942, pp.15–16

Hanson, V. D., 'Hoplite obliteration: the case of the town of Thespiai' in Carman J., and Harding, A. F. (eds.), *Ancient Warfare: Archaeological Perspectives* (Stroud: Sutton, 1999) pp.203–217

Hornblower, S., 'Thucydides on Boiotia and Boiotians', in Hornblower, S. *Thucydidean Themes* (Oxford: Clarendon Press, 2010), pp.116–138

Hodkinson, S., 'Land tenure and inheritance in classical Sparta' in *CQ* 80, 1986, pp.378–406

Howie, J. G., 'The *Aristeia* of Brasidas: Thucydides' presentation of events at Pylos and Amphipolis' in *Exemplum and Myth, Criticism and Creation: Papers on Early Greek Literature* (Prenton: Francis Cairns Publications, Collected Classical Papers no.3, 2012)

Krentz, P., 'The nature of hoplite battle' in *Cahiers Archéologica* 4, 1985, pp.50–61

Krentz, P., 'Casualties in hoplite battles'in *GRBS* 26, 1985, pp.13–20

Krentz, P., 'Fighting by the rules: the invention of the hoplite *agon*' in *Hesperia* 71, 2002, pp.23–39

Lazenby, J. F. and Whitehead D., 'The myth of the hoplite's *hoplon*' in *CQ* 46, 1996, pp.27–33

Lorimer, H. L., 'The hoplite phalanx' in *BSA* 42, 1976, pp.76–138

Manning, S., 'The history of the idea of glued linen armour' in *Mouseion* 17/3, 2021, pp.492–514

Pritchett, W. K., 'Observations on Chaironeia' in *AJA* 62/3 1958, pp.307–311

Roy, J., 'The mercenaries of Cyrus' in *Historia* 16, 1967, pp.287–323

Salmon, J. B., 'Political hoplites?' in *JHS* 97, 1977, pp.84–101

Snodgrass, A. M., 'The hoplite reforms and history' in *JHS* 85, 1965, pp.110–122

Tufano, S., 'The liberation of Thebes (379 BC) as a Theban revolution: three case studies in Theban Prosopography' in Marchand, F., and Beck, H. (eds.), *The Dancing Floor of Ares: Local Conflict and Regional Violence in Central Greece* (*AHB* Supplemental Volume 1, 2020), pp. 63–85

Tufano, S., 'Show trials and the opposition to Pelopidas and Epameinondas'. *Studia Antiqua et Archaeologica* 28/1, 2022, pp.245–263

Tuplin, C. J., 'Pausanias' and Plutarch's *Epameinondas*' in *CQ* 34/2, 1984, pp.346–58

Tuplin, C. J., 'The Leuctra campaign. Some outstanding problems' in *Klio* 69, 1987, pp.72–107

Wheeler, E. L., '*Hoplomachia* and Greek dances in arms' in *GRBS* 23, 1982, pp.223–33

Wheeler, E. L., 'The *hoplomachia* and Vegetius' Spartan drillmasters' in *Chiron* 13, 1983, pp.1–20